Raobeia Ken Sigrah and Stacey M. King

"Excellent study; very well-written!"
Grant McCall, Associate Professor of Anthropology, Sydney, Australia.

"Great collection of archival research and traditional history - This book is a great introduction to Banaban culture and history. Sigrah and King weave traditional history with archival research in a format that's accessible and interesting. A must-read for anyone interested in Oceanic cultures & history, especially those affected by mining operations and displacement during the colonial era".
Janice L. Cantieri, USA. National Geographic-Fulbright Fellow, Reporting from Fiji and Kiribati.

"This book is so well researched, written, and produced. The story is well told, but the visuals really help tell the whole story. Most anthropological books of a similar vein would include this information, but this doesn't read like a normal textbook. Perhaps, it's because the authors have emotional ties and understand Banaba on a deeper level. This is opposed to an outside author or academic coming in to write a book.
The history of Banaba is something that needs to be told".
Judge's Commentary: 27th Annual Writer's Digest Self-Published Book Awards. USA

TE RII NI BANABA

Backbone of Banaba

TE RII NI BANABA

Backbone of Banaba

Raobeia Ken Sigrah
and
Stacey M. King

Te Rii ni Banaba – Backbone of Banaba
Copyright © Raobeia Ken Sigrah and Stacey M. King.
All rights reserved.

Second edition 2019.
Published by Banaban Vision Publications
PO Box 1116 Paradise Point. Qld. 4216. Australia
www.banabanvision.com

A catalogue record for this
work is available from the
NATIONAL LIBRARY OF AUSTRALIA   National Library of Australia

ISBNs:
Paperback: 978-0-6485462-2-1
Hardback: 978-0-6485462-4-5
Ebook: 978-0-6485462-0-7

Cover designed by Stacey King

This book is a second revised edition of the history of the Banabans
from an indigenous perspective. Cultural information contained in this
book is endorsed by Banaban Clan elders involved in this history. The
authors have provided information sourced from original documents,
photographs and interviews either owned or kindly donated to the
authors. All other reference material has been sourced as quoted.
Internal diagrams were created and/or supplied by the authors.

Raobeia Ken Sigrah
www.raobeiakensigrah.com
Stacey M. King
www.staceymking.com

First published 2001
Institute of Pacific Studies, University of the South Pacific, Fiji.

Raobeia Ken Sigrah
1956–2021

My Champion, My Hero, My Warrior

"From the moment we both stepped foot on your homeland Banaba, we knew our ancestors had brought us together 97 years later to right the wrongs of the past.

How could the two of us, from such different worlds, give up everything we had known.

The days we spent together exploring the homeland, during the day and under the magical power of the moon combined the spiritual connection of both our ancestors and drew us closer.

Only our Banaban elders understood the importance of our shared passion to rehabilitate your devastated homeland and fight for the Banaban cause.

You may have left me here on earth, but you told me before your passing that your work for your people was complete.

Now you will return home with your ancestor Teimanaia in the days ahead. I will be with you on your last and final journey.

Your name will live on in history as a true Banaban warrior and proud descendant of his people, who gave your people the Greatest Gift:

> *To hold your head high and be forever proud of being BANABAN and ensure Banaban identity is never lost but passed on for future generations".*

"Stacey's Farewell", Raobeia Ken Sigrah's Memorial Service, Gold Coast Australia, February 2021

"Banaba
For the land that we love
And to what we have lost
Will remain in our hearts ... forever."
Raobeia Ken Sigrah

"Banaba,
I bukin te aba ae tangiraki
Ao ibukin bwaai aika atia ni bua mai iroura
Ana tei matoa uringakia I nanora... naki toki."
Raobeia Ken Sigrah

"Ken, we may be learned professors and have
degrees, but the knowledge you have about your
people can never be found in Academic writings
or the best universities, for this knowledge
comes from the very people themselves."
Dr W. Kempf, Rabi Island 1997

Contents

Photographs

Figures

THANKS

We thank Banaban elders and clan members who gave their knowledge and encouragement for writing the first history from a Banaban perspective and endorsed the writing of this book. All the Banaban clans involved in this history have sanctioned the work of this book. With the elder's permission, their findings are now finally published. Sadly, most of these elders have passed away since the first edition's publication. Some of the topics covered here are culturally sensitive; therefore, the trust the elders and clan members have placed in us is much appreciated. We hope this work meets their expections.

The completion of this book has been made possible with the advice and assistance of many

1. Raobeia Ken Sigrah and Stacey King with Harry and Honor Maude, Canberra (Kitaguchi Collection 1997).

people from different cultural backgrounds. We would also like to sincerely thank the following honoured I-Matang (European) friends who supported this project in many ways.

Harry and Honor Maude supported the preservation of Banaban culture and provided us with copies of their unpublished research papers and photographs. Dr Ronald Lampert came out of his retirement to drive 200 kilometres to meet with us in Canberra. He donated all his research material, including photographs, slides and maps of his Te Aka dig.

Professor Jack Golson arranged for the return of Te Aka artefacts and ancestral remains to the people. Ewan Maidment from the Pacific Manuscripts Bureau (PAMBU/PMB) was involved in locating Te Aka archaeological files and artefacts at ANU for us. He arranged interviews and maximised the effectiveness of our time in Canberra. Monica and Peter at the PAMBU office always greeted us with friendly, welcoming faces. Thanks to Professor R. Gerard Ward from the Department of Human Geography, Research School of Pacific and Asian Studies at ANU. He assisted with a grant being awarded from the Norman McArthur Memorial Fund towards the publishing of the first edition. For drawing a Banaban map for this book,

2. Dr Ronald Lampert and Raobeia Ken Sigrah looking over maps at ANU, Canberra (Kitaguchi Collection 1997).

2

thanks to Neville Minch from the Cartography Unit, Research School of Pacific and Asian Studies, ANU. Thanks to Linda Crowl, Publications Fellow, Institute of Pacific Studies, at the University of South Pacific, who supported this project and assisted in the publication of our first edition in 2001.

Thanks to Claire and Bill Murray, who offered moral support and Claire assisted in editing our first drafts. Our good friend and renowned Pacific historian, Max Quanchi, provided valuable advice and assisted with our second edition in 2019.

Frank Miller donated his father's *te itai* table, handmade on Banaba in 1927, back to the community on Rabi. Colin Hinchcliffe located research material in the United Kingdom. Dr Alun Hughes in Wales and Avi Gold in Israel commented on our work. They continue to research the lost Banaban language. Manabu Kitaguchi, in Japan, helped to get Ken to Australia and travelled from Tokyo to join us on our epic research trip to Canberra. We appreciate the support and friendship of all these people, especially while Ken was living in a foreign land.

Kam bati n raba to you all!

We did not realise when we commenced work on this book that our research would lead to the discovery of precious and priceless artefacts and ancestral re-

3. Raobeia Ken Sigrah and Stacey King with Robert Langdon, author of the 'Scandalous Document' at ANU, Canberra (Kitaguchi Collection 1997).

mains from the sacred village of Te Aka. By the conclusion of this project, two separate collections, one held at ANU and the other by ex-BPC engineer Peter Anderson, were donated back to the Banaban people. It has been an honour for us to return these items, knowing that they will provide all Banabans with a tangible link to their heritage.

Now, more than a century after phosphate mining began stripping the Banaban homeland, we finally see the first repatriation of such treasured items. We are very proud to be associated with this historic moment in Banaban history.

4. Prof Jack Golson releasing Te aka relics to Raobeia Ken Sigrah (Kitaguchi 1997).

INTRODUCTION

Heritage and Ethnic Identity of the Banabans

Raobeia Ken Sigrah and Stacey M. King

Once covered with coconut palms and surrounding waters teeming with fish, Banaba consists of 595 hectares in the Central Pacific, almost on the equator; latitude 0.50 south, longitude 169.530 east. Originally settled by the Te Aka people, two successive waves of migration created the Banaba we know today. This small isolated island is the tip of a submarine mountain that stands alone, 180 kilometres from its nearest neighbour Nauru. The rest of the world seems to have forgotten it, but the Banaban people have not. The Banabans struggle to survive under two separate Pacific Island nations, and it is crucial that their heritage and ethnic identity are preserved for future generations.

On 28 August 1900, Albert Ellis from the Sydney Office of the British based Pacific Islands Phosphate Company arrived on Banaba, or Ocean Island as it was known in colonial days. Ellis discovered that the island was one of the richest deposits of phosphate rock ever found at that time. He immediately negotiated a deal with the innocent Banaban people to mine their island for the next 999 years for £50 per annum. Mining began in 1900. Japanese forces invaded Banaba in August 1942, and the Banabans suffered greatly

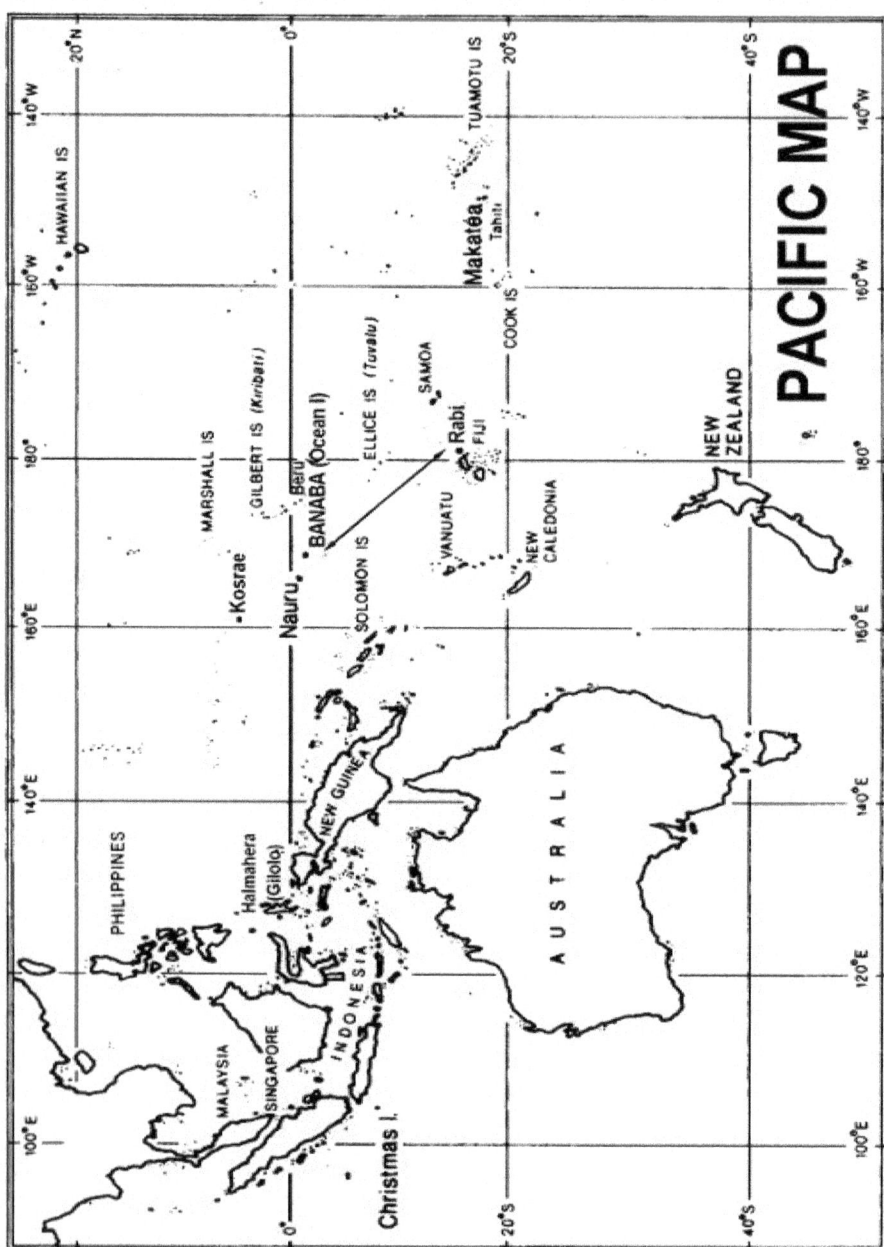

Figure: 1.1. Pacific Island Map

from starvation and other atrocities over the next three years. Most of the community was forcibly removed to labour camps on other Pacific islands: Kosrae, Nauru and Tarawa. A contingent of one hundred and sixty Banaban and Gilbertese workers (during Colonial times, the people were known as Gilbertese, but when the country of Kiribati gained independence in 1979, its people became known as I-Kiribati). These young men were regarded as the fittest and best fishermen and were left behind to supply food for the Japanese troops. They were murdered two days after the war was over. For eighty years, Banaba had been rapaciously mined. Now only 20 hectares remain unmined. Forests of tall coral pinnacles, with some rising to a height of 18 meters, make the island's interior impassable. Masses of rusting mining machinery lie rotting under the hot equatorial sun. A small community lives on the island. Their presence serves as protection against anyone ever taking the island away from them again. The Banaban people now find themselves scattered between their greatly diminished homeland and the faraway Rabi. The Republic of Kiribati governs Banaba. Rabi is governed by the Republic of Fiji.

Raobeia Ken Sigrah is a descendant and clan spokesman for Te Aka and other Banaban clans, a role acknowledged by his elders. The secrecy surrounding Te Aka up to now has prevented the recording of their history. Ken had experienced hopelessness and despair, even spending time in 1979 with fellow Banabans in a jail cell on Banaba itself, when they stood against the further destruction of their homeland by the ever-powerful British Phosphate Commission. The Banabans on Rabi and Banaba now find little of their homeland left unmined. They have lost most of their language. They have seen the plunder and removal of sacred artefacts and relics from village sites. But after a century of abuse and neglect, the tangible links to the past remain. Daily life on Rabi reflects cultural ties to the homeland. From birth until death, customs, events and rituals are founded on identity as Banabans within family clans. Bonds with beloved Banaba, land, water caves and terraces are still keenly felt and cherished and will be passed on to Banaban children wherever they might be until the end of time. This is Banaban heritage! They may be financially poor, but Banabans are spiritually rich.

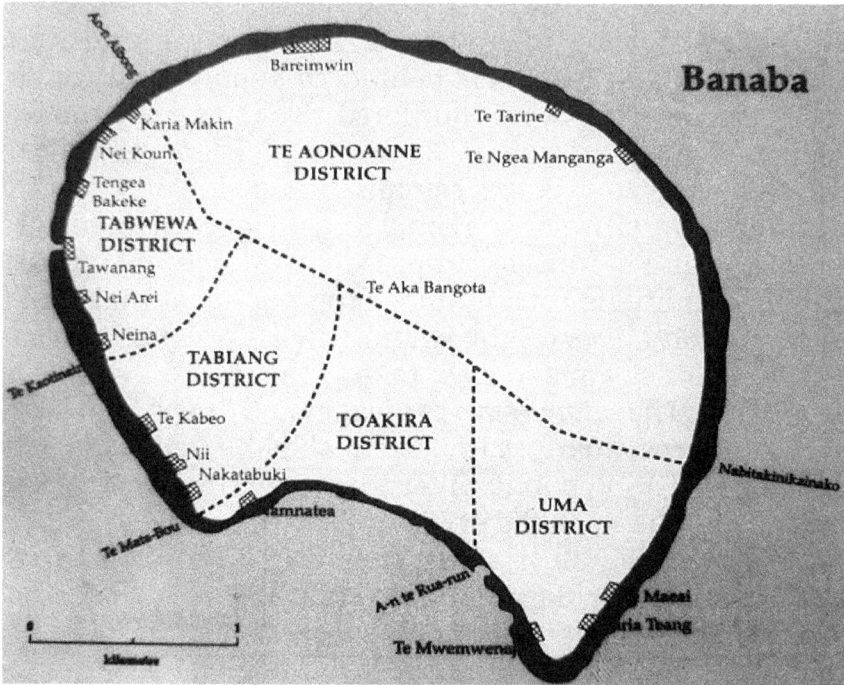

Figure: 1.2. Banaba map, Cartography Unit (RSPAS ANU).

Stacey's personal connection to Banaba stretches over four generations, starting with her great-great-grandfather Henry Williams, who arrived in 1901. He was followed by her great-grandfather John Williams in 1905, her great-grandmother Ella and her grandmother Hazel who was just five years old. Hazel would meet and marry Thomas O'Sullivan, Stacey's grandfather, on the island in 1922. Stacey's history and the history of mining on Banaba are entwined. However, it was not until the discovery in 1989 of her family's old photographs from this early part of Banaban history, that the stories told to her as a young child came to life.

Among Pacific historians, only Maude and Maude (1932, 1994), Lampert (1968) and Peter Anderson (1963) have touched on the subject of Te Aka people. In 1932, the Maude's confused their limited information on the indigenous inhabitants of Banaba with the later history of the Mangati clan, who were descended from the Auriaria clan (as explained further in Chapter 9). The Maude's mistake is understandable, considering the secrecy and silence surrounding Te Aka clan. When Ken and Stacey met Harry Maude in Canberra in November 1997 and heard that Ken was from Te Aka clan, his first words were *'te moa ni kainga!'* (the first hamlet!). He then went on to say that during his time as Lands Commissioner on the island in 1932, while he was researching traditional Banaban history, it was virtually impossible to get information about the Te Aka because of the code of secrecy. The stories of Te Aka people are timeless and have been passed from generation to generation despite the invasions of foreigners and the discovery of phosphate. Because of the secrecy surrounding this clan, this book challenges many previous writings recorded on Banaban history, especially those of Arthur Grimble, former Resident Commissioner for the Gilbert and Ellice Islands (now the independent nations of Kiribati and Tuvalu), and other historians of Kiribati. Ken, who is a descendant of Te Aka clan, obtained approval from the clan elders on Rabi for this project.

This book would not have been possible without their consent as it covers very controversial and taboo subjects relating to matters such as genealogy, ceremonial rites and village sites. Today Te Aka site covers about one-fifth of a hectare and is like an island in the middle of the mined-out interior amidst a forest of limestone pinnacles. On a trip to Banaba, Stacey was fortunate enough to accompany Ken on an excursion to Te Aka as the first I-Matang to visit this sacred site since mining ceased on Banaba in 1979. The incredible difficulties in negotiating and climbing through this dangerous region of the island only seemed to add to the experience of arriving at Te Aka itself. It is a strangely beautiful, eerie place, so silent, left unmined amidst so much destruction.

The authors hope this work clarifies Banaban identity and corrects accounts that align Banabans solely to Kiribati origins. The photographic collections support and document a uniquely Banaba way of life that existed until the Banabans were forcibly removed from their homeland in 1943 by the Japanese. The archival collections contain a wealth of material that has never been published and provide a broader view and aspect of Banaban history. The authors have bequeathed their original collections to the community on Rabi as their legacy in the belief that it will benefit all Banabans in the struggle to preserve Banaban identity in the uncertain and challenging years ahead.

5. Mining around Te Aka site in 1965 (Lampert Collection).

PART ONE:
TE AKA

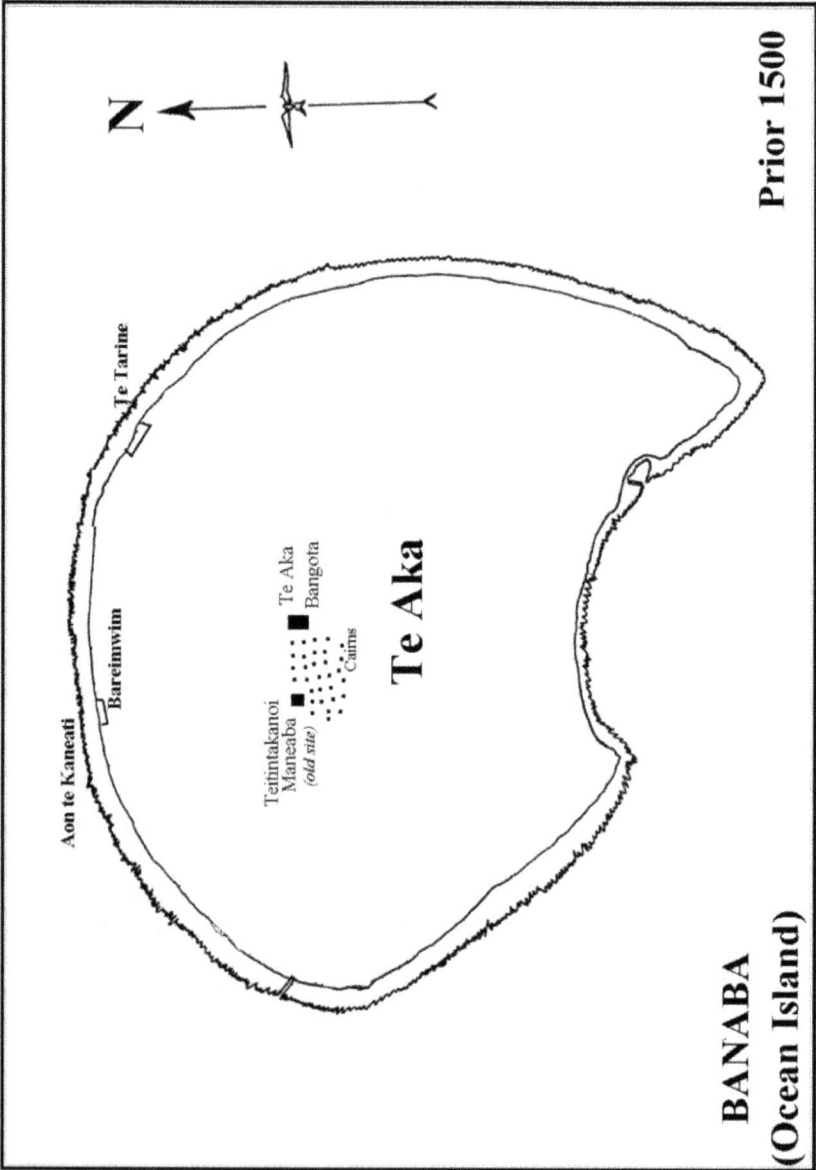

Figure: 1.3. Banaba map prior to 1500 – Te Aka (by R.K. Sigrah).

1: INDIGENOUS PEOPLE OF BANABA

With discrete knowledge and self-contentment, Te Aka clan who were known as sorcerers, regarded Banaba as the centre of the world. They had feelings of freedom and superiority at the very core of their awareness and nucleus of being Te Aka. These feelings still exist in the minds of Banabans today. The word Te Aka means 'the first hamlet', a small group of dwellings inhabited by members of the same family. Commonly referred to in the Banaban language as *'te moa ni kainga,'* this was the place where the senior elder of Te Aka clan resided (see Glossary). Te Aka people view the senior elder of the clan as the person who singularly has the right to guide his people in settling land disputes, as well as in organising burials, marriages, sports and community functions. Leadership within Banaban society is based on a patriarchal system rather than an inherited chieftainship, as often reported by previous historians. (Webster, 1851; Grimble, 1935; Ellis, 1936, as cited in Maude & Maude, 1932, 1994).

Te Aka hamlet was the focus for cultural rites and ceremonies. Because Te Aka practised sorcery, it is still considered taboo to mention even the name of this sacred place. The belief is that the power of Te Aka magic lies in secrecy; therefore, to utter the name will bring a curse upon that person.

Te Aka were land dwellers who knew nothing of ocean seafaring and whose stage of social evolution differed from that of people who arrived during later invasions. Te Aka clan legends support this view (see Chapter 3). The Te Aka had an affinity with the land and the fringing reefs, separate from other Pacific Islanders who are more renowned for their skills in trans-Pacific navigation. The nearest island is Nauru, 180 kilometres to the west. Early European accounts said Banaba lies in an area of the Pacific known as 'no man's land.' Whichever way Te Aka came to Banaba, the island remained remote, close to the equator and with strong equatorial currents. Maude and Maude (1975) stated it was indeed a place "... from which there was no return" (p. 5). In 1994, the Maude's concluded,

> "on linguistic evidence we are told that the first settler on both the Gilberts and Banaba came from Vanuatu (the Banks Group or Efate?). A computer simulation involving ten canoes leaving the Reef Islands of the Banks Group in January resulted in two reaching the Gilberts and one Banaba, the rest going on to the Marshalls ... we can be fairly sure that what Irwin calls the orthodox view of the settlement of eastern Micronesian Islands is at least probable."
>
> Maude's evidence for this statement is found in Bellwood, 1979; Grace, 1964; Irwin, 1992; Grimble MS n.d. as cited, in Maude & Maude, 1994, p. 105.

How do we know Te Aka are the Indigenous People?

The Te Aka clan believe they were the original inhabitants of Banaba. While this issue is difficult to prove by orthodox means, key features of Banaba life and historical facts support this belief:

14

- Te Aka had a distinct appearance and physical stature.
- Te Aka worship of the sun as their totem (Chapter 2).
- Te Aka myths and legends support the claim (Chapter 3).
- The land division of Banaba supports the claim in terms of Te Aka land ownership and their site of the sacred cairns.

6. *Te Karanga*, dancing costumes, including wigs (T.J. McMahon 1919).

The Te Aka people are known to be physically different from all other Banabans. Other evidence is the earlier use of special Te Aka wigs made of thick, black, crinkly hair in the performance of *te karanga* (war spear dance). As the source for this unique type of hair vanished in later years, coconut sennit fibre was used to duplicate this aspect of Te Aka culture (see Photo 6). "They are described as being small bodied, squat, crinkly-haired, large-eared and black-skinned and were skilful in sorcery" (Maude & Maude, 1932, p. 263).

Te Aka ancestors had long jaws, with many of their skulls well preserved in sacred family *bangota* (ancestral shrines) right up until the Banabans were forcibly removed from the island during the Japanese occupation in World War II. There are two sources for this information:

> "They are apparently burial mounds, and at one situated under a mango tree near the site of the former *maneaba* in the hamlet called Te Aka one could see the skulls of both the long-jawed and the short-jawed people through gaps between the stones: at least as late as 1903. Evidently, the Melanesians had inter-married with later arrivals but were still distinguishable by the shape of their jaws" (Maude & Maude, 1994, p. 106).

> "... the skulls referred to are under a low stone cairn and could be seen through gaps between the stones. They were skulls of both 'the long-jawed and short-jawed people.' The cairn was named te Burita, which has the meaning ... 'an enchanted place, dangerous to visit' (Bingham 1908:79) and was situated under a mango tree near the *maneaba* at Te Aka. It was said to be still extant as late as 1963, apparently until the ground surface beneath the tree was bulldozed flat so that workmen's huts could be erected in the shade" (Lampert, 1965, p. 3).

The place of the Burita cairn that Lampert refers to is also known as a sacred site where two large *teitai* (*Calophyllum inophyllum*, also known as the ship trees to Te Aka people) grew. One of the trees is called te Burita, which is the name of a war canoe in one of the Te Aka legends, and the other tree is called te Itimoa, meaning 'first lightning' (Chapter 3).

The Nucleus – Teimanaia

In Te Aka's clan oral history, Teimanaia is considered the godfather, the senior elder of the clan and the very nucleus of Te Aka people. He is renowned throughout history as a 'warrior' and defender of the people. Teimanaia is recorded in Ken Sigrah's family genealogy chart as being sixteen generations ago, which at an average of twenty-five years for each generation, takes Te Aka records and Teimanaia's existence to around the 1500s. However, Te Aka believe their lineage goes far beyond that date (Figure 1.7 in Chapter 4). Records confirm that fifteen generations ago, three Te Aka family groups lived in individual family hamlets. All aspects of culture and tradition were at an inter-family level during this period.

Rituals and Sorcery

In oral history, the Te Aka clan were known to be "peaceful people, who had no concept of cannibalism" (Maude & Maude, 1932). Te Aka clan ritually buried their dead and were "powerful in sorcery, a power they possessed through the worship of their ancestral skulls" (Ellis, 1936; Grimble, 1921; Lampert, 1968). The practices were a shock for invading parties, survivors in drifting canoes or runaway convicts fleeing from convict ships on their way to Australia or Norfolk Island, or beachcombers when they came across Te Aka people for the first time. One of Te Aka legends tells the fate of one of these parties. Imagine entering a *mwenga* (house) in Te Aka and seeing a basket of human bones, retrieved from burial sites, prepared by washing and anointing, and hanging from the roof beam. No wonder Te Aka were viewed by Europeans as savages.

Most visitors to Banaba in the 1800s were Europeans from America and England aboard whaling ships, and evidence of ancestor worship on Banaba was prominent in their accounts. The assumption of 'cannibalism' began at that time. In 1851, John Webster, a passenger aboard the schooner *Wanderer*, observed Banaban men wearing their most valuable ornaments, a necklace made of human teeth. In a log entry dated 3 June 1872, the captain of HMS *Barrosa* stated that several canoes came alongside their ship at Banaba to greet them. One canoe had a human skull lashed to the outrigger, and when they asked the islander for information about the 'skull hunters', no information was forthcoming. It is probable that this man's ancestor had been a great fisherman whose skull was a powerful amulet that empowered his descendant's fishing skills, bringing him great fortune and protection from all perils at sea.

More evidence of ritual burials and ancestral worship of Te Aka was uncovered years later in an archaeological dig of the site in 1965. R.J. Lampert from the Australian National University uncovered the remains of two skeletons. He wrote, "The cranium is completely missing, yet the vertebrae are intact and fully articulated right up to and including the atlas bone ..." Lampert's discovery indicates that Banaban people had sacred burial rituals and traditionally worshipped their ancestors. The skulls were kept as the link for Te Aka to communicate with their *anti*, spirits (see Chapter 2).

Later Arrivals in Banaban History

After Te Aka had settled Banaba, it was invaded twice. The first partitioning of Banaba was known as - *te moa n raeaki* and is commonly known as the arrival of the Auriaria clan. In 1932, Maude and Maude argued that members of this new clan were,

> "...tall, fair-skinned people who, according to the evidence shortly to be published by Mr Grimble, came in a migrating swarm from Gilolo and its neighbouring islands in the East Indies and overran the Gilbert group. A portion of this host, whose ancestor was Auriaria, landed on Banaba and succeeded in overcoming the inhabitants" (p. 264).

Te Aka clan records confirm this invasion, dating it back sixteen generations. Auriaria, in modern times, is considered the head of the Auriaria clan of Tabwewa district. From written recordings, we can place the time of the invasion as around the sixteenth century (see Part Two). From this period, inter-clan participation began, and a new culture evolved. The first invaders brought new customs, new aspects of culture and new blood through marriage to Te Aka people.

Introduction of I-Kiribati culture

Years later, the second partitioning of Banaba, known as *te kauoua n raeaki*, happened with the arrival of a woman called Nei Anginimaeao from Beru Atoll, and her party:

> "Whether this tradition is true or not, Nei Angi-ni-maeao came with her husband to Banaba, bringing with her a great many of her Beru relations led by Na Kouteba her brother, Na Mani-ni-mate, and Nei Te-borata" (Maude & Maude, 1932, p. 265).

Genealogical records suggest this invasion occurred thirteen generations ago, in the latter part of the seventeenth century. The Auriaria clan invited these driftaways to stay and make Banaba their home.

Te Aka records identify four early elders or leaders. Three of the leaders formed a new clan and district. They were Nei Anginimaeao, another woman Nei Teborata, and a man Maninimate. This partitioning of Tabwewa district into three new districts was the most crucial aspect of their arrival. The other man in the party, Kouteba, did not begin a new clan or district but married into Te Aka clan through a woman called Nei Teanibuti. Because of the sorcery that still existed at the time of this later settlement, the newcomers feared to utter the words 'Te Aka' in case they became cursed. The name of the northern region was changed to Te Aonoanne district, meaning 'that place'!

The conflict over Banaban identity

The foundation of Te Aka clan as a separate identity from the other clans on Banaba and later arrivals from Kiribati has long been a focus of argument among the Banaban people, and one which, in the later part of the 1970s during the Banabans' struggle for independence, conveniently fell on deaf ears. Even Maude contradicts himself in his writings, stating that the Banabans were a unique race while referring to only customs and legends that the I-Kiribati introduced to Banaba after the arrival of Nei Anginimaeao.

In 1975, Maude made a statement, 'The Relationship between the Banabans and Gilbertese', to the late Chairman of the Rabi Council of Leaders, Rotan Tito, and tabled as evidence in the civil lawsuit against the British government. In his statement, Maude endorsed the origins of the Banaban people:

> "The evidence shows that the autochthones population of Ocean Island was not Gilbertese ...

The real answer to the question of whether the Banabans are or are not Gilbertese lies, however, in the fact that regardless of racial origins, language and culture, they have never been included in the geographical or political sphere of the Gilbert Islands.

> In this inter-looking [sic] world of the Gilbertese, Ocean Island and the Banabans, situated far to the west, had no part. Forgotten in Gilbertese tradition, unrecorded in the Gilbertese genealogies, it may be doubted if a single Gilbertese Islander was aware of the existence of the Banabans at the time of their first contact with Europeans. Ocean Island was no more part of the Gilbert Islands than Greenland was part of

Norway a century or two after the Scandinavian voyages had ceased. Like Nauru, it was a dead-end reached by occasional driftaways from the Gilbert Islands, but from which there was no return.

It would seem honest to recognise that Ocean Island was, in fact, incorporated as part of the Gilbert Group solely by a unilateral decision on the part of the British Government in 1900, subsequent to and consequent on the discovery of lucrative deposits of phosphate on the island."

The skeletal remains taken from Te Aka site by Lampert and examined by G.C. Schofield from the Department of Anatomy at Monash University, Melbourne, also indicate that Te Aka people were in no way related to the I-Kiribati. "This is a right-sided femur from an adult female. The bone is NOT obviously Polynesian" (Lampert, 1968, p. 17). In the mythology of the southern atolls of Kiribati, it is well documented that the forefathers of their people came from Samoa, giving them a Polynesian heritage.

Maude supports this theory in his 1975 statement, even claiming Grimble had the same opinion:

"At a later date, to the best of my recollection in 1935, Mr P.D. Macdonald, now Public Service Commissioner, Fiji, and I conducted a series of standard anthropometric measurements on those Banabans considered by themselves to be of stock unmixed with Gilbertese blood. These numbered 70 in all and though the results cannot be regarded as in any way conclusive they did appear to suggest a difference in certain facial measurements and indices when compared with a control group on Beru. At all events, it was commonly asserted by the late Sir Arthur Grimble and others that a typical Banaban was distinguishable in physical appearance from a Gilbertese, and this I consider to have been the case in

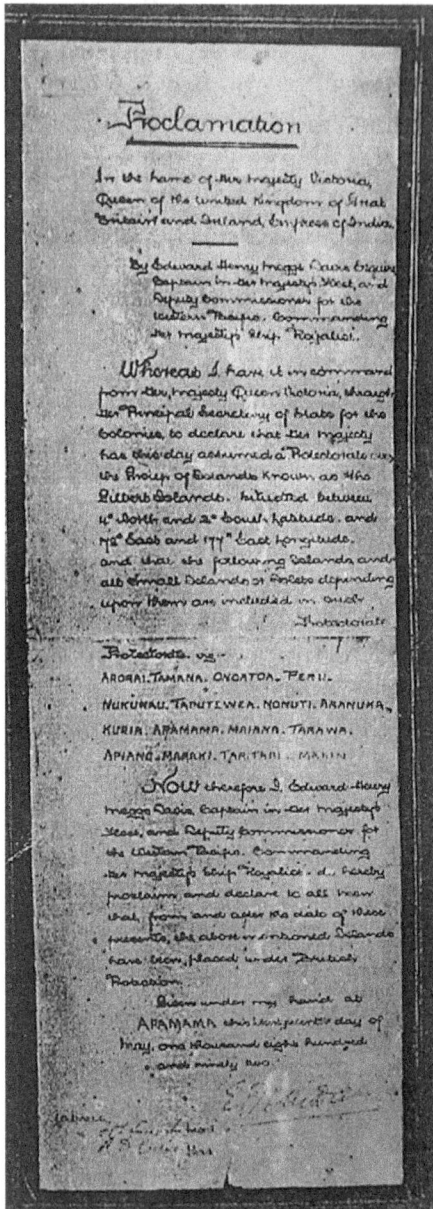

Figure: 1.4. Handwritten proclamation 1892 Gilbert and Ellice Island Colony.

a number of the older generation, whose features appeared quite distinctive."

Maude also explains how he became convinced about the separate Banaban identity:

"The view that the Banabans were Gilbertese was indeed uncritically accepted by myself during my early years of residence in the Gilbert and Ellice Islands Colony, and it was only after detailed study that it became apparent that, like almost every community the world over, they, in fact, represented a racial mixture, in which the Gilbertese component was a relatively recent overlay on a basically non-Gilbertese stock; and that in any case the Banabans never had at any time formed a part of the Gilbert Islands, whether geographically, politically or through social cohesion" (Maude, 1975, statement).

Others have conveniently distorted or ignored Banaban history to suit the politics of the times or the financial needs of foreign powers.

22

PROCLAMATION

In the name of Her Majesty Victoria, Queen of the United Kingdom of Great Britain and Ireland, Empress of India.

By Edward Henry Meggs Davis Esquire, Captain in Her Majesty's Fleet, and Deputy Commissioner for the Western Pacific. Commanding Her Majesty's Ship Royalist.

Whereas I have it in command from Her Majesty Queen Victoria, through Her Principal Secretary of State for the Colonies, to declare that Her Majesty has this day assumed a Protectorate over the Group of Islands known as the Gilbert Islands. Situated between 4 degrees North and 3 degrees South latitude and 172 degrees East and 177 degrees East longitude and that the following Islands and all small Islands or Islets depending upon them are included in such Protectorate.

Protectorate viz: -

ARORAI. TAMANA. ONOATOA. PERU. NUKUNAU. TAPUTEWEA. NONUTI. ARANUKA. KURIA. APAMAMA. MAIANA. TARAWA. APIANG. MARAKI. TARITARI. MAKIN.

Now therefore I, Edward Henry Meggs Davis, Captain in Her Majesty's Fleet, and Deputy Commissioner for the Western Pacific. Commanding Her Majesty's ship Royalist do hereby proclaim and declare to all men that, from and after the date of these present, the above mentioned Islands have been placed under British Protection.

Given under my hand at APAMAMA this twenty ninth day of May, one thousand eight hundred and ninety two.

Signed: E.H.M. Davis

Witnessed: (2) Unknown Signatures.

Figure: 1.5. Text version proclamation 1892 Gilbert and Ellice Island Protectorate.

WESTERN PACIFIC HIGH COMMISSION.

ANNEXATION OF OCEAN ISLAND, OTHERWISE PAANOPA.

By His Excellency Sir GEORGE THOMAS MICHAEL O'BRIEN, Knight Commander of the Most Distinguished Order of Saint Michael and Saint George, Her Britannic Majesty's High Commissioner for the Western Pacific.

[L.S.]   G. T. M. O'BRIEN.

THE Secretary of State for the Colonies having issued to the Pacific Islands Company, Limited, a Licence for the collection of Guano and other fertilising substances from OCEAN ISLAND, otherwise PAANOPA, it is hereby notified that the provisions of the Pacific Order in Council, 1893, and of such of the Queen's Regulations made in accordance therewith as apply to the islands of the Gilbert and Ellice Protectorate are extended to all persons living or being within the limits of the said Island, which from this date shall be included within the jurisdiction of the Resident Commissioner and Deputy Commissioner of the Gilbert and Ellice Islands Protectorate aforesaid.

Whereof let all men take notice, and order themselves accordingly.

By Command,
M. KING,
Secretary.

Office of the High Commissioner for the Western Pacific,
Suva, Fiji, 28th November, 1900.

Suva: Edward John March, Government Printer.—1900.

Figure: 1.6. Copy of official annexation of Ocean Island otherwise Paanopa, 28 November 1900. The contract to mine phosphate was first dated 3 May 1900, six months before this official annexation of the island.

2: TOTEM AND *KAUTI* (MAGIC RITUAL)

The totem of Te Aka is the sun. It is the very foundation of Te Aka spiritual belief, invoked through special rituals or sorcery, called *tabunea* in the worship of their ancient gods. The Te Aka believe and trust that from nature, the sun is their main source of power and the very source of life itself. The Te Aka invoke their sun totem when the need arises and during certain days of the lunar cycle. These particular rituals can correspond to the time of sports and certain cultural events, such as Banaban boxing, frigate bird snaring, tuna pole fishing, and performing the *karanga*. The totem's powers can also be called upon to assist with aspects of personal life, including seducing a lover, cursing or killing an enemy, healing the sick or bringing rain.

A Distinctive Totem on Banaba

Te Aka people were from a "fire cult," Maude and Maude (1932), meaning that they worshipped the sun or fire, which was a very different practice from later inhabitants. Te Aka were the only people on the island to have the sun as a totem. Maude inaccurately defined their gods as Na Areau (male spider) and Na Tabakea (male turtle). He associates them with a fire cult. The other Banaban clans worship animals or fish: Na Tabakea is from certain hamlets within Tabwewa district; Na Areau is from the descendants of the Auriaria clan. Another totem, Nei Tituabine (female stingray god), is from the clans which descend from Nei Anginimaeao. These totems are also worshipped in other islands of Kiribati and were introduced into Banaban society through the arrival of Auriaria and Nei Anginimaeao from Beru, in traditional legends from the Kiribati group. The people of a particular clan claim to be descended from their totem, which is usually an animal or plant form. In their belief, their people evolved from their totems over the generations. Therefore, clans with these types of totems have a natural bond and affinity to their symbol. They believe they can draw energy, healing, protection and even magical powers from their totems to destroy or restore life.

Practising *te Kauti* – Enhancing powers with ancestral skulls

Because of the secrecy of Te Aka magic or *kauti*, it was forbidden to talk in detail about the rites involved. Here are descriptions of some essential elements at a general level. The Te Aka clan believe that the magical powers from their totem can be made even stronger by using ancestral skulls to perform certain rites and rituals. During Maude's first visit to Banaba in 1932, he mentions the fear and superstition surrounding the small black folk or autochthones from the central plateau and how strongly the other Banabans feared them and their powers of sorcery:

> "A portion of this host, whose ancestor was Auriaria, landed on Banaba and succeeded in overcoming the inhabitants, 'casting them into the sea,' though they had a wholesome fear of their sorcery ... However, it would appear from local tradition that not all of the black folk were killed for a remnant appear to have been driven to the central plateau of the island ...

Until a few years ago the people of Mangati lived on the uplands above the present village of Tabwewa village and in their territory may still be seen the cairns of rough stones which local tradition states to have been connected with the fire-worship of the autochthones" (Maude & Maude, 1932, p. 264).

Maude also states that the Mangati no longer lived in the place in question, but his description perfectly fits the indigenous Te Aka. By 1947, from a BPC land survey of what all Banabans consider as their accurate land holdings, records clearly show the boundaries of the hamlets involved (Chapter 9). It was common knowledge that Te Aka site included sacred cairns. Archaeologist Lampert (Chapter 29) and retired BPC surveyor and engineer Peter Anderson (Chapter 32) verify our view.

Learning the Ways of Men

This totem plays a vital role in the initiation of young men. At puberty, the boys are sent to the house or quarters made especially for this purpose. These quarters belong to the eldest male member of the clan, who is usually a great-grandfather or great-grand-uncle. He is respected in the hamlet as the tutor and teaches the customs of men, such as boxing, fishing, snaring frigate birds and *kauti*. The sun totem is used as the primary link to perform these rituals. The young men are taught to believe that the powers they invoke from their totem will reflect on all the upcoming events in their lives and the lives of their family, including the traditional duties they will need to perform according to custom. If they fail to pass the initiation or trials, these boys will never be considered men and will not be able to take up any role of authority within the family clan. Unable to perform the essential rituals associated with *kauti*, their place within Te Aka society would be questioned.

Women's role in performing *tabunea*

Only women perform certain *tabunea* rites, mostly related to making magic oils for healing and all matters of daily life, such as healing a sick child, seducing a lover, or gathering water. Unlike men, they do not worship at the terraces but attend the family's *bangota* to evoke the power of their ancestors. Like the men, they look to their elders (female elders in this case) to lead and teach them in these special rituals. The men also rely on the women's expertise to make their *bunna* (sacred garland made of certain leaves) and oil for their sacred rites.

Rules when performing the rites

The taboo rites of the Te Aka are still performed and passed down today as decreed by custom. Only the family that has the inherited right to perform them can speak in detail on this taboo subject. The following rules apply to the rites:

- Men are not allowed to sleep with women for three days before the rite is carried out.
- Women who are menstruating are not allowed to touch or participate in any part of the ritual or ceremony involving anything to do with the totem.
- The rites should be performed only between three and five o'clock in the morning. If the sun has already risen, then it is too late to conduct the ceremony.
- The performance of the actual rites should be known only to the participants. No one else outside the group should be aware of the event. This is why the term 'taboo' is used to describe the rites.

Material needed for the rites

Certain materials are gathered in preparation for the rituals.

These items should be safeguarded and put inside the home of the individual in charge of conducting the rite. They are essential for evoking the magical powers of the *anti* (spirits):

- The leaves of certain medicinal plants, such as *te uri* (*Guettarda speciosa*), which also has a fragrant white blossom and *te kakoko* (first shoot of the coconut leaf). Today *te non* (*Morinda citrifolia*), found on Rabi, can be used for its potent medicinal qualities in these rites.
- Other roots can be used according to the needs of the ritual to be performed.
- Scented coconut oil that has been specially made for the rite and not used for any other purpose.
- The most essential material for the ritual is an ancestral skull, which evokes the full spiritual power of the items mentioned above. Without the skull, the ritual is still possible but will not be as strong or powerful.

How to recognise someone conducting *kauti*

During the performance of *kauti*, the man will wear a *te mao* (*Scaevola kownigi*) leaf in his pierced earlobe. *Te mao* plant is a bushy shrub found amongst rocks around the shoreline. It is usually yellow and used for local medicine. The ear is pierced, generally on the same side as the performer's preferred hand, which is typically the right side. He wears the leaf on this side to signify that he is conducting *kauti* for an upcoming boxing tournament or other competitions, such as frigate bird snaring or tuna pole fishing competitions during later times. Wearing the leaf in both ears signifies that he is in the process of *maie kauti* (dancing magic ritual). Wearing this leaf is an essential aspect of the ritual as it signifies to the women and other members of the district that this man is currently performing *kauti* magic and cannot be interrupted. Everyone in the community, including the women and children, knows how the performer should be treated according to tradition. Menstruating women must keep away from him so that they do not weaken the power he is evoking from the spirits.

7. Te Tabo ni Kauti, private terrace for *te kauti* ritual (Williams Collection 1901–1931).

The Link Between Te Aka and their Ancestral Powers

Te Aka oral history refers to the special powers of one man named Teimanaia, who Te Aka revere as their main source of magic power. His magical feats are legendary.

He is known as a great warrior who defended his clan and his island during reported invasions before the arrival of the Auriaria clan. Because of Teimanaia's standing within Te Aka society, succeeding generations of Te Aka people preserved his skull after his death.

After generations of reverent care, a European, Dr Gould, took the skull away from our people. BPC records show he was the Medical Officer of Health for the Ocean Island Government jointly with the BPC duties between 20 May 1918 and 1933.

According to Ken's grandparents, the doctor learnt of Teimanaia's skull through one of his Banaban workers, Tekiera, who was working under Dr Gould as a dresser. Tekiera was one of Te Aka clan himself and broke clan secrecy by telling his employer of the existence of Teimanaia's skull and how it was much larger than other human skulls that

8. Dr. Ebon C. Gould removed Teimanaia's skull from Banaba 1933 (passport image).

were kept. Dr Gould became fascinated with the story and asked Tekiera to bring the skull to him. Tekiera must have wanted to please his employer and removed the skull without permission from the clan's sacred *bangota*. On his farewell night, Dr Gould allegedly used trickery to get Tekiera drunk enough to allow the doctor to take the skull away. From that moment in history, everything is said to have changed. In Banaban philosophy, only when Teimanaia's skull is returned to its rightful resting place back in the homeland of Te Aka will the prosperity return.

A ray of hope?

The following story comes from the descendant of Namoti, who was one of the elders of Te Aka clan. Namoti had the right to make the sacred *bunna* and oil, which his descendants still make today. The family continue to have strong spiritual ties to the powers of Teimanaia. Teimanaia's skull was removed from the land of a man called Tanaera, which was in the hamlet of Teinangina. The man's brother was Tekiera, the man responsible for giving away the skull from the family's *bangota*. In 1961, Tanaera's son Tuteariki had a dream where Teimanaia came to him in spirit form and told him that his skull was taken to the United States. Tuteariki recounted how the tears would fall from the sockets of Teimanaia's skull when he heard people say that his skull looked like an animal's. Because of this story, the Te Aka clan believe Teimanaia's skull is on public display in an American museum. To date, all efforts to confirm this belief have been unsuccessful. The Te Aka clan hope that through the publication of this story, Teimanaia's skull will be found.

Note: Doctor Gould's movements after he left Banaba with Teimanaia's skull have been traced back to Australia and the United States. After extensive investigations, the whereabouts of the skull has not been located. The search continues.

3: MYTHS AND LEGENDS

Banabans have recorded their traditional history through oral methods. Part of typical family life is for *te unimane* (old men) and *te unaine* (old women) to sit around in their leisure time and recall the stories or myths and legends of Banaban heroes and their feats of courage. These various stories contain the history of the Banaban people. Because they have been passed down from early times, generation after generation, some of the myths and legends have evolved and changed. Such stories are a rich source of information. For example, how Te Aka on Banaba was invaded by the Auriaria clan from Gilolo in the Indonesian archipelago (Halmahera), and Nei Anginimaeao and her party from Beru in the Kiribati Group were allowed to settle on the island (Maude & Maude, 1932, 1994).

Over the years, the cultural source of each tale has become confused, causing misunderstandings for our young generation and threatening Banaban identity. Academics, governments and others assume the Banabans are culturally just an extension of the I-Kiribati. From the time that Nei Anginimaeao and her party arrived from Beru, I-Kiribati culture began to affect Banaba. The introduction of missionaries to Banaba saw another significant change to the culture, with the first Bible translated and written in the

9. *Uma ni kauti*, small day shed and *mwenga*, house at Tabwewa terrace (Doutch Collection 1914).

Kiribati language. This was the beginning of the end of the unique Banaban language (Chapter 23). After the discovery of phosphate on Banaba and the influx of so many I-Kiribati and Tuvaluan workers, intermarriage increased, making the cultural differences harder to define. Despite all these outside influences, Banabans have claimed a distinct culture and identity.

For the first time, the myths and legends of Te Aka clan are recorded in written form to ensure that these precious parts of ancient oral history are preserved for posterity. These must not be confused with other clan legends that are retold in later chapters.

The Secrets of the Water Caves

Although the date of this event is unknown, Te Aka legends

tell of one of the worst droughts to befall Banaba, when people were desperate for water. One of the men from Te Aka clan was sent out to look for water, and before he left, the magic ritual was performed to help this man on his important journey.

As this man walked around Banaba, it became apparent that no water could be found anywhere on the island. So, he called to the four spirits from the four corners of the world and asked them to help him with his task. One of the spirits came to him in the form of *te manai* (land crab). He noticed the crab's legs were wet and instantly knew the crab had been in the water. He followed the crab to a rock. When he lifted the rock, he found the opening to a cave and went in. When he crawled in, his way was blocked by a large *te aii* (coconut crab). The spirits told him his way was barred to the cave because he was a man and only women were permitted to enter. The spirits also told him that the woman should be naked and adorned only with a *bunna* around her neck and anointed with coconut oil. The woman should carry a dry coconut leaf for her flaming torch to see her way in the cave, and two coconut shells should be tied together so she can sling them over her shoulder or arm. She must leave *te bunna* on a particular rock so that the coconut crab would allow her clear passage down to the water level in the cave. He returned to the village. The women followed his instructions. They found water and were able to survive the drought safely. That was how the first *bangabanga* (water cave) was discovered.

The cave where this event is said to have happened is called Na Motinriri and is owned by the descendants of Te Aka clan today. Since the first discovery of *bangabanga* on Banaba, the people have discovered entrances to more caves. Each new cave was on private land holdings and had its own history. These *bangabanga* could supply water for approximately twelve months. Due to phosphate mining, many of these sacred caves were destroyed, and a significant part of history was lost forever through the bulldozer's blade.

Te Tabunea (Magic) to Bring Rain

One of the greatest fears of Te Aka in the olden days was drought, which brought death. When the dry season befell Banaba, people took it as an omen of impending catastrophe. They began to worry, would it be the year the drought would hit the island, how long would it last, and how could they best survive it?

A legend recalls the *tabunea* or special powers of 'bringing rain' for the Te Aka people after all the drinkable water from the *bangabanga* was gone, and the rain clouds dropped their precious water far offshore. So, the story begins: Nei Kabuta was the daughter of Na Itirakabuta (See Chapter 4, Figure 1.7). She had two older brothers: the eldest was Na Raobeia, and the second was Na Moti. According to the legend, if drought struck, the people went to see the old man Na Itirakabuta in his hamlet and told him they were desperate for water. They brought their offerings to him according to custom: coconut shell to carry water, food, pandanus mat, or any other item acceptable as a gift. Then Na Itirakabuta took three days to prepare everything before the actual *tabunea* could be evoked. The old man then called his three children and, with their help, performed the following ritual. Nei Kabuta was seated while the eldest brother, Na Raobeia, cut the ends of her long hair. The younger brother, Na Moti, caught the hair, for it was taboo for it to touch the ground. The secret of evoking this *tabunea* lies in the ritual that the old man performed, but the cutting of Nei Kabuta's hair triggered *te anti* to cause the rain to fall. Once the hair was cut, the rain fell, life returned to normal, and the feasting and celebrations that followed were the focus for the Te Aka people.

This rite is not performed unless all else has failed and is a matter of life or death. A saying in our language, *'Ea baka karaun Nei Kabuta!'* means 'Kabuta's rain has fallen!', an idiom for 'Life is back again!' In modern times our young people may quote the saying, but they may not know the meaning or that it comes from a Te Aka legend. It is not uncommon to overhear an elder, especially old women proud of this ancestral story, to whisper as rain begins to fall, *'Ea baka karaun Nei Kabuta!'* It has become a way of thinking that to talk about rain is to talk about life itself, a sacred subject to Te Aka.

Studying the growth rings on old coconut trees on the island supports the theory that droughts occurred in seven-year cycles. Historians such as Maude and Maude 1932, and Ellis 1936 document a Great Drought in the late 1870s, just before the arrival of te I–Matang and the discovery of phosphate on the island.

The Feat of Teimanaia

Te Aka legend states that before Auriaria and his clan came to Banaba, a group of people from an unknown destination tried to land on the island. As the large seafaring canoe came near Banaba with seven passengers aboard, two women and five men circled the island to see if Banaba was inhabited. They approached the northern side of the island to a place the Te Aka called Bareimwim, where people launched their canoes. They noticed a lone man standing on the seashore. He was tall and dressed in a war costume. They realised Banaba was inhabited and wondered how they could best negotiate with this man to safely land. They thought the safest move was to send one of the women in their party to sweet-talk the man into letting them land. As soon as their canoe entered the passage, the man on shore walked forward to meet them at the edge of the reef. The woman jumped out of the canoe and approached the man. Before she could utter a word, he struck her with a single blow from his club and killed her. Where she fell on the surrounding jagged reef, her body changed into beautiful white sand. This location, called Nei Tabikebike, means Miss Sandy Spot.

The other people in the canoe realised that they had to fight for their lives. One of the men jumped out of the canoe and began to fight with the man on the reef. He was also struck dead, and his body took the form of a rock in the shape of a shark's tail. This rock was called Na Bukiinibakoa, which means Mr Shark's Tail. The surviving woman jumped out of the canoe and tried to escape from the man on the reef. She was also struck dead. Her body turned into a rock in the shape of a woman's fringe of hair called Nei Korobaro, which means Miss Fringe.

The next man made his way past his fallen companions but also failed to reach the shoreline. After being struck dead, his body also turned into a rock, this time in the form of Na Bobubua, which means Mr Knee Striker. Knee strikers are rocks in the Bareimwim canoe passage, which sit just below the water line at mid-tide. Many people walking along this passage have had the painful experience of hurting their knees on these rocks.

The third man suffered the same fate in endeavouring to get to the shore. Where he fell, his body turned into the rock form of Na Katokirama, which means Mr Forehead Striker. Again, this simple word explains the overhanging rocks found on this part of the beach on Banaba.

The fourth man was turned into a rock called Na Ngongoaku, Mr Backscratcher. The last man made it right to the edge of the shore, to a place called Teinangina, which is the boundary of the first land belonging to Te Aka people. He suffered the same fate as his fallen companions, and his body took on the form of a rock with the shape of an exposed or opened backside. He was called Na Ureki, meaning Mr Open Backside.

Today on Banaba, all these rocks can still be found at Bareimwim canoe passage, with the same names. They stand in a line along the passage and show where the individuals are said to have fallen. According to Te Aka mythology, the person fighting these invaders was none other than our ancestral father, Teimanaia.

How Na Kouteba from Beru Married into Te Aka Clan

Legend says that when Nei Anginimaeao and her driftaways (three other people) from Kiribati arrived on Banaba in a canoe from Beru in Kiribati. While she formed the Tabiang clan, Nei Teborata formed the Toakira clan, and Na Maninimate formed the Uma clan. The fourth person, Na Kouteba, married Nei Teanibuti of Te Aka clan.

Te Aka genealogical charts support this legend. The story endorses the clan's belief that Nei Teanibuti is a descendant of Te Aka people. Her marriage to Na Kouteba is the first-time outside blood was introduced to the clan. It also confirms that Na Kouteba had no birthright to the inherited roles of Te Aka people. His children, however, through their mother's side, inherited the birthright to continue the spiritual and clan roles of the Te Aka (see Chapter 4). Na Kouteba's relationship with Te Aka through marriage is a significant facet of the legend, which has caused much debate among the Banabans, even in Kiribati. In modern times people have tried to distort history by claiming that Na Kouteba was the ancestral leader of Te Aka people. Kouteba only joined Te Aka clan through marriage and has no ancestral blood relationship to the original inhabitants of Banaba.

Learning New Skills from the Invaders

The people of Te Aka were reputed to be primitive people, less advanced than the later invaders and settlers. They were greatly feared for their powers of sorcery, yet their isolation from the outside world made them timid and shy. The first known invaders, the Auriaria clan, brought with them many new customs, ideas and inventions. Although Te Aka did not readily mix with these new arrivals and kept a discreet distance, they were intrigued by what they saw. The following legends retell what the Te Aka observed from their hiding places and tried to copy them.

The first trip abroad for Te Aka

One day some of the Auriaria clan prepared to sail away from Banaba on their big canoe. When Te Aka saw the Auriaria travelling away, they returned to their hamlets in the central uplands of the island and thought about beginning their own journey. They collected a party from their district and prepared food and provisions for a sea journey. Instead of travelling in a canoe, they climbed two big *te itai*, the two largest trees found on the northern coastal side of Banaba in the region of Teinangina. They believed they could travel away from Banaba by sitting upon these big trees. The trees were about 800 meters from their hamlets. Peter Anderson (1963) also referred to these special trees as "*teitai*, ship tree of Te Aka people." They sat for months. Before the trip, they had said their *tia kabo* (goodbye) and had shed farewell tears just as they would have for any long journey. With word from their people that the other party had arrived back, they gladly went back to their hamlets to the delight of their loved ones. Their triumphant return finished with great rejoicing and feasting as if the journey had happened.

Body surfing the waves

Another new experience for Te Aka was to witness the invader's body surfing. They realised this practice was great fun and were keen to learn this new skill. Because they could

40

not travel down to the shore for fear of meeting face to face with the new invaders, they decided to body surf on dry land. They noticed, in Tabwewa district where the new invaders had settled, that when a surfer had ridden a sound wave, the spectators shouted, *'E maoto naona!'* (his waves have broken!). They decided that someone should demonstrate and called for an instructor. He climbed the roof of the highest building in the district. Which happened to be the *maneaba,* and slid from the top of the roof to the ground. The spectators complimented their rider by calling out, *'E maoto naona!'* Unfortunately, their poor rider had broken his neck on landing, but this was part of the new sport for Te Aka spectators. Everyone enjoyed the game, and victims who were hurt or died during the event were regarded as heroes.

How to use fish traps

The Te Aka people witnessed some of the Auriaria clan using fish traps made from sticks. The fishermen took the traps out to sea, weighed them with a large rock, and sunk them below the water. The witnesses decided to give the rest of their people a demonstration of this new fishing skill so that they could gain experience with it. They took one of their men down to the shore, tied a rock to his feet, then carried him out to the reef's outer edge and let him sink beneath the waves. All the spectators then returned to their hamlets in the uplands. They waited for news from observers near the Auriaria camp that their fishermen had brought back their catch from the fish traps. When Te Aka learned of their return and the amount of fish caught, they knew it was time to return to the seashore and check their fish trap. They pulled in their fish trap and found that the human bait had gone. It was a moment of great rejoicing, for the Te Aka believed that the fish trap had proved a perfect invention, for the fish had enjoyed eating the bait.

Swaying trees dance

The swaying tree dance legend shows how Te Aka people started integrating with the Auriaria invaders. A young Te Aka man became engaged to a girl from the Auriaria clan. The wedding day was usually decided by the seasons of the moon, with the engagement period central in the preparation of the bride and groom for the wedding ritual. Following the introduced customs of the Auriaria people, Te Aka were told that their young man should go to the girl's family in Tabwewa district during this period to learn the customary dance to perform during the wedding ceremony. This practice was new to Te Aka, but they agreed to accept this proposal so that the wedding ceremony could proceed. Each day the boy had to leave home and make his way from Te Aka down to Tabwewa on the coast.

One day the young man was late leaving home. Halfway down the track, he realised he was hungry, so he decided to stop and sit down in the shade of the big *te itai* trees to eat the meal his family had prepared for him. As he sat there, the afternoon breeze began to pick up, and he noticed the smooth swaying of the tree branches around him. Because he already had lessons in the new forms of dancing, it came to his mind that these new dances looked like the movement of the trees in the breeze.

At this point, he began to dance, imitating the swaying trees around him. Another thought dawned as he practised his dancing, why go all the way down to Tabwewa when he could practice here closer to home? He was already uncomfortable travelling so far from home and having to mix with so many outsiders, something he was not used to from his upbringing in an isolated environment. Over the next three days, he spent each day dancing in harmony with the trees, convinced that he was learning the proper dance needed for his upcoming nuptials. He was satisfied that he had saved time and effort and that his prospective in-laws

42

would be proud of his efforts. On the fourth day, the girl's parents sent word to Te Aka village that this young man had not shown up for his practice sessions. On hearing the news, the young man's elders could not understand what had happened to him each day. They demanded to know where he had been for the past three days. The young man replied that he had been practising his dancing in harmony with the trees between the two districts. They told him that the dancing trees could not be his tutors, as they were never part of the original agreement for the wedding plans. They made him return to the proper practice session, and he could not understand the anger of the girl's parents when he believed he was doing them such a favour.

This legend was retold by one of the elders whose wife is a descendant of the young man in the story.

From the information provided by the elders, the dances of Te Aka people were war dances introduced after the arrival of Auriaria clan. These war dances are called *te karanga* (war spear dance), and *te karanga are e uarereke* (war club dance) (see Chapter 12).

Te Karanga Are E Uarereke (The War Club Dance)

Te karanga are e uarereke is a Te Aka re-enactment of the land disputes that began after the arrival of Auriaria. The dance is performed only by men, usually in pairs. Even though it is an aggressive dance style, it has no connection with the war spear dance, *te karanga*. The war club dance imitates two men arguing and fighting over land boundaries (Appendix 10). In the *te karanga*, all the dancers interact in complicated movements to imitate a full–scale battle. The dancer in the *te karanga are e uarereke* holds a war club in both hands, and the object of the dance is to strike the partner, who blocks the blows with his club. It is a well–timed, well–choreographed dance with intricate moves performed only with the opposite partner. The music backing for this dance comes from the chanting and stamping of the feet of the dancers.

There is very little known regarding the dances of the Auriaria clan. They were regarded as seafarers and warriors. Their cultural influence eventually merged with Te Aka clan, especially after a few generations of intermarriage. Many more dances were introduced to the Banaban people after the arrival of Nei Anginimaeao nearly a century later. Banaban dancing on Rabi has evolved from its original war dances into more flowing movements, especially among women. The men have adopted more aggressive movements based on self-defence. Their actions could compare with what we see in current forms of martial arts in western society.

These four simple tales above are only a few of many Te Aka stories that provide firsthand experiences of how an ancient people first came into contact with a different culture. These stories support the view that the indigenous Te Aka were different from those who evolved in later times.

4: GENEALOGY

In Banaban ancestral belief, genealogy is integral to traditional life because it is crucial to the clan's legal system. This system is the basis of everyday life at the hamlet level and for complex issues such as settling land disputes and inter-clan rivalry. In Banaban society, for a person to earn the respect of others, they must be acquainted with all aspects of tradition and culture. A person can only achieve this knowledge by knowing his or her family's genealogy and the position and duty that individuals hold within society inherited at birth. In other words, to know one's genealogy is to know one's birthright, thus one's identity, within the complex structure of the Banaban clan system.

Clan roles and duties are performed to exact standards and in defined ways. From special occasions to seemingly menial tasks, participation depends on lineage. Duties include garlanding the strangers, calling games, holding village meetings, and catching fish. In olden times, particular clans were responsible for how the village was run and maintained. For instance, one family within a clan was in charge of trimming the leaves on the roof of the district's *maneaba* (community meeting house). Another family within the same clan was responsible for picking up the leaves and clearing the pathways within the hamlets. A third family could have the specific duty of cleaning the floor and pandanus mats within the *maneaba*. Other families could not get involved or interfere with these defined duties.

Today, a visitor to a Banaban hamlet might feel the urge to assist an elderly man or woman struggling to clear a path. Offering assistance, however, goes against the intricate workings of Banaban culture. To provide help for that person is to insult the individual's family, who is proud of their inherited duties. In Banaban tradition, all duties and responsibilities are highly regarded, signifying position within the clan and society.

Clan duty as a birthright

When the first child is born in a clan, he or she inherits the right to perform the duties of the mother's and the father's sides of the family. If the father, for instance, is a trimmer of the *maneaba* leaves and the mother is the sweeper of the *maneaba* floor, the eldest child of the couple has the right to perform both tasks but can only undertake one duty at a time. The offspring in the same family will also inherit the same duties but at a different level. The eldest child is always regarded as the leader and organiser for the rest of the siblings. That is why, in Banaban culture, great respect is always shown to the elders. If a family neglects one of its duties, their clan has to resolve the matter. If the elders find a person guilty of neglecting the duty, then the elders will have to discharge him or her from this duty so that the whole clan is not disgraced and ridiculed. Automatically, the next brother or sister within the family will inherit the role. If there is no sibling, the role is given to the first cousin within the same clan structure. This same philosophy applies to married couples who may come from different clans. If the husband, for example, has neglected his inherited duty, a wife from another clan cannot take over his role. The discharge of the role is an inherited birthright.

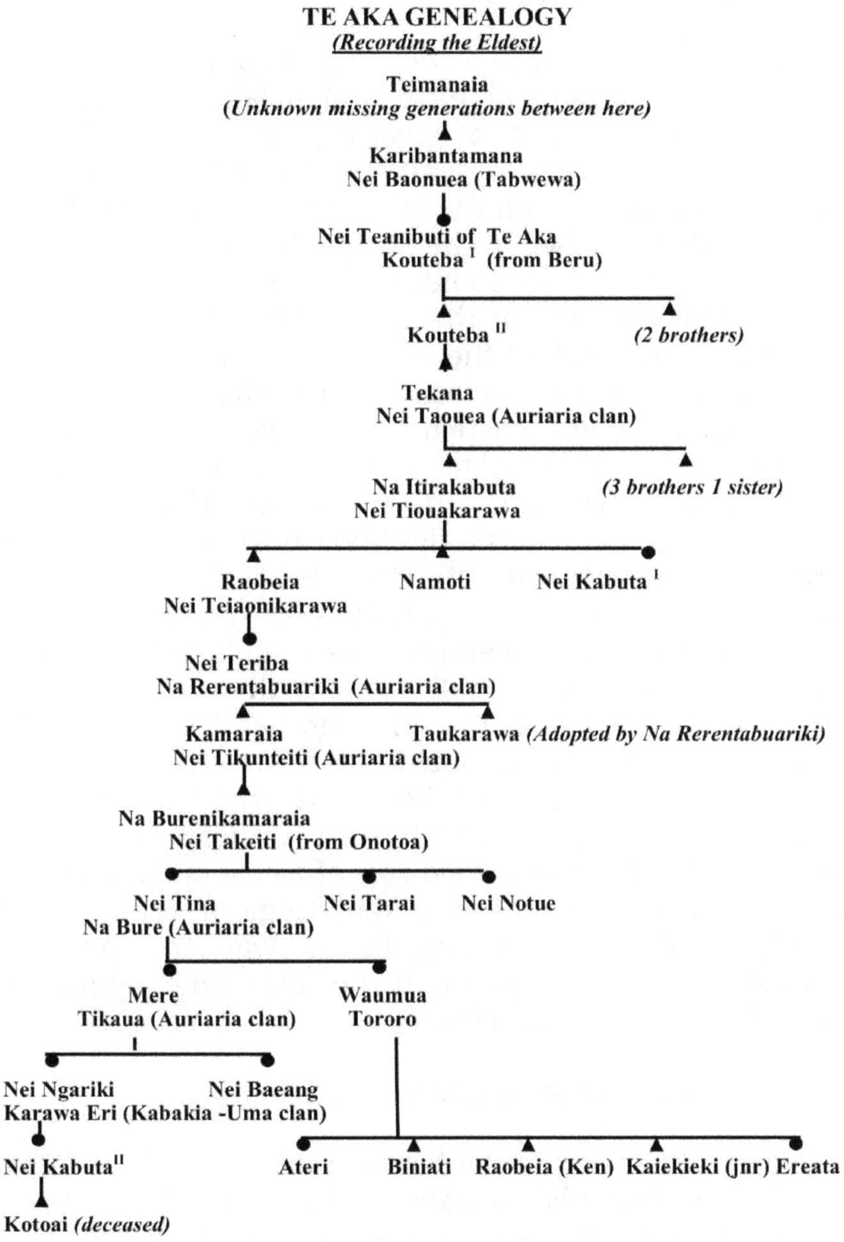

TE AKA GENEALOGY
(Recording the Eldest)

Teimanaia
(Unknown missing generations between here)

▲

Karibantamana
Nei Baonuea (Tabwewa)

●

Nei Teanibuti of Te Aka
Kouteba [I] **(from Beru)**

▲   ▲

Kouteba [II]   *(2 brothers)*

▲

Tekana
Nei Taouea (Auriaria clan)

▲

Na Itirakabuta   *(3 brothers 1 sister)*
Nei Tiouakarawa

▲   ▲   ●

Raobeia   **Namoti**   **Nei Kabuta** [I]
Nei Teiaonikarawa

●

Nei Teriba
Na Rerentabuariki (Auriaria clan)

▲   ▲

Kamaraia   **Taukarawa** *(Adopted by Na Rerentabuariki)*
Nei Tikunteiti (Auriaria clan)

▲

Na Burenikamaraia
Nei Takeiti (from Onotoa)

●   ●   ●

Nei Tina   **Nei Tarai**   **Nei Notue**
Na Bure (Auriaria clan)

▲   ●

Mere   **Waumua**
Tikaua (Auriaria clan)   **Tororo**

●   ●

Nei Ngariki   **Nei Baeang**
Karawa Eri (Kabakia -Uma clan)

●

Nei Kabuta[II]   ●   ▲   ▲   ▲   ●

▲   **Ateri**   **Biniati**   **Raobeia (Ken)**   **Kaiekieki (jnr)**   **Ereata**

Kotoai *(deceased)*

Figure: 1.7. Te Aka Genealogy (by R.K. Sigrah).

The role of a clan spokesman

The clan spokesman must listen to and confer with his clan elders, whether women or men, and speak for them during clan meetings. It is a duty of great responsibility. Only a man can inherit the position of clan spokesman. If the eldest in the family is a woman, all the inherited roles of that clan will go to the eldest brother in the family. If she does not have a brother, the duty will go to her nearest male cousin. Women are respected as elders of the family and the clan, but they cannot speak on behalf of the clan at important meetings.

The men are given this task because when arguments and debates become heated, fisticuffs between two men can ease the tension. For these reasons, the traditional game of boxing is a highly respected sport. Any boxing resulting from a clan meeting is not regarded as a fight but as a traditional process of claiming identity and defining roles, following set rules (Chapter 6). As soon as the bout is over, everyone is back to normal without any ill feelings, and usually with the added excitement of the event still surging through their veins. There is no real loser, as the one who has lost the match is also viewed with great respect because he stood up to fight for his cause and what he believed was right. Banabans are not a warring people, and physical altercations are soon resolved. To hold the respected role of a clan spokesman, it is also essential to have accurate knowledge of genealogy and be skilled in the art of boxing. In this way, the spokesman can speak with authority and, at the same time, be prepared to defend his position physically.

Recording the Detail of Family Genealogy

In the past, the eldest in the family, whether male or female, recorded the family's genealogy, then passed it down at death or, if the elder was no longer capable of performing the duty for health reasons, to the next in line. When recording genealogy, it was of utmost importance to record the exact details of the placing of kin according to their birth year. Ken Sigrah's family recorded genealogies for sixteen generations. If on average, a new generation comes every twenty-five years, Ken's documented lineage probably goes back to the 1500s (see Figure 1.7). Because of Teimanaia's almost god-like status within the clan, there is no actual record of his family. Only his precious skull and his legends provide the link to Te Aka people, right through to the present day.

After Teimanaia, we have no idea how many generations have vanished before the recording of the next person on Te Aka family tree, Karibantamana. He was the first man to have his wife recorded on the family tree. In Ken's role as historian for major clans, he has been trained to uphold the vital placing of individuals within the clan's genealogy charts. One of the major pitfalls in modern Banaba society is to neglect these essential details.

For example, wrongly placing a younger sibling before an older one can alter the inherited role or duty of the descendants significantly, causing consternation for many generations to come. We may see even greater mistakes made when the sex of a person is recorded wrongly. Women and men in Banaban society have similar names, and a person's gender is defined through the preceding word of *Nei,* denoting a woman, and *Na* denoting a man. Mistakes in recording the sex can cause disputes within a family and clan.

Inheritance Through Adoption

Child adoption in Banaban custom indicated a family bond where a child was the centre of affection between two families. An adopted child should have a land share from the birth parents to secure his or her future return to the family. Without land, the child cannot be involved in any of the birth family's affairs and has no physical or moral ties to the birth family. If the child inherited land from the adopted family, then this child had a right to be involved in all matters regarding this family's affairs. If the adopted child owned lands from both birth and adoptive parents, then the child had the right to be involved in matters concerning both families, such as land settlements, cultural duties and genealogical discussions within the clan.

In earlier times, different forms of adoption had various purposes and meanings. Adopting a girl signified one's need for a water gatherer from the caves. Because Banaba has no surface water, the women's primary task was to visit the sacred caverns and bring out coconut shells filled with precious water. Adopting a boy signified one's need for a fisherman.

The adopted child received the best a family could give, such as land shares. Attention was given to the child because he or she will have the critical role of water gathering or as a fisherman within the family structure. After the two parties agree on the adoption, and the child is taken away by the adoptive family (generally, it is still within the same clan), it is customary that the birth parents have no right to reclaim that child as their own. However, the child can visit them if the adoptive parents agree.

Adopted children and the right to land ownership

	1	2	3
	Banaban Land Owner	Adopted Child of Foreign Origin	Adopted Child of No.2 also of Foreign Origin

According to tradition, if Adopted Child No. 2, in the above diagram, bears a child of their own, this child has the right to inherit land passed on from Land Owner 1. If Adopted Child 2 bears no child and adopts another (Child No. 3) also of foreign origin, Adopted Child No. 2 has no right to give

Adopted Child No. 3 land inherited initially from Land Owner 1. The only exception is when the *utu* (immediate family or next of kin) of Land Owner 1 agrees, then a large adoption feast and celebration will be held to commemorate the inheritance, which legalises the process within Banaban society.

Using *Te Rii ni Banaba* (The Backbone of Banaba) to Settle Disputed Claims

Genealogy reveals the customary roles in the family and clan and precise knowledge of land boundaries. In Banaban philosophy, these three interlocking pieces of information are known as *Te Rii ni Banaba*: three essential points that are the only earthly 'possessions' a Banaban has. In today's western society, we judge a person's wealth by their material possessions. Banabans believe a person's wealth is their spiritual wealth and wellbeing - *Te Rii ni Banaba:* Genealogy, Role and Hamlet.

This three–point philosophy means that if a person claims to be the speaker of Te Aka clan, first, he needs to establish his identity to claim the right to take up this duty. Second, he must prove that the original hamlet that his ancestors came from on Banaba has the inherited right of clan spokesman. Similarly, if a person steps forward to claim land on Banaba, he or she needs to be able to provide evidence of genealogy and their inherited clan role. If the land on Banaba does not match up with these other essential facts, then that person's claim is false.

Today on Rabi, this three–pointed philosophy is fundamental in settling claims. Much debate can rage, especially over matters concerning land or official duties, but in the end, answering these three simple questions can easily put these matters to rest:

- *Katea rikim?* Recite your genealogy?
- *Tera taum?* What is your family's inherited role?

51

- Arana am Kainga! Name your hamlet!

At a clan meeting, they work through these questions in the order given, and if any point does not match with the preceding one, then the claim is lost. If a claimant cannot provide the correct answer to these three critical questions, the person is not permitted to speak in the meeting. If they make the mistake of speaking first and are challenged regarding these three questions and fail the test, they could be asked to leave the meeting. That is why *Te Rii ni Banaba* is such a critical issue.

Determining an acceptable marriage

For marriage between two families to be accepted, the engaged pair cannot be related to each other within three generations. Cousins four generations apart may marry. While elders do not permit close relationships, in exceptional circumstances, they allow second cousins to marry to strengthen land holdings, inherit specific family duties, or expand the clan. Family bonds are so strong that sometimes, marriages are arranged to hold and build family unity. Arranged marriages are very important within Banaban society.

Genealogy: Past and Future

With the modern world's influence likely to impact future generations, Banaban elders have to uphold the teaching of genealogy as the very essence of Banaban identity and ensure it is never lost. It is easy to be influenced by western society, and vital to always consider and respect genealogy as a significant factor in decision-making. With these principles in mind, Banabans can benefit from modern technology and, at the same time, preserve their traditional heritage. Banabans have suffered 80 years of exploitation from phosphate mining, and then in 1945, elders had to manage the resettlement on Rabi. This decision was probably the only thing that saved the people. If they had decided on the alternative, which was to disperse Banabans throughout Kiribati and other Pacific Islands, it surely would have seen the extinction of the Banabans people. The move to Rabi brought new adversities. In a new environment, with cold winters, cyclone seasons, and mosquito-borne diseases, many old and young died. They were left in army tents with two months' rations and were told – there was plenty of spring water, groves of swaying coconut trees, pandanus, and a multitude of cattle and wild pigs. No one explained that the cattle were riddled with tuberculosis. Banabans were not farmers, and the pigs were indeed wild. They had never known the art of hunting, only fishing. They welcomed the idea of no more droughts, but no one told them about the dangers of drinking contaminated water in the tropical dry season.

When looking back at what Banaban elders faced, we realise what great courage they possessed after being forcibly removed from their beloved homeland, interned by the Japanese forces, scattered across the Pacific in enforced labour camps, and then forced to live in a new environment. How weakened physically they must have been after such an ordeal, yet maintaining their genealogy helped them transpose their cultural identity to a new land.

How did Banaban elders cope with such adversity? They watched their people die around them from pneumonia and dengue fever. Their meagre army tents did not protect them against the cyclonic rains that lashed the island. The Banaban elders took an entirely new step, outside the customary structure of the clan system, of coming together to decide and plan the future of their people. They determined they had to return to their traditional clan system to survive. The first step was to bring back as many cultural practices as possible to this new environment. The clans gathered, and the elders instructed them to settle Rabi in the same village hamlets and social structure they had on Banaba. Their decision was the turning point in the survival of the people. It is hard to imagine where the Banabans would be today if the pioneers had not made this major decision.

Life on Rabi has never been easy, and people have struggled. They have very little material wealth, but unlike many other dispersed and exploited peoples, they have culture and traditions as their strength. This inner strength that every Banaban seems to carry is achieved by a strong sense of identity, genealogy and birthright. The governments of the United Kingdom, Australia and New Zealand, which formed the BPC and were responsible for the ultimate devastation of the homeland, never recognised that Banabans had such perseverance. To Banabans, the battle to see justice finally achieved will continue to be passed down for generations to come. Genealogy is the link that allows Banabans worldwide to feel the bond of being a Banaban deeply embedded in their souls.

5: CUSTOMS AND CULTURE

Births, Puberty and Marriage

Traditionally, Te Aka have associated rituals and customs with all the significant events through a person's life: birth, puberty, marriage, older age and eventually death.

Not much is known about Te Aka birth rituals. Most of these customs originate after the arrival of Auriaria and Nei Anginimaeao clans. Te Aka myths and legends do not mention this topic.

Banaban elders state that from the time of a girl's first menstruation, she was considered a woman, ready to take a partner and begin her adult role within the community. Until her marriage, the family safely guarded her virginity so that she would not dishonour them or suffer rejection and abuse by her partner and his family. The first menstruation was a significant event celebrated by all the clan. During the first three days, the girl was kept isolated. The woman elders in her family taught her how to be a woman and how to look after herself. Then a large celebration was held, signalling to the rest of the community that the girl was now a woman and had to be respected. For example, men practising *te kauti* are made aware of her new status, as her presence could weaken the power of their ritual.

There is only basic knowledge of the traditional role of women in Te Aka society. It was imperative for each family group to have a girl child to be their water collector and to prepare the food for the family meals. Women were also responsible for weaving the pandanus into mats, coconut leaves into baskets, spinning coconut fibre for cords, and plaiting grass skirts. Making special ceremonial wigs from hair preserved from deceased ancestors was also a woman's duty. Finally, they had an important role as attendants during the sport of traditional boxing.

A male's role within Te Aka society was similarly essential. The male was responsible for feeding his family by fishing daily and defending his family and island during invasions. Only men could conduct *te kauti*, practise boxing, and snare frigate birds.

Only two references were found regarding courting and marriage in the

10. Banaban girl, nearing puberty (Williams Collection 1901–1931).

early times. First, a Te Aka legend tells of a young Te Aka boy's engagement with a girl from the Auriaria clan from Tabwewa district. This event occurred around AD 1500. Second, when Nei Anginimaeao arrived with her party from Beru, one of her fellow travellers, Kouteba, married a woman called Nei Teanibuti from Te Aka hamlet in approximately AD 1673. Before these later events, there is no recorded evidence of whether Te Aka married. However, elders teach that life-long partnerships were formed with only one partner. It was forbidden to commit adultery or take another partner (in contrast to the later records of other clans, which indicated men took more than one wife).

The role of an elder

An elder in Te Aka family is the most respected and considered the most knowledgeable leader of the family. A

11. Banaban woman with *te ati ni mate*, wooden pounder, preparing pandanus (Miller Collection 1908–1939).

family seeks wisdom and guidance from elders in all matters of culture and tradition and in times of family dispute or hardship. There were five different levels of elders. As a person reaches each new level, he or she gains even more respect from the community:

1. *tibu*, meaning grandmother or grandfather, when the grandparents are still young and active (usually late thirties and forties);

2. *tibu toru*, when the grandparents can still look after the grandchildren but cannot participate in heavy or strenuous work, especially in carrying grandchildren for long distances (usually aged around the late forties to fifty years);

3. *tibu mamanu*, when the grandparents are not expected to be involved in daily work. They usually are involved in the simple tasks of feeding and looking after their great-great-grandchildren (usually aged in their late fifties to sixty years);

4. *tibu babako*, when these old elders are expected to sit back and be waited on by their immediate family and loved ones. Their only duty within the family is to pat their very youngest grandchildren to sleep: *babako* means 'to put into the lap' (usually they are in their seventies and eighties);

5. *tibu taratara* is the most sacred stage of an elder's life in Banaban tradition. To attain such an age is noble within the clan. At this age, the old one can only lie down all day, watching the small children and life go on around them. Other community members come to visit and pay their respects, knowing that what little time these elders have remaining on earth is precious.

These traditional customs regarding Banaban elders are still relevant today. Unfortunately, partly because the mining years introduced western foods that changed the traditional diet, many elders never reach the exalted age of *tibu taratara*. Those who do are still held in the highest regard.

Death ritual (embalming)

When a person died it was essential that the body was well preserved and treated with respect. First, the body

12. Banaban woman, scraping coconut (Miller Collection 1908-1939).

was kept in the family *mwenga* for three days of mourning. Then the body was taken to an elevated hut made specially to house the dead. The eldest female relatives, such as grandmothers and great-aunts, continually oil and rub the body. The ritual oil used during this embalming process was made from fresh *te bwaa* (coconut oil) and mixed with leaves such as *te ngea* (*Pemphis acifula*), *te ren* (*Tournefortia argentea*), and the roots of plants called *te non*. Sections of dried coconut flesh with the harder brown shells removed were used as pads to rub the oil into the body. This process encouraged the flesh to fall away from the bones as quickly as possible. The bones were then gathered and placed under the slabs of the Te Aka *bangota*. Some bones were kept in a basket in the family *mwenga* according to the family's requirements for making tools, such as ribs used for weaving shuttles, finger or toe bones for fishing hooks and teeth for treasured family necklaces. The remaining bones, sometimes but not always including the skull, are anointed and preserved in the embalming oil, stacked neatly in the family's sacred cairn, or kept separately for *tabunea* and *kauti.*

Te Aka cairns and *bangota*

The Te Aka kept the remains of their dead in cairns that consisted of a wide slab of stone. It was supported off the ground by three other stones to a height of approximately 23 centimetres. These cairns were usually situated in a sacred area called a *bangota.* Much more than just a sacred shrine, *bangota* defines a whole site of ancestral cairns containing a multitude of remains. It was not until the later invasions that ritual burials were introduced. The most treasured relics were stored in *bangota* above ground; thus, they were the first casualties of the bulldozer's blade. Retired BPC surveyor and engineer Peter Anderson also found evidence for this practice

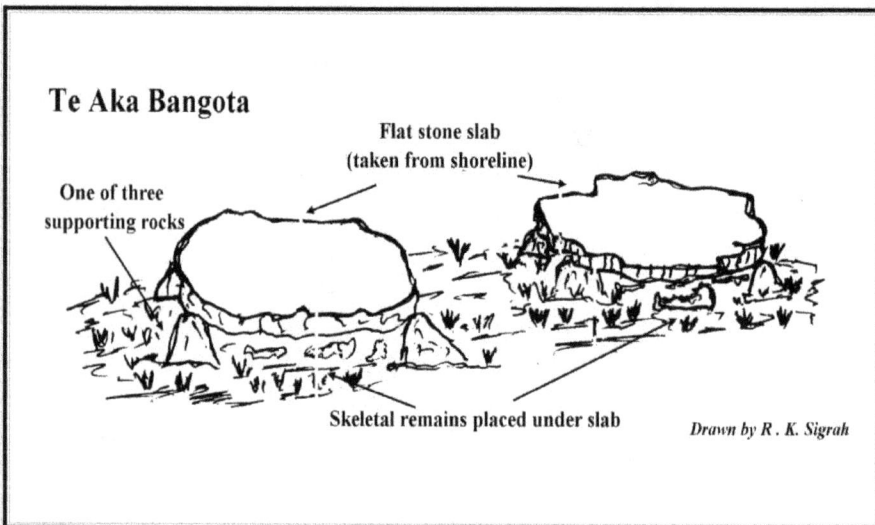

Figure 1.8. Te Aka *bangota* (drawn by R.K. Sigrah).

with his discovery of many Te Aka artefacts before the area was mined (see Chapter 31).

When Ken Sigrah's grandmother, Nei Tina, was a young girl on Banaba, she used to go to this sacred site at Te Aka *bangota* (shown in Figure 1.8) with her grandfather, Kamaraia. They would remove the bones or skulls from under the rock slab, oil and garland them with fresh flowers and then return them under the slab. The area was well cleaned and maintained, with old dried garlands carefully taken back to the family home for use in making sacred oils. These old dried flowers were believed to carry great magical powers from their ancestors. The last time she went to this sacred place was just before the invasion of the Japanese forces.

Today, the area is severely damaged, with the top surface being taken away in preparation for mining, while some of

13. The mined-out area looking towards Te Aka site. The mining at this site creased after the sudden, unexplained death of the BPC overseer (R. Lampert 1965).

the surrounding areas have been destroyed by the phosphate diggings (see Photo 13).

Land and Land Ownership

When only Te Aka lived on Banaba, they were one big extended family, owning the entire island. Divisions or boundaries over the land were not known to exist during this period, and Te Aka were free to wander over the island as they chose. There was no need to inherit land and, therefore, no disputes over land ownership. After the Auriaria clan's first invasion, the first partitioning of the land took place. Te Aka were forced back to the central and northern side of the island after the Battle of Tairua (see Chapter 8). From this time, disputes over land ownership and inheritance began.

Bangabanga (water caves)

A Te Aka myth gives the first account of the discovery of the *bangabanga*. It was one of the most critical events in Banaban history, given the absence of surface water and cycles of drought on the island. Before Auriaria's invasion, everyone shared the caves under the strict supervision of the elders. As the legend recounts, the *bangabanga* was always considered a place strictly for women, with the presence of men considered taboo. Following the later arrivals, the *bangabanga* on Banaba eventually fell under individual land ownership and were considered a valuable form of property.

Daily Life – Sources of food

Banaba means 'land of rock', and all over the island are strange limestone configurations that protrude from the natural formation of the land. Between these rocks were rich deposits of guano. The Te Aka were not tillers of the soil but gathered from the land and the sea. When the island was not suffering from drought, it was densely covered in coconut trees. Other essential food trees grew mainly along the coastline. They included *te tou* (Pandanus), *kunkun* (*Terminalia catappa*, wild almond), *mangko ni Banaba* (wild mango), *te mai* (breadfruit) and the fruit of *te non* (commonly known as noni throughout the Pacific and, also found on Rabi). Besides the birds that nested there, crabs were the only other creatures living on Banaba. *Te aii* was a coconut crab, while *te manai* was a land crab that lived down by the seashore. Te Aka never killed these crabs for food. All Banabans, right up until they left the island in World War II, considered these creatures sacred. The giant coconut crabs were a great delicacy to the I–Kiribati and Tuvaluan labourers working for the BPC at the turn of the twentieth century. Like the island's natural canopy and hundreds of coconut trees destroyed through mining, *te aii* declined and eventually were thought to have disappeared. However, during a visit to the island in 1997, many land crabs were present. The rocky shoreline was alive with *te*

14. Inside a *bangabanga,* water cave (Williams Collection 1902–1931).

kamakama (sea crabs) despite 80 years of mining. It is heartening to see these crabs still thriving.

Fishing was restricted to the fringing reefs surrounding the shoreline, which were alive with fish. There was no need to venture further. There are no oral records regarding styles of outriggers from earlier times. Te Aka were land dwellers, not seafarers, so their fishing skills were limited. Later they acquired new skills from the seafaring invaders. Myths and legends tell of the Te Aka's lack of open-ocean fishing and seafaring skills. Te Aka were expert in fishing for octopus, sea eels, lobsters, sea crabs, and fish that frequented the myriad reefs along the entire coastline.

Adornments

An adornment for Te Aka male elders was a necklace made from the teeth of their beloved ancestors. Each tooth carried a tale that related to his ancestor. The elders used these necklaces during storytelling to tell the family's stories and preserve Te Aka genealogy oral history. The men also made necklaces and wristbands of seashells that had been finely bored and ground. These had no magic or historical purpose but were used as body adornment and were ideal gifts for a young man to give to his fiancée. During *kauti,* the leaves of *te mao* (*Scaevola kownigi*) were used by the men as earrings. Men and women wore adorned with frigate bird feathers. They twirled these adornments in their crinkly hair, which held it in place while they did their daily chores. They oiled their bodies instead of wearing clothing as natural protection against the elements. Flower garlands were worn for ornamentation and perfume.

6: SPORT

The role of *kauti* magic, *Te Itau ni Banaba* (Banaban Boxing)

The Te Aka clan consider Banaban boxing as their most popular sport. The sport combines *kauti* as well as an individual's strength. Closely interwoven into Te Aka culture, competitive boxing is a fierce competition between the families of the clan and is different from settling disputes by altercations during everyday decision making. The elders' duty was to see that males were trained from a young age and qualified to represent their family in the event. The sport of boxing has a unique place in Banaban hearts, for it allows strong young men and women to show their abilities and elevate their clan within Banaban society. A loss also reflects on the loser's clan elders and family, causing shame and even putting the family in an awkward position.

Every Banaban male boxer must be acquainted with *kauti* to possess more spiritual powers than his opponent. (We discuss women's participation in boxing later in this chapter). *Te kauti* is involved in boxing training over three days, conducted on family terraces where the *uma n roronga* (young man's sleeping quarters) were located, away from the distractions of the rest of the family. This training also involves specific rules, which can be taboo for a boxer to break:

1. Men must keep away from women during this period.

2.   Menstruating women must not touch food, eating utensils, sleeping mats or anything that belongs to the training boxer.

3.   The boxer must perform his morning worship rituals from 3 a.m. to just before sunrise. The rituals are one of the most critical aspects of training, allowing the boxer to connect with his ancestors and gain power from their spirits.

During the three-day ritual, the boxer must condition his mind into believing he can win and convince his elders that he is indeed capable of the task. If his elders have any doubts during this period, they will delay the date of the next match. In this way, they protect the boxer from possible loss and his family from the associated shame.

Stages of training

At **birth**, the first thing the elders claim from a male child is his umbilical cord, that is, the piece of dried cord that falls from his navel a few days after birth. They then preserved and formed it into a wristlet for boxing training rituals and tournaments. An adult boxer wraps this wristlet around one wrist, usually on the left (not the working hand). He wears it during the training ritual and tournaments. This wristlet is an essential part of the boxer's armour when he goes into a fight. It is also believed that the child who provided the wristlet will grow up to be a boxer of the same standing, so the boxer is motivated to win the fight for the sake of the child's future. This is why the leading boxer of the day looks amongst his relatives' offspring for a suitable candidate who will be trained to be the family's future boxer. As a respected boxer, if none of his offspring shows any promise, he has the right to adopt any male child he chooses and train him as his successor. He does not have to give the child anything, such as land titles or inherited family or clan duties, for the child has inherited the sought-after position of the *tia itau* (boxer).

At **puberty**, the first lesson on boxing begins. The boy learns oral history and begins to attend tournaments as a spectator. He also begins his lessons in *kauti* and is taught the reasons why women cannot be part of the training ritual. At this stage, too, the boy is taught other aspects of culture pertaining to puberty.

The youth commences his first practical lessons during his **teenage** years. The trainer begins to strengthen the young man's body and mind for his future role. He learns the intricate stances and techniques of the boxer. He must harden and condition his fists by continually punching specific rock slabs down at the terraces, which are considered sacred. The elders and trainer work together to train the young man, introducing him to the magical rituals. At the end of this stage, the young boxer is well conditioned and fully aware of his future responsibility to defend his family's honour or represent the clan in future bouts.

On reaching the **age of 18 to 20**, the boxer is ready to compete in his first bouts.

After 20 years of age, training from his elders is over. He now has the right to adopt a child and begin the training cycle of the boxer all over again. He is now respected and looked upon as a man because he has earned the title of 'boxer.' His comments can be sought during family or clan meetings, and the elders will value his opinions.

Forms of boxing stance

Te Butu (**Thumb Thrust**). In this stance, the closed fists with the thumb thrust out are held in front of the body, bending downwards at navel level. The legs are slightly flexed, and the feet are placed slightly apart. From this position, the hands quickly strike the opponent's face. The most important part of the fist is the thumb. The boxers who prefer to use the *te butu* grow their thumbnails as part of their natural armour.

Te Uma (**Home**). One arm (the 'guard arm') is held in the raised position at forehead level, while the other arm is held at the side at waist level and used for punching. The forward leg is slightly flexed while the back leg is thrust back for support. This move is referred to as the 'killing' punch. The strike from this position is delivered by the spin and full rotation of the body. It should be done in a rapid motion to catch the opponent off guard.

Te Katabara (**Open**). Both arms are held high at forehead level, while legs are slightly flexed with feet apart. The fists are moved in quick circular movements, with the aim to hit the opponent on the side of the ribs and the face. The move is the most popular and commonly practised stance on Rabi today.

Te Tiribenu (**Shadow Smash**). Women use this stance if they need to box. The fists are held in front of the body at chest level. The legs are straight, and the feet are slightly apart. From this position, the woman strikes out in a sideways motion, bringing the front of the fist in contact with her opponent. The continual rotating moment of the hands blocks the opponent's blows.

Materials

Te bana (boxing gloves) for men are woven from coconut fibre. Initially, the knuckles of these gloves had spikes attached taken from the porcupine fish in surrounding reefs. These spikes were later replaced with small shells and stones found along the seashore. Since the 1900s, only plain coconut fibre gloves have been used. Herbs and ointments are an essential part of boxing to cure the boxer's injuries. Magic oil is another part of his armour guarding the boxer and his sister or cousin, who acts as his second in the competition. The oil made from specially scented coconut oil is empowered by *kauti* with *tabunea.* According to tradition, the best sorceress within the clan can only make this oil when the

15. *Te bana*, boxing gloves, made with coconut fibre
(King Collection).

strongest *tabunea* is needed.

The oil is considered a powerful defence to ward off the equally strong magic powers of the opponent. The boxer is covered in the oil before he begins the bout. It protects the body from the impact of the blows as they slide off the skin's oily surface. Without these herbs and ointments, the boxer would feel as though he has been sent out to box without any protection, immediately putting him at a disadvantage.

The rules of Banaban boxing

1. The first boxer to touch the ground is the loser.

2. No ill feeling should enter the game; it must be regarded as a competitive sport only.

3. While age does not count, the boxer's relationship with the opponent's family does. In the days when only Te Aka resided on Banaba, bouts were between adopted brothers and cousins. In later times, potential opponents extended to cousins from other clans and districts.

4. Elders organise the date of the matches.

69

5. The secrecy surrounding boxing techniques and the *kauti* must be maintained.

Women in boxing

At the same time, young men are receiving full-time boxing training; young women are trained in the art of the *tabunea*. These women must be either the fighter's sisters or closest cousins, and they must attend to any injuries he suffers during the match. These injuries can sometimes be so damaging that his whole face is distorted or badly gashed from the spikes of the gloves.

In the oral history of Te Aka, women's medicinal powers were great indeed. Eyes hanging from sockets, torn-off ears, broken jaws, and battered noses and lips were just some of the injuries that these women could remedy skillfully and almost instantly. Although women usually do not box, they are also taught the art, so they can meet other women in a match if required. Such circumstances arose if their brother or cousin was injured from unjust play, and the clan called for a match against the victor's female attendant to try to recover the honour of their family and clan. Such a challenge was only possible if the elders deemed the opponent's moves unfair, so these rules usually spurred the men to compete at their best and to honour and protect their sister or cousin from ridicule if accused of foul play.

At the end of a tournament, if a boxer was injured from unfair play, and his sister or cousin also lost their match, the only option left was for the family to take them home and train another younger family member to compete and regain the family honour. Although male or female losing boxers were not given a second chance at that same event, they could compete at later tournaments to regain their family's lost honour. In the meantime, the whole family felt that their male and female contenders did their best and could accept the loss. The loss also encouraged the trainers and elders to study and improve their training regime. Another significant ritual and chapter of Banaban history changed with the arrival of the Europeans and an imported labour force to work the phosphate diggings.

When they saw *te bana* (boxing gloves), they viewed the boxing as brawling.

Outsiders could never understand the complexities of Banaban boxing, the ritual that it involved and the social standing that the boxers had within the community. The missionaries banned

16. Tame frigate bird on perch (Doutch Collection 1914).

traditional boxing matches, and then a ban was enforced by colonial laws in the later years. Boxing on Rabi as a sport tried to make a comeback, but the game is now not encouraged because the elders who controlled the game and knew the associated training and skills have passed away or are very elderly. However, within the Te Aka clan, some of the descendants consider themselves very fortunate to still have a family member with the specialised skills of the traditional Banaban boxer.

Te Kabwane Eitei (Frigate Bird Snaring)

Although no one can identify who invented the game, Te Aka men practised frigate bird snaring for generations. Oral history recalls that Te Aka people were playing it well before Auriaria and Anginimaeao clans arrived. The sport died out from the impact of phosphate mining on the island and the destruction of the bird's natural habitat. Te Aka people have always believed that frigate birds, like themselves, were the first inhabitants of Banaba; therefore, they greatly respected these creatures. The game of frigate bird snaring had two purposes. One was to gather the valued long black feathers for adorning the crinkly hair of Te Aka people and, after the arrival of Auriaria and the Battle of Tairua, feathers for adorning the war dance spears in *te karanga* and the dancer's headpieces. However, the primary purpose was an exciting sport where men competed to snare and tame the most birds. The person who owned the most birds was recognised as the best and respected for that unique skill. The materials used in this sport were as follows:

1. Long sinews of coconut fibre twisted into fine, strong strings 9 to 12 metres in length. Each string was securely tied to a stone weight through a hole made at one end.

2. *Te baobao* (tall wooden frames) built high off the ground were a resting place for the tamed birds. A good supply of fresh fish was essential to feed the birds during the taming process.

The two main phases were first to catch and then secondly to tame the frigate bird. A competitor snared birds by swinging a long coconut fibre string, weighted down with a stone tied to one end, in a circular motion to build up speed and then tossing it high into the air to wrap around the bird in flight. The bird was then pulled down to earth.

Once snared, the wild birds were secured by the leg on a long string and attached to *te baobao* on the terraces around the seashore. Here they were well fed with freshly caught fish

TAME FRIGATE BIRDS, OCEAN ISLAND

17. Tame frigate birds sitting on *te baobao*, tall wooden frames, on Banaban terrace (Postcard 1910).

and continually handled until they became tame. The birds were marked with a string on their leg or their feathers. Once sufficiently tamed, they were released every morning to fly off in search of food. The bird returned at dusk to its owner, who waited on the terrace. When wild frigate birds returned with them, the game of bird snaring began again. The men also knew the art of 'calling the bird' so that their birds returned on command.

18. *Te Karanga*, dancing costume and pandanus cap (Maude Collection 1920–32).

19. Raobeia Ken Sigrah performing *Te Karanga are e Uarereke*, on Rabi 1975. (Source: Dean, B).

7: MUSIC AND DANCE

Music has always been an essential part of the culture and is used for storytelling. Banabans have used oral history and dances to record important historical events over the generations. Traditional Te Aka music and songs seem to have disappeared so that today little is known of them except for *te karanga*, which offers a snippet of the Banabans past way of life. *Te karanga* is known as the war spear dance because long wooden spears are an integral part of the dance. It developed as a war dance to commemorate the various invasions of Banaba over the years. It is not used to incite the people to war; in fact, it has the opposite meaning.

Te karanga is the last dance style that relates to the separate existence of Te Aka people. The words *te karanga* come from an old dialect, just like a few words in the dance. Although the elders that remembered the meaning of the old Banaban words have now passed away, when the dance is performed on Rabi, it still uses the words to hold on to this part of Te Aka heritage.

Different styles of *te Karanga*

Te karanga differs in movement and singing from other well-recognised Banaban dance and music styles. The dancers use a chanting singing style while performing, which is not melodious. Two straight lines of dancers face each other in pairs. Aggressive in style, the dance begins with the dancers moving their spears and stamping their feet while the chanting continues. Lines of dancers weave in intricate patterns in and out, just outside the reach of the swirling spears. It is a dance only for the well trained.

Invaders have influenced Banaban dances and music with styles that are in sharp contrast to the hard–aggressive actions, the stamping of feet, the war cry and the chanting of *te karanga*. One legend tells how Auriaria and his clan first influenced dancing by introducing soft flowing movements, which Te Aka perceived as the swaying of trees.

In modern dances, men use defensive solid movements adopted from the original war dance, although their actions are now more flowing like birds they have seen in flight. The women complement the strength of the male dancers with soft and gentle swaying hips and intricate hand and head movements. These movements also represent the movements of birds, especially the frigate bird.

The costume used for *te karanga* differs from that used in other, more common dance styles. In former times, headpieces, body ornaments, coconut leaf skirts, and spears were made in skilful patterns that were only found among the early Banaban people.

The **headpiece** designed by the Banabans was a plaited pandanus strip adorned at the base with seashells and woven with frigate bird feathers in an upright position. Only after the second invasion and the introduction of Kiribati culture to the island did people begin to wear a helmet type of cap made from plaited pandanus and tied under the chin with coconut sennit. This helmet is occasionally used in modern times during special performances of *te karanga*. Early photographs confirm that Banabans were still wearing handmade wigs. These wigs were initially made of human hair but, in later times, were made from shredded coconut fronds dyed black to imitate the long crinkly hair of Te Aka ancestors, a characteristic greatly prized. The headpiece used today, *te* *bau,* is similar to the original design. It, too, has a headband plaited from pandanus and decorated with frigate bird feathers and seashells, while it also includes delicate decorations made from the pandanus leaf.

20. Banaban dancing group on Rabi 1992 (King Collection).

The **neckpiece** consists of two items. The first piece is called *te enta*. Its base is made of finely woven pandanus sinew, about one centimetre wide, with its length measured according to the diameter of the wearer's neck. In the centre is an amulet cut out from a seashell, usually a red coloured cone shell. The second piece is called *te kakii* and is usually made of plaited human hair (usually from a female relation). Banabans believe this piece is the focus of magic powers for the wearer. The combination of these two ornaments signifies power, courage and protection for the wearer.

The **bracelets for arms, wrists and ankles** are made in a pattern and design that match the neckpiece. The base is made of plaited leaf ornamented with seashells and human hair, from the top of the rib cage to the top of the stomach. Its edges are trimmed in a U shape.

Te ramwane is the **cross–piece ornament** for men that is made of plaited pandanus, seashells and human hair and fitted across the chest under the left arm and over the right shoulder.

The **belt**, *te bure*, is made of the plaited pandanus leaf and ornamented with seashells surrounded with human hair. Its width is 7 to 10 centimetres, while its length is measured according to the wearer's waist size.

The **dancing skirt**, *te riri*, was traditionally made of dried and treated coconut leaf, held together and fastened with a coconut fibre string. In later times, the skirt was made from *maunei* (treated grass) instead of coconut leaves.

The **dancing spear** is the most important aspect of the costume. It is not considered a weapon and is only used when performing *te karanga.* The spear is made from *te ngea* (*Pemphis aifula*, coastal bloodwood useful for making tools and weapons) and decorated with frigate bird feathers tied to the spear in a pattern of coconut fibre strings.

Initially, only men performed *te karanga,* but today girls are permitted to perform the dance and wear a similar costume, with the addition of a pandanus bra. The elders must see that every performer is suitably attired, and they can forbid a dancer from participating in the dance if the costume is incorrect.

The performance of *te karanga* is the most exciting event for the performers. From the outside, observers may not see the excitement involved, but to Te Aka people, *te karanga* is part of their culture. In performing it, they recite their history by chanting and acting as if they were at war. For the Te Aka spectators, the experience brings both excitement and envy. Watching *te karanga* performed is like witnessing the actual battle and adds to their excitement.

Arthur Mahaffy, in 1910, during his six-month stay as Acting Resident Commissioner on Banaba, recorded details of a *te karanga*:

> There is, however, one very curious and beautiful dance which I have never seen elsewhere. The performers are drawn up in two lines facing each other, and each dancer is equipped with a staff about six feet long, decorated with feathers and coloured streamers. A long recitative is sung by the leader, at the completion of which the two lines of dancers engage in a most complicated set of figures, passing in and out through the spaces between the performers with wonderful precision. As each man passes his neighbour, he raises his staff above his head and clashes it against the next one in absolute unison. The effect is very fine, and figure follows figure in great variety, always preceded by the chanting of a recitative.
>
> The dress of the dancers is also peculiar: they wear upon their heads conical caps woven of coconut leaves, and from their waists, almost to the ground, hang petticoats made of the same leaf. They have necklaces of shells and flowers and are profusely anointed with coconut oil. During a pause in the dance, the women who are not themselves taking part in it bring bottles of oil, which they pour over their husbands, brothers, or friends in the most liberal way. This is a form of extravagance, which 'places' the anointers and anointed as among the richest of the population (p. 13).

Te kauti was the most important aspect of dancing, as it gave the protection of the *anti* (spirits) to every participant. The elders decided when *te karanga* was performed, and the dance group leader decided when to begin *te kauti*. Four days from the performance date, the men were sent to an *uma n roronga* at the Bareimwim terrace. For the next three days, they would practice *te karanga,* going to bed at sunset and waking up at three to four o'clock in the morning to perform *kauti* and evoke the *tabunea*, when the *anti* was known to be the most powerful. Their diet at this stage consisted only of *te takataka* (a piece of coconut) and water for every meal, believing that the less the performers ate, the clearer their mind would be during their performance. (Young people today neglect this part of the ritual).

The power of the dance

Since the introduction of Christianity, there has been a demise in the use of *te kauti* in dance performances. However, the practice is not lost altogether, with one dance group on Banaba today incorporating *te kauti* within its dance performance.

For the dancer to feel the power of the *te anti* surging through his or her veins is a great experience. Even today, the spectators can be overcome by the powers regenerated during the dance. The air surrounding the energetic dancers seems to be filled with an electrical charge, and even I-Matang, who have been at these events, have commented that they could feel the hairs on their arms stand up from the power of the performance. The dancers scream and yell as they release the powers of *te anti.* Sometimes the pressure is so high that dancers collapse or must be carried off during the performance.

For the uninitiated, it is hard to explain the strength generated from such powerful *tabunea* during these performances. However, one clear illustration comes from Ken's family members, his aunt, Nei Mere, who was the wife of a well-known Rabi elder clan speaker from te Karia clan, Tikaua Taratai. Shortly after World War II, while performing the *batere* on Nauru for the American soldiers, she suffered a heart attack from the excitement and died.

The Banabans believed that she was so overcome by the spirits of the dance that her body could not take it. She tried to contain her feelings and did not release the emotions that were building up inside her. She was only in her twenties (see photo 21). Banaban traditional dances are connected not only to their history and identity but also to the very spirits of their ancestors. Through dance, Banabans believe the spirits of their ancestors will live on.

Note: Ken Sigrah was a retired dancer who has followed the *kauti* ritual leading up to dance performances. For the three months before the group's performance at the opening of the Sydney Opera House in Australia in 1972, they practised the *kauti* ritual, including the special diet and preparing their costumes in proper succession.

21. Mere Nabure (who died on Nauru while performing the *batere* for American soldiers) (n.d., Miller Collection).

22. Banaban elder wearing *karanga* dance costume early 1900s (Source unknown).

PART TWO: AURIARIA

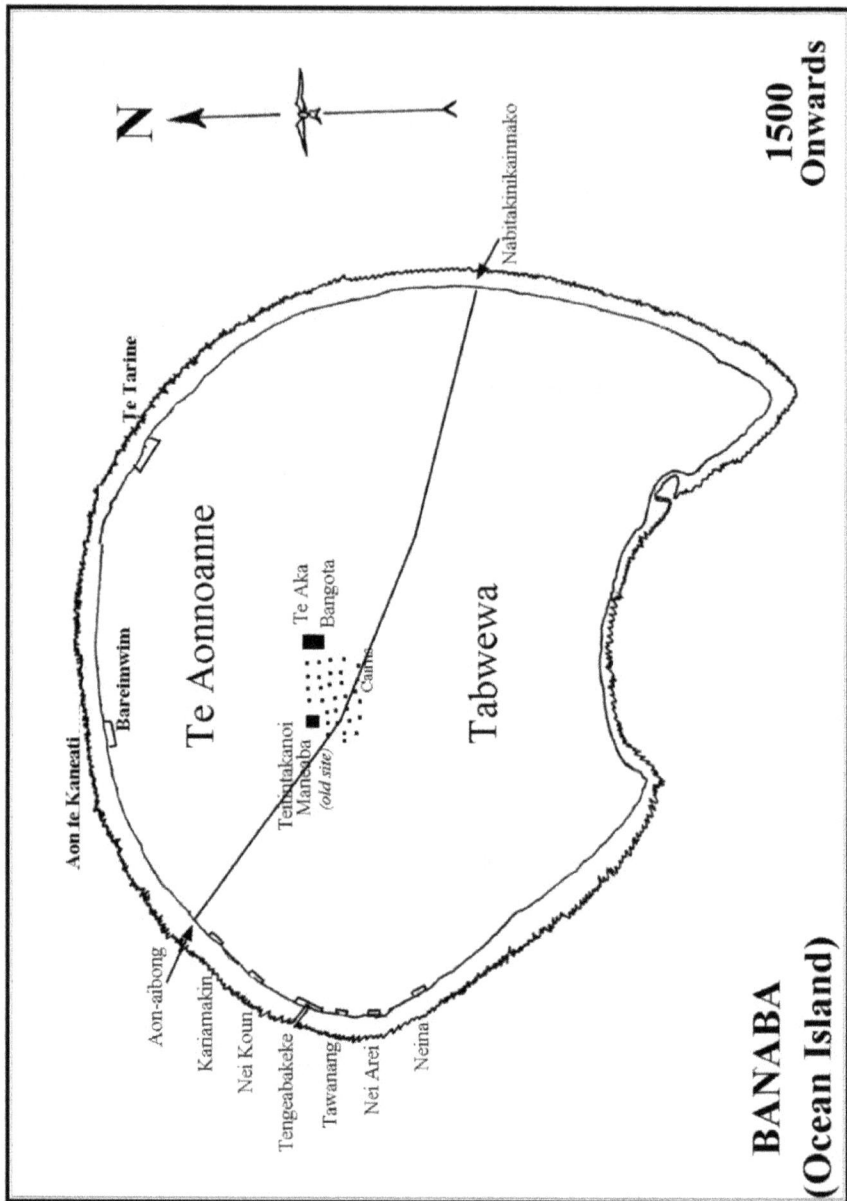

Figure: 2.1. Banaba from 1500 – first invasion (by R.K. Sigrah).

8: THE FIRST INVASION OF BANABA

According to Banaban records, the first invasion of Banaba was by Auriaria and his party in the late sixteenth century. To the Auriaria clan's descendants, he was his people's godfather or deity. He was known as Auriaria te Tabu (Auriaria the Holy). The other people who travelled with him were Tabuariki, Bakatau, Taunteang, Bare, Baia and Kautabuki, and the party also included a woman named Nei Tematenang. These people came to be regarded as demigods. Auriaria and his party originally came from Gilolo in the East Indies, now known as Halmahera, a part of Indonesia. They left Gilolo in a *baurua* (large ocean-going outrigger canoe) called Bakarerenteiti, which means 'the lightning strike.' Auriaria's first destination, after by-passing Banaba, was Nikunau, an island in the southern region of the Kiribati Group. When he landed, he named the place Tabutoa and erected a *maneaba* called Itinikarawa, meaning 'heavenly lightning'. It is said that his plans to prolong his stay on Nikunau were interrupted when his sister, Nei Aokabu, arrived with a second party from Gilolo. She was in love with two men in her party, Taburimai and Taburitongoun, whom the people of Nikunau would later call their ancestral godfathers. According to custom, Nei Aokabu's arrival at

AURIARIA GENEALOGY
TABWEWA DISTRICT
(Recording the Eldest)

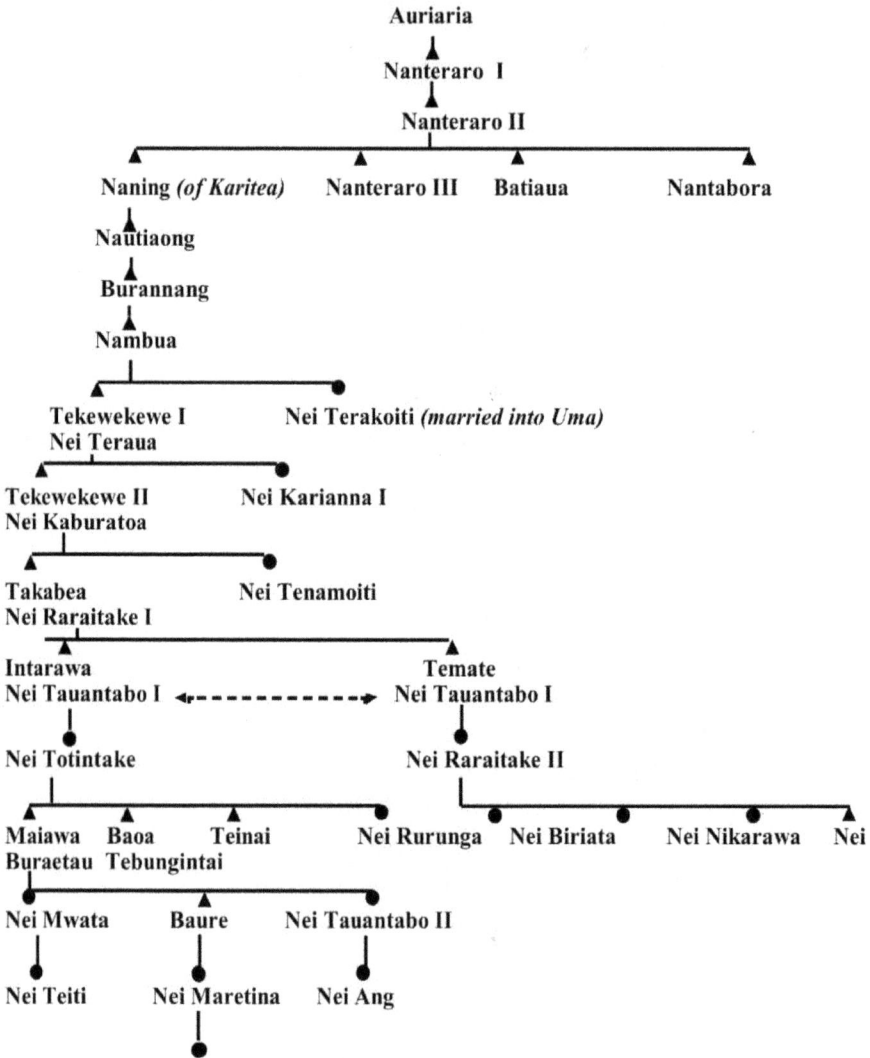

Auriaria

Nanteraro I

Nanteraro II

Naning *(of Karitea)*	**Nanteraro III**	**Batiaua**	**Nantabora**

Nautiaong

Burannang

Nambua

Tekewekewe I
Nei Teraua   **Nei Terakoiti** *(married into Uma)*

Tekewekewe II
Nei Kaburatoa   **Nei Karianna I**

Takabea
Nei Raraitake I   **Nei Tenamoiti**

Intarawa   **Temate**
Nei Tauantabo I ◀------▶ **Nei Tauantabo I**

Nei Totintake   **Nei Raraitake II**

Maiawa   Baoa   Teinai   **Nei Rurunga   Nei Biriata   Nei Nikarawa   Nei**
Buraetau Tebungintai

Nei Mwata   Baure   Nei Tauantabo II

Nei Teiti   Nei Maretina   Nei Ang

Figure: 2.2. Auriaria genealogy Tabwewa district (by R.K. Sigrah).

Nikunau put Auriaria in a difficult position. Out of respect for his sister, he gave her all his land on the island and moved on to seek new land for himself. During his brief stay on Nikunau, he did not produce any offspring. He left behind his sister, her two lovers, the *maneaba*, a stone monument known as 'stone binoculars' commemorating his arrival, and traces of land partitioning. While it is not known if the above events in Auriaria's myth are historically accurate, it is known that Auriaria te Tabu left Nikunau and sailed to find a new island he named Ubanabannang. By deleting the initial 'U' and the final 'nang' we are left with *Banaba*, which translates in Kiribati to 'the land of rock', the name in use today.

The Battle of Tairua

After Auriaria and his party landed at Tabwewa canoe passage on Banaba, they realised the island was already inhabited. They met with strong opposition from Te Aka people. According to oral history, this is known as the epic Battle of Tairua: Tairua means foreigners or outsiders. Auriaria and his party were experts in warfare. They defeated Te Aka, driving them back to the northern region and creating a land partition right across the middle of the island. The northwest boundary was marked from a place at the shoreline called Aon Aibong and up over the plateau to the southeast shoreline called Nabitakinikainako. Auriaria had already decided to settle at Tabwewa and began dividing the area into hamlets among his people. Clan records do not include the names of all those in the invading party nor the total number involved. Even though the shy and secretive Te Aka were defeated at the Battle of Tairua, it took many years for them to accept the new invaders and for social interaction to begin.

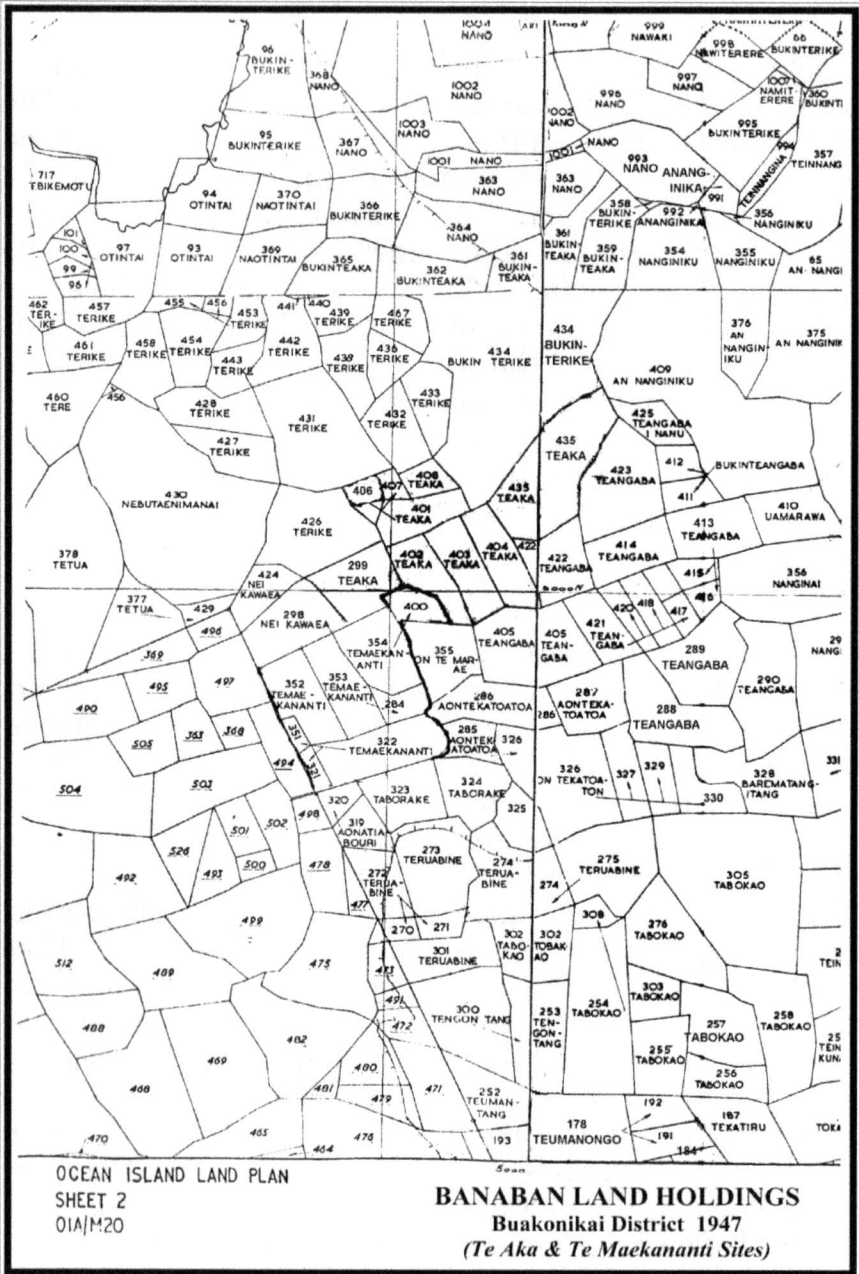

Figure: 2.3. Te Aka and Te Maekananti sites 1947 (BPC Official Map).

9: ESTABLISHMENT OF TABWEWA DISTRICT

Once the Battle of Tairua was over and the new boundary line set, Auriaria named his side of the island, Tabwewa district. According to legend, the hamlet of Aurakeia was where he first resided. In later years, his great-grandchildren began to set up family hamlets. Auriaria's grandson Nan Teraro II divided the original hamlet of Aurakeia equally between his sons. Naning called his hamlet Aurakeia of Karieta, the upland region of Tabwewa district. His other son, Nan Teraro III, called his hamlet Aurakeia of Karia, the lowland of Tabwewa district. The third to establish a hamlet was great-grandson Na Batiaua, who called his hamlet Te Maiu, also in the Karia. The fourth was Na Tabora, who was given two hamlets: Tei Namoriki of the Karieta and Aon te Bonobono of the Karia. All the people in these hamlets would become known as the Tabwewans from the Tabwewa district.

The Roles of the New Clans

The establishment of the new clans meant each developed individual roles and duties. Naning and Nan Teraro III were considered the elders and clan speakers of their respective hamlets. They were also responsible for settling land disputes and all other matters within their districts. They shared the duties of 'welcoming' and boarding foreign vessels that called on the island and organising dancing and sports, especially the *karemotu* and *katua* games (Chapter 12). Na Batiaua was the only one with the power and duty to prepare the sacred *bunna* and to garland the stranger or visitor when they arrived. Without this *bunna*, strangers or visitors were not permitted to land and were regarded as enemies. When Na Tabora stayed at his upland hamlet, Tei Namoriki, his role was to oversee the conducting of *katua* and *karemotu* games in the Karieta. When he resided at his lowland hamlet of Aon te bonobono in the Karia, his role was identical for that region, and he had the authority to oversee the formal process of setting up of the grounds for these games. He also had the role of sharing the food for both divisions during the games and whenever stranded fish was brought from the other villages to Tabwewa.

Te Aka and Mangati Hamlets

The story of the Mangati is another significant part of Auriaria clan history. The Maude's in 1932 and 1994 provided the only published mention of Mangati. However, they made several errors, which are examined in more detail in Chapter 16. In 1932 they wrote, "Indeed there is evidence suggesting that they have, to some extent, kept their separate identity to this day and that they are none other than the people of Mangati – the fierce people ...". Here he has confused people from Mangati hamlet with Te Aka clan. Another error in their statement was, "Na Kamta is the chief of Tabwewa" (p. 264). According to Banaban genealogy charts, Na Kamta was only an elder of the Mangati hamlet at the time of the battle over the cairns and was not descended from Tabwewa. His great-grandparents came from Uma hamlet, and both were given land in Tabwewa by the grandson of Auriaria.

The battle over sacred Te Aka cairns

The hamlet called Mangati, where Na Kamta settled was located within the boundaries of the new Tabwewa district sometime after the arrival of Nei Anginimaeao in the late seventeenth century. It was also close to the sacred site of Te Aka *bangota*, to which Te Aka clan still had access. Over the years, as the boundaries of Tabwewa began to expand, it also started to infringe upon this sacred site. What followed was fight between Te Aka clan and Na Kamta and his family from the Mangati hamlet. During this dispute, the descendants of Auriaria residing in Tabwewa helped Na Kamta by sending enforcements to help fend off Te Aka. The outcome of this clash resulted in Te Aka keeping their original boundaries intact along with access to their sacred site of Te Aka *bangota*. Maybe they were better prepared for the Mangati fight than they had been for the Battle of Tairua. *Te Karanga Are E Uarereke* (The War Club Dance) reenacts this event (see Appendix 10).

23. Tabwewa [Ocean Island], village (Postcard 1910).

Confusion over Te Aka and Mangati

There has been much debate and confusion over Te Aka and Mangati's boundaries. In a 1947 land survey (Figure 2.3), the British Phosphate Commission recorded at least nineteen individual pieces of land falling within seven hamlets. Because of the importance of these hamlets' locations and the misrepresentation of Mangati as Te Aka in history, it is essential to record the names of the seven hamlets – Te Rike, Nabutaenimanai, Te Tua, Teabanara, Terenaine, Te Tira and Tanrakenikarawa. Mangati and Te Aka have never shared a boundary.

Further confusion is found in Maude's 1994 recording of myths and legends told by Nei Anginimaeao's descendants. He describes the fierce Mangati people known for their expertise in magic. Maude mistook these people for the people of Te Aka. Maude said the sacred cairns at Te Burita

24. Tabwewa Canoe Passage (Miller Collection 1908-39).

were a dangerous and haunted place that everyone on the island feared. The Te Aka myths and legends retell the story of Te Burita, the place where the two large *te itai* grow, commonly known as the 'ship trees' (see Chapter 3). This area is situated on the other side of Te Aka *bangota* towards the northern coast. Both these areas are considered sacred sites and are found in the Te Aonoanne district that falls under Te Aka clan. The war canoe of Te Aonoanne district is also named Te Burita in honour of this second sacred site. Maude has wrongly identified these important locations as being under the Mangati clan. The site of Mangati hamlet is located further to the south in the Karieta (uplands) division of the Tabwewa district.

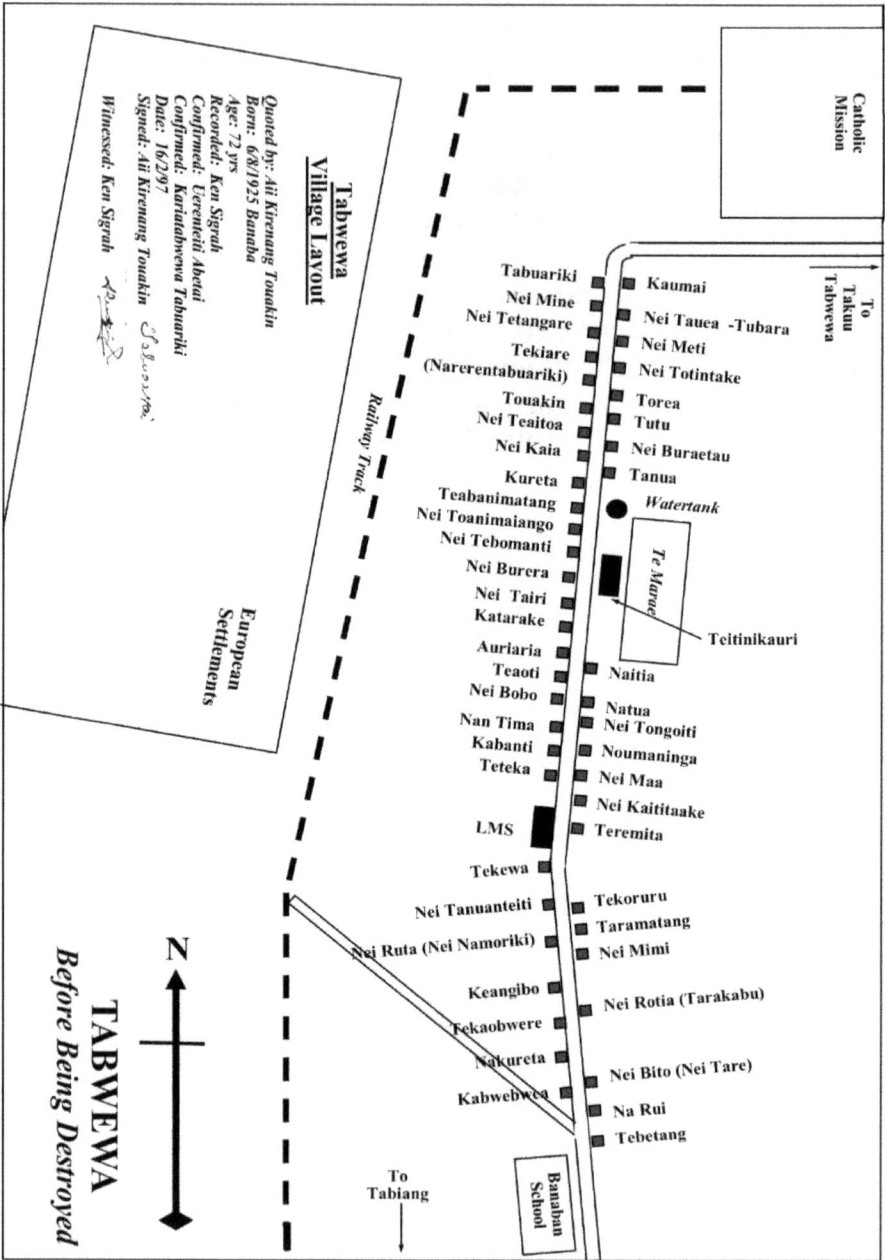

Figure: 2.4. Tabwewa Village layout before destruction (by R.K. Sigrah).

10: INTERPRETATION OF AURIARIA'S HISTORY

The totem of the Auriaria clan is said to be Tabakea (Turtle). The Auriaria people considered Tabakea a deity. It was strictly forbidden for them to fish or eat their sacred totem. It was only when Nei Anginimaeao arrived on Banaba nearly a century after the arrival of the Auriaria people that they witnessed the catching and eating of turtles without dire consequences.

From clan history, it is known that the Auriaria believed in life after death. They believed that to reach paradise, the deceased had first to pass through the gateway to the beyond. This gateway was obstructed by the evil spirit Nakaa and his large fishing net. A person could only get past this net with the assistance of the totem Tabakea who was also there to greet and guide them. Tabakea would only assist if he considered the person was good and pleased him. If the deceased had not appeased this beloved totem, he or she was permanently caught in Nakaa's nets.

There are different versions of Auriaria's history and beliefs because the original versions became confused with the other histories after the last invasion of Banaba by Nei Anginimaeao and her group from Beru in Kiribati. It should be remembered that Auriaria came from Gilolo in the East Indies via Nikunau.

The only written records regarding Auriaria's journey and arrival on Banaba come from Pacific historians Arthur Grimble and Harry Maude. They recount a slightly different tale to that of Te Aka oral history. Te Aka's oral history concurs with records that Auriaria passed through Nikunau on the way from Gilolo to Banaba but disagrees that Auriaria imposed Kiribati culture, as these historians claim. In a Kiribati myth, Auriaria is a demi-god (half man, half spirit) originally from Tamoa (Samoa) and, therefore, Polynesian. It is known from the history of Kiribati's southern atolls that many of their islands' early inhabitants were Samoans. Maude's 1932 writings confirmed that the second arrivals on Banaba were the tall, fair-skinned people from Gilolo in the East Indies who had already overrun the Kiribati Group. Over the years, with the publishing of the Kiribati version of the myth of Auriaria, more confusion emerged regarding the spiritual beliefs and totem of the Auriaria clan. In later chapters, the later arrival of Nei Anginimaeao (Part Three) demonstrates how her influence impacted Auriaria's early settlement in the Tabwewa District and the rest of Banaba. Today on Rabi, the Auriaria clan's descendants firmly consider themselves Banabans. This clan has for generations known and believed in their Gilolo ancestry and has never accepted the claims of their historical ties to Kiribati culture.

11: MYTHS AND LEGENDS

This chapter discusses three myths, and the Auriaria claims they were the first inhabitants of Banaba. Grimble and Maude documented the arrival of Auriaria to Banaba, but they based their records on the following Kiribati version of Auriaria's journey.

Myth A Banaban Creation:

"Auriaria was a giant who did not sail but was capable of walking across the water. He conquered all the islands on his way, including some of those in Kiribati. On reaching Banaba, he fell in love with a woman called Nei Tituabine, and they had offspring. She was said to be a Kiribati goddess. Because Nei Tituabine was said to have cheated on Auriaria, he became so angry that he took his walking stick or staff and capsized the whole of Banaba, so that it looked like an upturned canoe. This myth of the creation of Banaba states the belief that the first inhabitants sprang from Auriaria."

However, Te Aka were the indigenous inhabitants of Banaba, while Auriaria and his party were the first known invaders. To continue telling this myth is to dismiss the very existence of Te Aka. What is also known from Banaban oral history, now recorded in written form by Grimble and Maude, is that Nei Tituabine was regarded as a goddess brought into Banaban culture by Nei Anginimaeao and her group from Beru. Their invasion was a century after the arrival of Auriaria on Banaba. So, this myth does not match historical knowledge.

Myth B: The Myth of Auriaria, the Godfather

Today the elders of the Auriaria clan believe that Auriaria is the godfather of all Banaban people. The following myth explains:

> When Nei Anginimaeao and her party came to Banaba, they began to partition the land. Kouteba (Nei Anginimaeao's brother) went walking through Te Aonoanne district on the northern side of the island, thinking that no one else lived there. While he was looking for a place to leave a land marker near the seashore, he noticed something moving on the sand. He was curious, so he lifted the object and to his surprise found a *makauro* (hermit crab) talking to him. So Kouteba asked the *makauro*, 'Oh ... who are you, and where do you come from? I thought nobody was living here?' *Makauro* answered, 'So Kouteba, at last, you have noticed me. I want to tell you that my name is Auriaria and I own the whole of Banaba.' Kouteba told Auriaria of his journey in search of land and how his party had arrived on Banaba. Auriaria took pity on him and offered to help. He told Kouteba to follow his instructions carefully. The first thing Kouteba did was to take a wife. He was told to wait in a hiding place at a certain point of the reef where creatures who were half girl and half spirit swam. He was told to use a fishing net to trap one of these half-spirits, so that she could become his wife. He was instructed that once he had caught a wife, he should place her in a basket for three days in order for her to take on full human form. The first girl he trapped

was called Nei Bokeang. He followed instructions and placed her in a basket. On the second day, he became impatient and opened the basket. As soon as he did, Nei Bokeang escaped, as she was still an *anti n aomata* (half human, half spirit). She was never seen again. Auriaria met Kouteba again and told him to go back to the place at the reef and this time to try for Nei Bokeang's sister, Nei Teanibuti. This time when he netted Nei Teanibuti, he followed Auriaria's instructions and did not open the basket until three days had passed and Nei Teanibuti had turned into a real woman. Both she and her sister were said to be descendants of the Tabwewa people. Kouteba took her as his wife, and Auriaria gave him the right to inherit land known as Te Aonoanne. Kouteba settled down with Nei Teanibuti and had children. Through this myth, Kouteba came to be regarded as the first inhabitant of the northern region of Banaba, an inheritance given to him by Auriaria himself.

This myth confuses several historical facts. Maude and Maude, in 1932, stated that "Kouteba himself married one of the Tabwewans" (p. 267). However, Te Aka oral history and clan records show that Nei Teanibuti was a descendant of Teimanaia, the godfather of Te Aka clan (see Chapter 4, Figure 1.7). Moreover, Kouteba arrived on Banaba with Nei Anginimaeao nearly a century after Auriaria's arrival. Therefore, Auriaria had passed away well before that. From the description of the location and the mention of Te Aonoanne, it is evident that the land is that of Te Aka. It is also known that Te Aka had the entire northern district, including the shoreline, right up to the time of the Great Drought (early 1870s) at least. This period of upheaval was followed by the arrival of missionaries and the Europeans who began to mine in 1900. So, if Kouteba met a man in this myth, that man would have come from Te Aka clan. Once Nei Anginimaeao arrived, the land already held by the Auriaria clan on the southern side was split up between Nei

Anginimaeao and two other members of her party (Chapter 13). Even during this time of great upheaval, Te Aonoanne district on the northern side was intact. Through Kouteba's marriage into Te Aka clan, he took up his duty as an in-law, residing in this region. The secrecy surrounding Te Aka and the mere mention of 'Te Aka' was considered taboo, and the northern district was instead referred to as Te Aonoanne. To elevate Kouteba to the role of leader or godfather for this region is not supported by historical evidence.

Myth C: The Myth of Te toa Ma I-Matang

Peter Anderson recorded this myth on Banaba in 1941:

Auriaria, a powerful devil from Samoa, came upon Banaba and, not liking it, turned it over with his magic *te Ibi* stick (that is why the coral is found on top!). He then called Nei Tituabine from the land of Matang to live with him. Their descendants, the first Banabans, called Te Makauro (Hermit Crab), lived at Tabwewa. To keep out strangers, Auriaria commenced building a wall of coral around the Island, using his magic stick to carry the large pieces of reef ashore. (There is no reef within the bay between Ooma and Tabiang.) The giant Te Toa Ma I-Matang killed him and broke his magic stick because he wanted other people to come to the island. Auriaria was buried at Nangkouea near Ooma, whence the first trees came. His Terakunene stone may still be seen there. Then according to legend Te Toa Ma, I-Matang brought Tokiteba, Nei Anginimaeao and Nei Teborata from Beru (or Peru in South America or Boru in the Moluccas?) to Banaba. Running around the Island, they selected their land and formed the villages of Te Aka, Ooma and Tabiang, marrying with the Makauro people and naming the lands accordingly ... The island of Banaba is really an overturned turtle (*te oon tabakea*), and [this] is a purely Kiribati belief not shared by the Banabans.

Contentious points

Listed below are some of the contentious points in the myth of Auriaria creation, as recounted above:

- Where did Te Toa Ma I–Matang come from, and who is he?

Fact: There is no such giant in our recorded history. 'Matang' refers to a 'fair–skinned' person in society.

- Why was Auriaria referred to as a 'powerful devil' who was killed?

Fact: Auriaria is never referred to as a devil or spirit but as a human, a man who is considered the first invader of Banaba who settled Tabwewa district.

- Could the killing of Auriaria be an attempt to discredit his history and promote theories of later land settlement?

Fact: Throughout the Pacific, 'killing off' past heroes or invaders was a way of developing a new story to overwrite historical facts.

- Nangkouea is named as the place where Auriaria was buried.

Fact: This is impossible as Nangkouea was the first hamlet established within Uma district by Na Maninimate, who arrived with Nei Anginimaeao and her party nearly 100 years after Auriaria's arrival.

- There is no mention of forming the district of Toakira, but there is mention of Te Aka, Uma and Tabiang.

Fact: This myth was recorded at a much later period when the storyteller was unaware of the existence of Toakira and Te Aonoanne in Banaban history.

When Myths are not Backed by Historical Facts

Preserving these three myths throughout the generations was a simple way of telling the story of Auriaria's arrival to his descendants. The elevation of the Auriaria clan founders to a god-like status is common practice among the Banaban people. By stating Auriaria was the first inhabitant of Banaba, these myths have served the purpose of giving his descendants greater status than any earlier or later arrivals on the island. These myths were embellished even further after the last invasion of Nei Anginimaeao from Beru. From that time, because of Kiribati influences, it began to be claimed that Auriaria had come from Kiribati, with origins in Tamoa (Samoa). Therefore, from Polynesian ancestry rather than Gilolo (Halmahera) (Chapter 16). This story of the original settlement from Kiribati grew over the years that followed, especially when a Kiribati labour force was brought to work the phosphate mines on Banaba. Challenging these myths is the fact that physical evidence found in a Te Aka dig in 1965 proves the uncovered skeletal remains were not of Polynesian origin. The three myths demonstrate how stories were created to give the illusion of a stronger bond to Kiribati culture.

12: FISHING

For years after Auriaria and his group arrived on Banaba, they interacted with the indigenous inhabitants, Te Aka. Although for a long time, Te Aka preferred to keep to themselves. However, sports and marriage were major social influences that slowly established interaction between two old enemies. The Auriaria clan began to share their skills and knowledge of ocean seafaring and fishing with the Te Aka clan and gathered new skills from Te Aka.

Te Roa Ati (Tuna Pole Fishing)

One of the first sports introduced was *te roa ati*, tuna pole fishing. It was an essential skill to the Auriaria clan that they brought to Banaba.

Materials required

The Auriaria clan found the stalactites in the sacred *bangabanga* and, after close study, used the stalactites to carve fishing shanks, which they called *kaneati.* They then used small human bones or shells suitable as hooks and lashed them to the shank with fine sennit twine or plaited human hair. They attached a tail of fibre at the base of the hook to act as a lure.

Te abo (fishing line) was made of hibiscus fibre that was

26. *Te Bareaka*, canoe shed (Williams Collection 1901-31).

braided in a certain way, known as *te karo ten*, to form one long length. The line usually was about 30 centimetres shorter than the wooden fishing pole.

The wood for *te kain roa* (fishing pole) came from the wood taken from *te ngea* (*Pemphis acifula*). This timber was usually hard to find, especially in the straight lengths needed for the pole. Once a suitable branch was found, it was cut and treated over a fire. This process not only assisted in drying out the wood but also, it was said, added to the strength of the timber and its overall flexibility. If the branch was not straight, its thin end was tied to a tree, and a heavy weight was attached to the other end. It was left hanging in this position for at least a month or until it had straightened enough for use as a pole.

Use of *te kauti*

The Auriaria clan utilised the skills of Te Aka in sorcery and magic so they could be invoked in *te kauti*, especially for important sports such as pole fishing. The Auriaria already possessed their own powers of magic but now incorporated new ideas they were beginning to learn from Te Aka, especially through intermarriage and the birth of children who inherited the secrets and skills from both clans. The first and most important rule relating to pole fishing was the *te kauti* ritual and all its associated restrictions leading up to the event. *Te kauti* in this sport was virtually the same as other sporting events, except for *te bareaka* (canoe sheds) built at the terraces to house the outrigger canoes. The participants brought their canoes and all the equipment needed for the sport so that *te kauti* could begin. The ceremony took three days. They called upon the powers of the *anti* to bless and empower the participants and all their equipment. After *te kauti*, the sport was ready to begin. The

"A TOILER OF THE DEEP," OCEAN ISLAND

27. Banaban single *te waa*, outrigger canoe (Postcard 1910).

elders would arrange the date to coincide with the *bonito* (skipjack tuna) season, when large schools of these fish moved close to the shoreline, especially around the island's leeward side (later known as Home Bay). Representing his family or clan, each fisherman went alone in a single-seater outrigger. In later times, individual competitors represented their village. Because the deep water is so close to the shore, the spectators could line the higher ground around the coast to watch the game.

The objective was to be the last person in the game. As the fishing began, judges or referees watched each fisherman closely. A participant was disqualified if he accidentally dropped a fish. He was also disqualified if a fishing pole snapped or a fishing line broke. The competition proceeded until only one fisherman was left, and he was deemed the winner. At the end of the day, all the fish were distributed amongst the competitors' families to enjoy the feasting and recognition of the best fisherman. These games continued as long as the season lasted. There were no strict rules on who among the men could compete in this game. All men were considered equal. Therefore, all were eligible to compete. The season concluded with a celebration to recognise the overall champion for that season. Today Banabans still use the art of pole fishing on Rabi, utilising boats equipped with outboard motors. Some still use canoes. The skill and craft of canoe making will always be treasured within Banaban society.

Banaban Outrigger Canoes

After the arrival of the Auriaria clan and the introduction of their seafaring skills to Te Aka society, a distinctly Banaban outrigger canoe evolved. It had a raised and ornately decorated prows, as reported by Captain Mackay, of the Queensland Brig *Flora,* on his visit to the island in 1875. Here is his detailed description of the Banaban canoes:

"Their canoes are beautiful specimens of savage skill a

and mechanism, constructed wholly of small pieces of wood, neatly sewn together with sennit, made from the coconut fibre; each end is raised, with a curve about ten feet above the deck, beautifully carved and inlaid with pearl and tortoiseshell. In these frail craft, they venture many miles away from their island home; but notwithstanding their dexterity in managing them, a great number have been lost or blown away" (as cited in, Maude & Maude, 1994, p. 89).

In 1900, Albert Ellis also commented on the unique style of Banaban canoes:

"The high prows of these crafts and their fine lines made them both attractive and seaworthy. They were not dug outs but properly built with small *tamana* wood boards, laboriously hewn from local timber. No nails were were available, and in any case, the strong coconut sennit neatly laced along the plank edges was

28. Banaban *te waa,* three-seater outrigger canoe (Miller Collection 1908-1939).

107

more suitable, and better able to stand the shock when the canoes were dashed on the reef by the surf, as was inevitably the case at times. They were of light construction, and one capable of holding a crew of five could be readily carried down the beach and across the reef by two men. A canoe thus, manned would make good headway against quite a heavy sea and the strong equatorial current; it was an invaluable item in the Banaban equipment" (Ellis, 1936, p. 73).

The high prows were initially designed to cope with the large surf and swell that hit the edge of the fringing reefs. The prows helped save the canoes from taking in water as their crew skillfully maneuvered them through the waves. By the early 1900s, Banaban canoes were slightly different, with lower elevated prows of less than a metre. They were no longer decorated. After 1900 the imported labour force introduced different Kiribati and Ellice styles of canoes. Today on Rabi, the community has implemented a canoe making programme. The design is based on flat prows, as Rabi does not have the rough surf found around Banaba. When the programme started, the canoes were handmade using traditional tools and fine sennit coil. Now the demand has increased, and the craftsmen are making the canoes from modern materials such as marine ply, brass screws and strong fishing line for bindings.

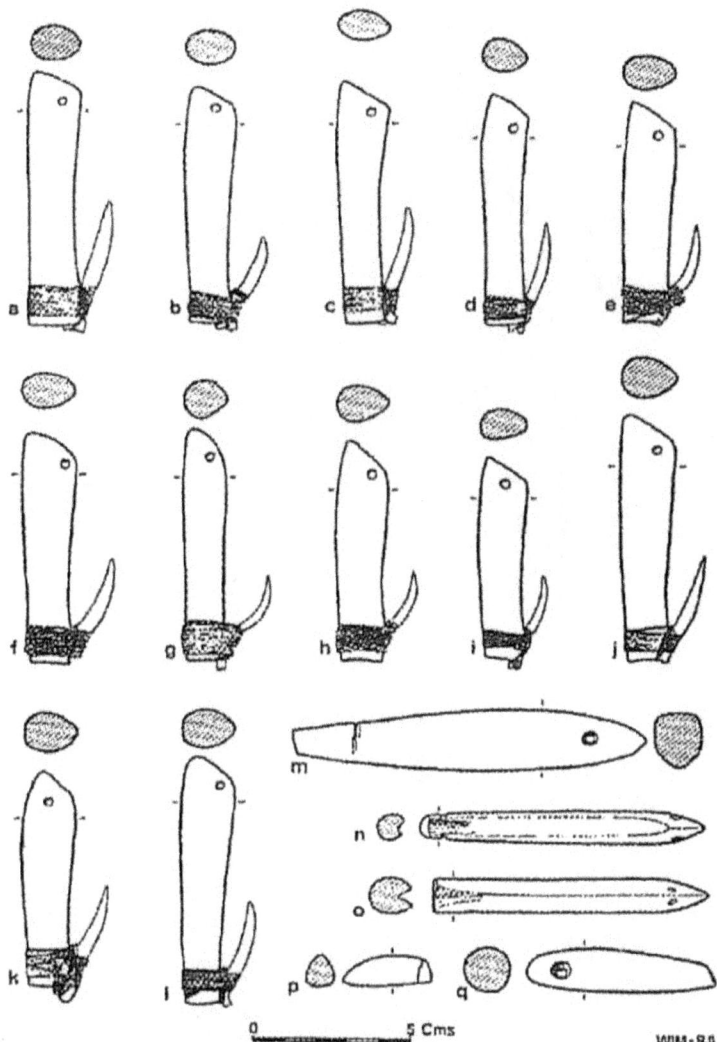

FIGURE 2

Fig 2: Legend

a to l. Complete hooks from the Maude collection; lateral view; hackles and lines have been omitted from drawings.
m. Unfinished shank from the Maude collection; lateral view.
n & o. Finished shanks from the Maude collection; dorsal view.
p. Part of unfinished shank from excavation at Te Aka Village, Ocean Island (publication forthcoming); lateral view.
q. Part of a finished shank from same excavation; lateral view.

29. *Te kaneati*, Banaban fishing hooks (H.E. Maude and Lampert 1967).

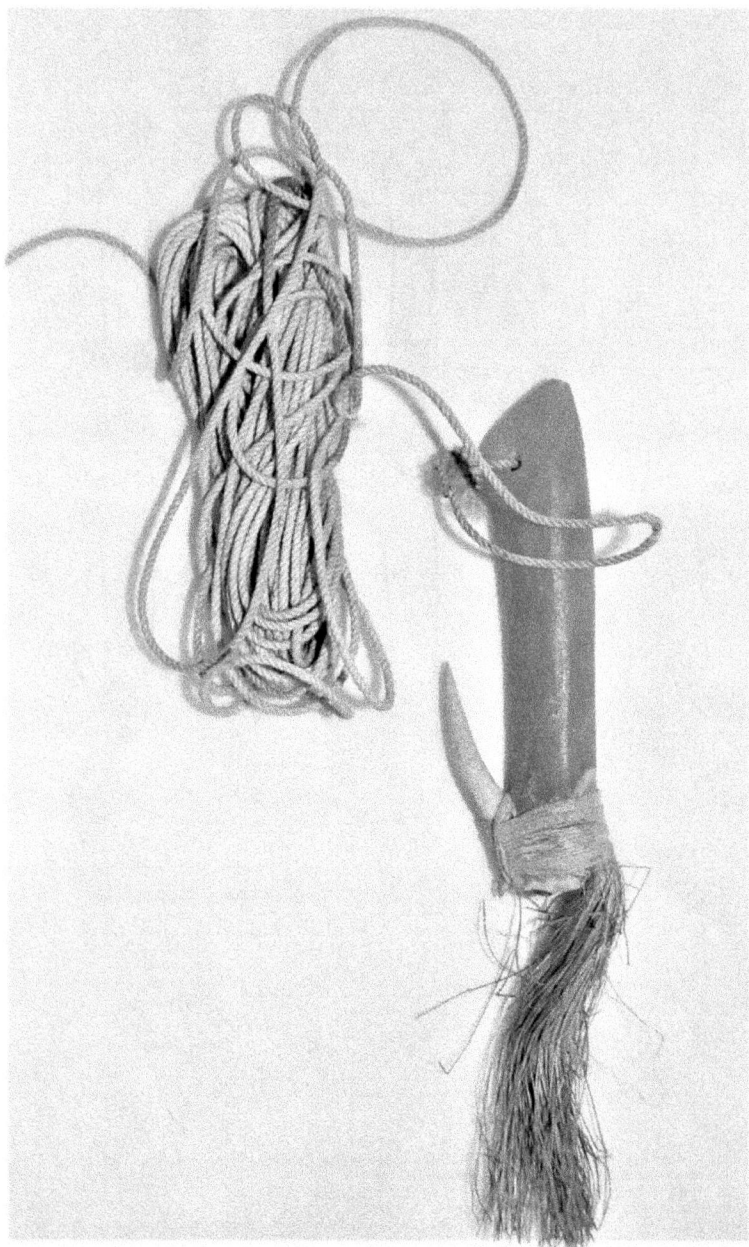

30. *Te kaneati*, Banaban fishing hook donated to British Museum by Arthur Grimble 1931.

PART THREE:
NEI ANGINIMAEO

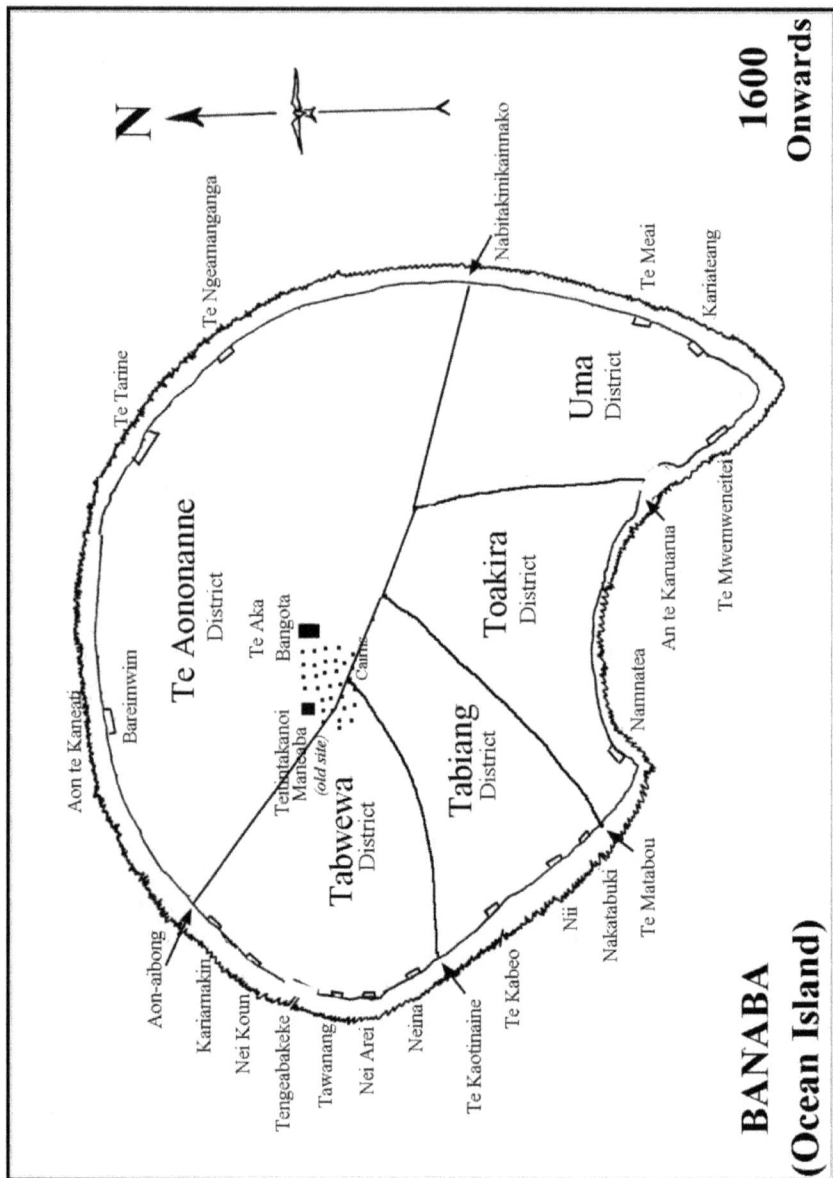

Figure: 3.1. Banaba from 1600 (by R.K. Sigrah).

13: THE SECOND ARRIVALS ON BANABA

According to Te Aka history, in the late seventeenth century, Nei Anginimaeao landed on the spot known as Aon te Ruarua in the southeastern area of the island, which is now known as Uma Village. The whole southern region of the island was already under the ownership of the Tabwewans (the descendants of the Auriaria clan). The Tabwewans permitted Nei Anginimaeao and her party to land. They arrived with many new skills that were much appreciated by Tabwewans. For the new group to stay and live on Banaba, they traded these skills for land. The Banabans call this process 'claiming the rights'; giving these skills was like entering into a permanent contract in which only the new owners could use the skill or knowledge. To Banabans, who knew nothing of money, skills were valuable and could be traded. On the northern district of Te Aonoanne, the Te Aka retained their land and somewhat separate traditions and identity.

A Modern Controversy over Past Events

In notes made by Grimble and later edited by Maude and Maude (1932, 1989, 1994), the most common of the landing of Nei Anginimaeao is based on an interview by Grimble with Nei Beteua, a direct descendant of Nei Anginimaeao:

"Nei Anginimaeao arrived on Banaba at the invitation of the Banabans, who were few in number and anxious to increase the population of the island. She brought with her many Beru relations led by Na Kouteba, her brother, Na Mani-ni-mate, and Nei Te-borata."

Maude added,

"... the newcomers proceeded to partition the island in an arbitrary manner, and the older inhabitants, quite over-awed, returned to their settlement on the flat seacoast land below Tabwewa" (p. 265).
"This partition of Banaba made by Nei Angi-ni-maeao is of great importance, as the boundaries of the five village districts thus fixed, stand unaltered to this day" (p. 266).

Te Aka clan records do not match Nei Beteua's claims in her statement to Grimble. Her claims raise the following questions:

1. Why would Nei Anginimaeao be **invited to come and settle on Banaba**? Nei Anginimaeao arrived on Banaba nearly a century after Auriaria. If there is any truth in the claim that Nei Anginimaeao arrived on Banaba at 'the invitation of the Banabans', as Maude recorded, it is strange that the Anginimaeao clan descendants hold no rights to any cultural events in Banaban society today (Chapter 15).

2. The **population of Banaba** was said to be low and needed to grow. Banaban genealogy charts suggest a relatively healthy population.

3. **Why was the Te Aka district of Te Aonoanne never partitioned**? After Nei Anginimaeao's arrival, only the southern districts held by Auriaria's descendants were divided into three portions.

4. Nei Beteua stated that the **older inhabitants were overawed** and returned to their settlement on the flat coast below Tabwewa and that the newcomers' then partitioned the island in an arbitrary manner. As far as Banaban oral history recalls, the Tabwewans were never overawed but negotiated land ownership in exchange for new skills, knowledge and rights which are still part of Banaban culture today.

5. Maude noted **five village districts**. This was true at the time of the partitioning by Nei Anginimaeao (Uma, Tabwewa, Tabiang, Toakira, Te Aonoanne). However, by the time of Maude's writing, there were only four districts. Te Aonoanne and Toakira had been merged to form Buakonikai.

6. Failure to acknowledge Te Aka. The Nei Anginimaeao's myth of partitioning fails to mention Te Aka because the name Te Aka was cursed and considered taboo. The new name Te Aonoanne (meaning 'that place') took its place. Also, Te Aka were not involved in exchanging rights and land on the southern coast and became marginalised.

The historical facts

Te Aka clan genealogy charts back up other historical accounts relating to Kiribati history and the arrival of Nei Anginimaeao in Banaba. On the genealogy chart of Na Kouteba (the brother of Nei Anginimaeao who arrived with her party), his position goes back thirteen generations. Working on twenty-five-year spans for each generation and estimating the landing of Nei Anginimaeao as approximately the mid-seventeenth century.

In Arthur Grimble's *Tungaru Traditions* (1989) regarding the Battle of Kaitu and Uakeia, he states that the two chiefs of Beru fought and conquered nearly every island in Kiribati. This date coincides with Banaban genealogy charts, and the event could have led Nei Anginimaeao and her group to flee in search of new land or become driftaways. In his sworn statement to the UK court in 1975, Maude's statement fits very closely with Banaban genealogy charts:

> "Much more is certain about the second party, led by Nei Angi-ni-maeao of Beru Island in the Gilberts. On genealogical evidence, this group arrived at Ocean Island about the year 1650 and may, therefore, be presumed to have consisted of refugees from the wars of Kaitu and Uakeia, which were in progress at that time. Other fugitives from these wars colonised Nui in the Ellice Group."

The Evolution of the Banaban People

During clan meetings on Rabi, elders have often questioned why modern historians have overlooked Banaban identity relating to the earlier times in Banaban history before the arrival of Europeans. This problem has arisen because Banabans have either remained unaware of the earlier invasions and settlements or relied on conventional European Colonial history written in recent times. The misunderstandings about the evolution of the Banaban people are because modern-day Banabans have relied too much on the Grimble–Maude version of Banaban history not recorded until well after 1900. There has been a misinterpretation of Te Aka as the original inhabitants of Banaba and the later influence of Auriaria and Nei Anginimaeao. A further misconception has been that these two new groups of arrivals did not take over the island or impose Kiribati culture. In fact, for two hundred years, a blending of cultures and customs took place and created a new and uniquely Banaban identity. It is imperative to recognise that Nei Anginimaeao's and her party's arrival involved breaking away from their original ties to Kiribati.

The earlier invader, Auriaria, also had moved away from his original culture and origins.

Auriaria and Nei Anginimaeao came to Banaba. They neither owned land there nor had a genealogy linked to it. Regardless of their motives for arriving at Banaba, "Banaba was a place of no return" (statement, H.E. Maude, 1975, p. 5). They soon claimed land through war or arbitrary negotiations over land in Nei Anginimaeao's case. Thus, from early on, they began to form bonds with Banaba, providing them with a place in Banaban history. These new arrivals certainly brought their own cultures with them. Their interactions with the indigenous inhabitants, Te Aka, have contributed to the rich culture of the Banaban people we know today. Every Banaban should be able to trace his or her family genealogy to at least one or two of these three main clans; Te Aka, Auriaria and Nei Anginimaeao. These are the blood ties of a Banaban.

ANGINIMAEAO GENEALOGY
TABIANG DISTRICT
(Recording the Eldest)

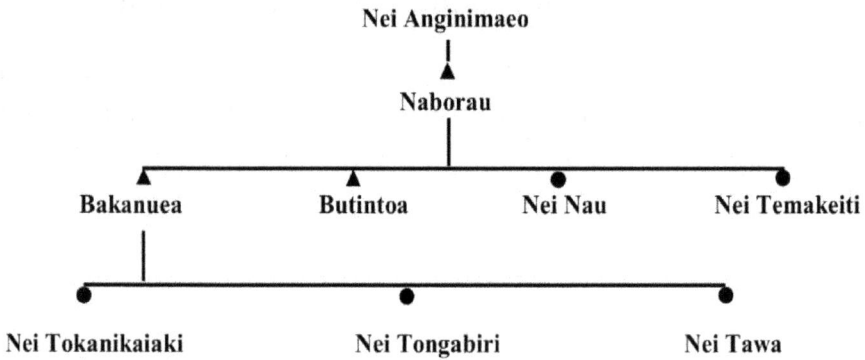

Nei Anginimaeo

Naborau

| **Bakanuea** | **Butintoa** | **Nei Nau** | **Nei Temakeiti** |

| **Nei Tokanikaiaki** | **Nei Tongabiri** | **Nei Tawa** |

(All have descendants on Banaba and Rabi today)

Figure: 3.2. Anginimaeao genealogy Tabiang district (by R.K. Sigrah).

14: OLD AND NEW BOUNDARIES

Some boundaries, notably on the northern Te Aka side of Banaba, did not change with the arrival of Nei Anginimaeao. However, on the southern side, her arrival led to three new districts. All of Nei Anginimaeao's party were invited to stay by the people from Tabwewa district (Chapter 16). The Tabwewans gave land to three of the party in exchange for various 'rights and skills.' This chapter examines the districts or villages, Tabiang, Uma, Toakira and Tabwewa.

Tabiang District

Nei Anginimaeao was given land next to the Tabwewans' primary location. This new district she called Tabiang, which was the name of her *maneaba* on Beru. The western boundary line of the district commenced at the seashore at a place called Te Kaoti-n Aine, meaning 'the woman's arrival.' On old maps drawn by Maude, the place is called Te Kouti-n Aine, which translates to the Kiribati word for 'a small mat worn about the shoulders.' (Grimble and Maude make a similar mistake when referring to *te kauti* magic ritual, which they often spelt as *te kouti*). Banabans know that their ancestors named this place to commemorate Nei

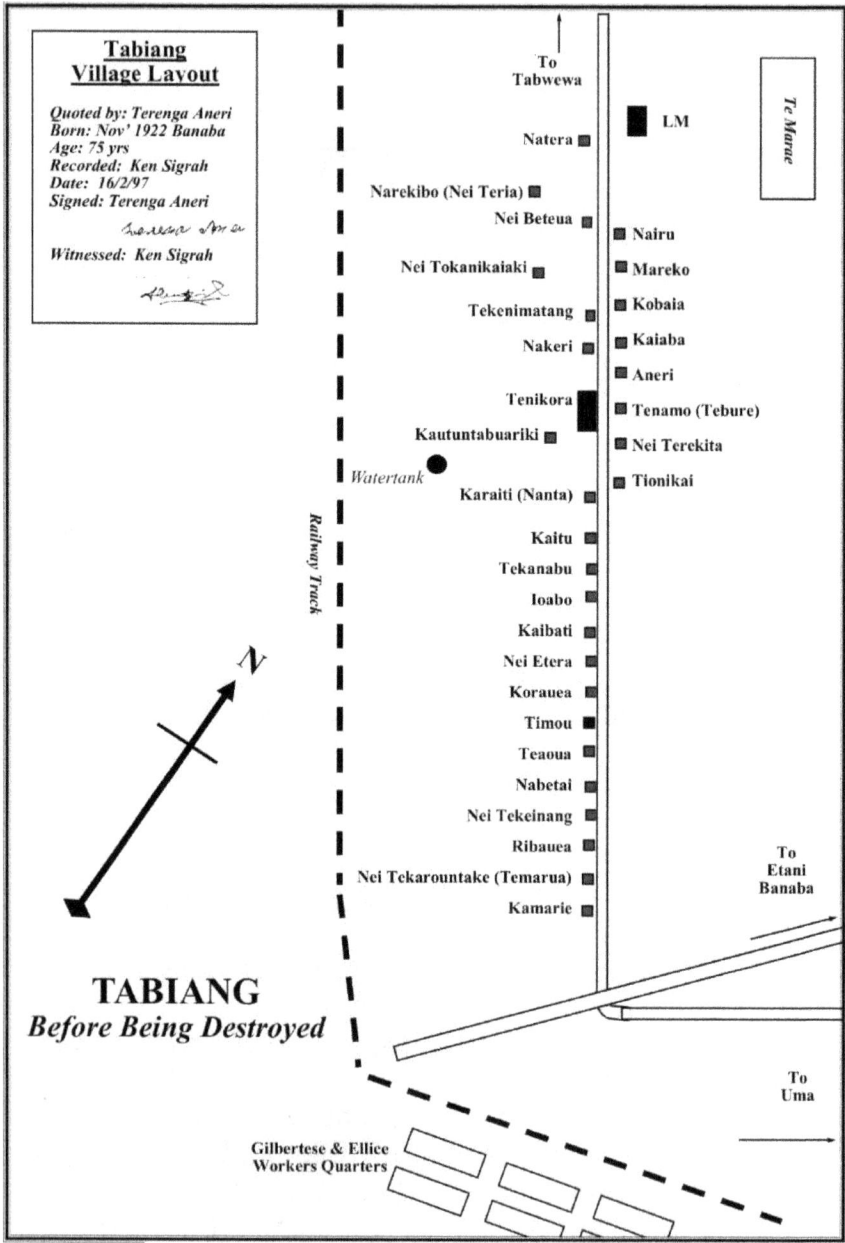

Tabiang Village Layout

Quoted by: *Terenga Aneri*
Born: *Nov' 1922 Banaba*
Age: *75 yrs*
Recorded: *Ken Sigrah*
Date: *16/2/97*
Signed: *Terenga Aneri*

Witnessed: *Ken Sigrah*

To
Tabwewa

Te Marae

Natera ■   ■ LM

Narekibo (Nei Teria) ■

Nei Beteua ■

■ Nairu

Nei Tokanikaiaki ■   ■ Mareko

Tekenimatang ■   ■ Kobaia

Nakeri ■   ■ Kaiaba

■ Aneri

Tenikora ■   ■ Tenamo (Tebure)

Kautuntabuariki ■   ■ Nei Terekita

Watertank ●   ■ Tionikai

Karaiti (Nanta) ■

Kaitu ■

Tekanabu ■

Ioabo ■

Kaibati ■

Nei Etera ■

Korauea ■

Timou ■

Teaoua ■

Nabetai ■

Nei Tekeinang ■

Ribauea ■

Nei Tekarountake (Temarua) ■

Kamarie ■

To
Etani
Banaba

Railway Track

N

TABIANG
Before Being Destroyed

To
Uma

Gilbertese & Ellice
Workers Quarters

Figure: 3.3. Tabiang Village layout before destruction (by R.K. Sigrah).

31. Pathway through Tabiang (Williams Collection 1901–1931).

Anginimaeao's arrival. The district extended along the coast just before the southern point of the island to a place called te Mata-Bou (New Face or Eyes). The boundaries extended to the island's crest through to the boundary of what was now called Te Aonoanne district, where Te Aka clan lived on the entire northern side of the island (see Figure 3.1).

The district's three terraces along the shoreline were called Tekabeo, Nii and Nakatabuki. The first *maneaba* was named Te Kiakia n Tabiang. The name changed in later years to Te Nikora.

The names of Tabiang **hamlets** were as follows:

Ata-ni Banaba	Buariki	Nakieba
Bare Bongawa	Buki	Nanimanono
Bare Buiairake	Etani Banaba	Neingkambo
Nei Rao	Tabo ni Buota	te Aba n Aine

Nukuao	Tabon te Marae	te Aba Nimate
Oraka	Taiki	te Aba Uareke
Tabiang	Tangin-te-ba	te Kammamma
Tabo Matang	Tarakabu	

Banaban elders before World War II recorded these hamlets and the ones named in later sections. Maude and Maude's 1932 list of hamlets places some of them under the wrong district, mainly in the upper and lower lands of the Tabwewa district. However, the list largely correlates with Te Aka oral history and the names passed down by Banaban elders.

Toakira district

Another woman in Nei Anginimaeao's party, Nei Teborata, was given an area of land that she called, Toakira. The boundary extended from the new Tabiang district at the shoreline of Te Mata-Bou and took in most of the southern seashore right up to a canoe passage in the fringing reef known as A-n te Rua-rua which translates to 'below the pit.' This name describes part of the shore where Europeans would build a boat harbour in the 1900s. To the north, this new district extended to the boundaries of Te Aonoanne. The *maneaba* Te Toa situated close to the northern boundary, further up the hill. The district had two terraces, Nam Natea and Tabo-n te Rengerenge, which means 'the edge of the cliff.'

The names of the **hamlets** of Toakira district were:

Nakieba	Teai Manreburebu	te Roko ni Borau
Nei Tang	te Bubunai	Toakira Maeao
Niniki	te Kamaruarua	Toakira Mainuku
Tangin Teba		

TEBORATA GENEALOGY
TOAKIRA DISTRICT
(Recording the Eldest)

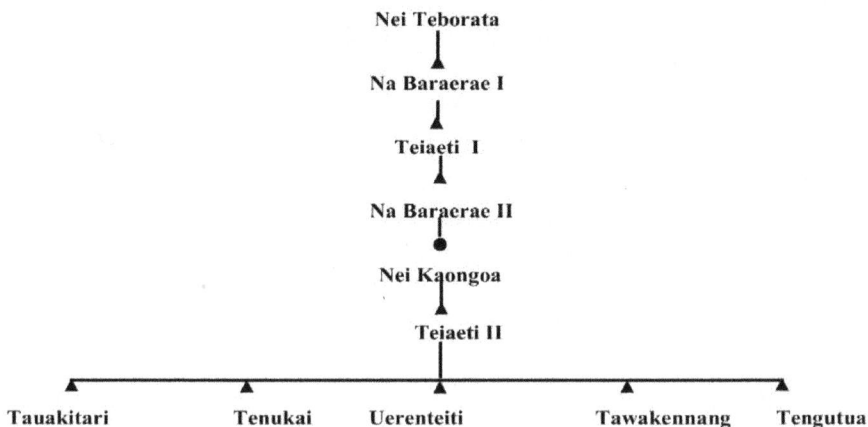

Nei Teborata

Na Baraerae I

Teiaeti I

Na Baraerae II

Nei Kaongoa

Teiaeti II

| Tauakitari | Tenukai | Uerenteiti | Tawakennang | Tengutua |

(All have descendants on Banaba & Rabi today)

Figure: 3.4. Teborata genealogy, Toakira district (information provided by Banaban elder Eri to Harry Maude).

Uma district

Na Maninimate was given the southeast portion of the original Tabwewa region. He called it Uma, meaning 'lagoon side of the island.' In reality, Banaba has no lagoon of the type found in Kiribati, but this area is considered the most sheltered region of the seashore. The western coastal boundary began from the Toakira district boundary at Ante Ruarua and continued right around the eastern coast to Te Aonoanne boundary at Na Bitakinikainnako. There were three terraces in the district called Te Mwemweneitei (the upward flight of the frigate bird), Te Kariateang (the waiting of the wind) and Te Meai. The *maneaba* was called Te Tokanimane, 'the seat of the man'. Much later, the most recent *maneaba* to be built in this district was called Te Kaotine Engiran, meaning 'uprising of England.'

The **hamlets** in Uma district were:

Aoniman	Nuka	te Mangaua
Aon te Marae	Rarikin te Kawai	te Maneaba
Atan te *maneaba*	Taboiaki	Tonga ieta
Bareterawa	Tabonteaba	te Tarine
Bwibwintora	te Bangan U	te Toka
Nangokouea	te Rawainano	te Umani Mane
Naruku	Terawaieta	te Wae
Nariakaina	te Reineaba	

The remaining areas of Tabwewa district

After this partitioning, the Tabwewans still had land in Te Karia and Te Karieta divisions. The Aurakeia is the head hamlet and falls between these two divisions.

The **hamlets** in te Karia division were:

32. Uma village early 1900's (A.J. Hobbs Collection 1932).

MANINIMATE GENEALOGY
UMA DISTRICT
(Recording the Eldest)

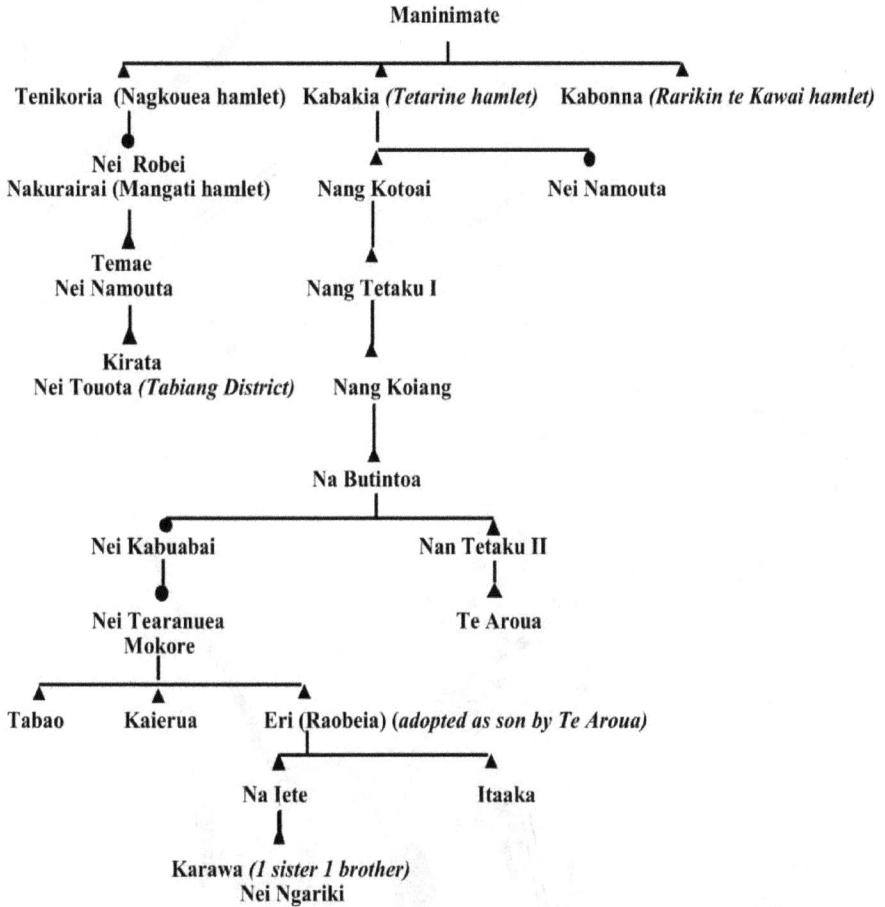

Maninimate

Tenikoria (Nagkouea hamlet) **Kabakia** *(Tetarine hamlet)* **Kabonna** *(Rarikin te Kawai hamlet)*

Nei Robei
Nakurairai (Mangati hamlet)

Nang Kotoai **Nei Namouta**

Temae
Nei Namouta

Nang Tetaku I

Kirata
Nei Touota *(Tabiang District)*

Nang Koiang

Na Butintoa

Nei Kabuabai **Nan Tetaku II**

Nei Tearanuea
Mokore **Te Aroua**

Tabao **Kaierua** **Eri (Raobeia)** *(adopted as son by Te Aroua)*

Na Iete **Itaaka**

Karawa *(1 sister 1 brother)*
Nei Ngariki

Figure: 3.5. Maninimate genealogy – Uma district (by R.K. Sigrah).

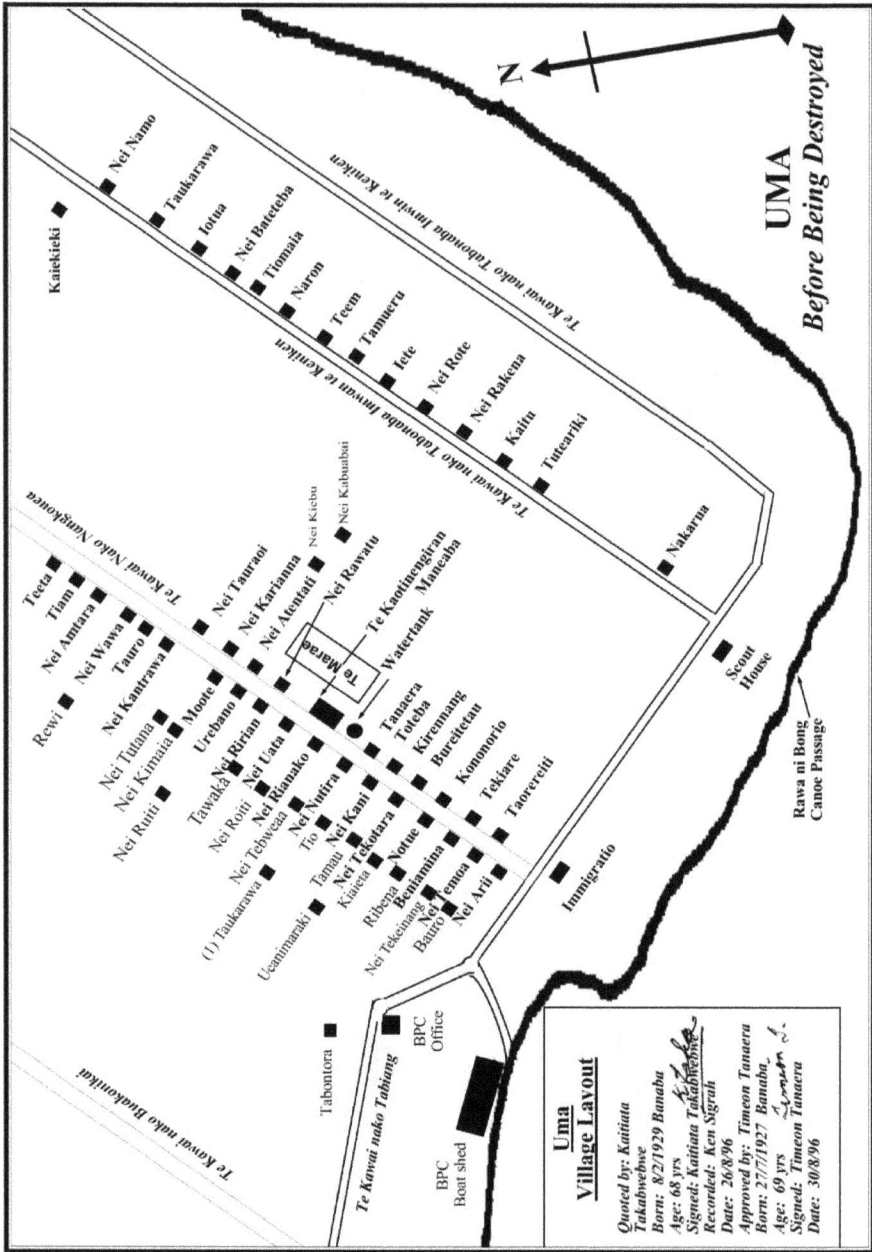

Figure: 3.6. Uma Village layout before destruction (by R.K. Sigrah).

Aobike	Ao-n te marae	Tabongea	Tekerau
Aurakeia	Kabi-ni marata	Taekarau	te Maiu
Ao-n tebonobono	Namanai		

The **hamlet**s in te Karieta division were:

Aurakeia	Mangati	Tei -Namoriki	te Kainga
Karibariki	Marakei	te Irua	Uma-ni-kainako
Karongoa	Tabon te marae		

Na Kouteba's marriage

The new arrival Na Kouteba married Nei Teanibuti from Te Aka clan in the newly named Te Aonoanne district. He resided in Te Aka hamlet within Te Aonoanne District, and his descendants inherited land through his wife's family. This marriage is recorded in Te Aka genealogy.

Maude and Maude, in 1932, incorrectly identified the clan that he married into when they stated, "Na Kouteba himself married one of the Tabwewans who, as will be seen later, retained many rights and privileges over the rest of the island" (p. 267). Maude and Grimble derived their information mainly from the elders from Tabwewa, Tabiang and Uma, who emphasised their own history and legends that had evolved up to the European arrival. As already discussed, Te Aka had been mistakenly identified with the Mangati people and were named as people of Tairua when no such place existed (Chapter 16). Even Na Kouteba's story has been twisted to say that he married a woman from Tabwewa when, in fact, his genealogy, which has been passed down through his marriage to Nei Teanibuti, who was a direct descendant from Teimanaia, the godfather of Te Aka clan.

Throughout the history of the 'giving of rights' and the partitioning of Banaba in to five separate districts, Te

127

Aonoanne district remained virtually intact. This period spans four centuries, from the time of Auriaria's invasion in the late sixteenth century through to the arrival of the Europeans in 1900. Throughout this period Te Aka and all other hamlets of Te Aonoanne retained rights to their lands.

The **hamlets** of Te Aonoanne district were:

Aon Atiabouri	te Ababa	te Maekan Anti
Aon te Katoatoa	Te Aka	te Maranikaomoti
Bakatere	te Angaba	Terike
Norauea	Teinangina	Toka Mauea
Taborake	te Katuru	

Note: Although Te Aka people were the original inhabitants of Banaba at the time of Auriaria's arrival after the battle of Tairua, they were forced to the northern side of the island, and the survivors settled into fourteen hamlets. The name Te Aka was retained for one hamlet regarded as the spiritual and ancestral home of the Te Aka people. The *bangota,* the sacred cairns, were located in this hamlet.

Each District's *Uma n anti* (Spirit House)

The *uma n anti* is the building where elders from the clans of the district meet to discuss and make plans for that district. From this place, the elders then take their decisions to the district *maneaba* to put their ideas before the whole community of their district.

Maude describes the *uma n anti* as being used for magic and ceremonial purposes. He comments that these buildings were more akin to large communal eating houses in which everyone had their *boti* (sitting place). His observations contradict Banaban traditional understanding that the *uma n anti* or spirit houses were considered taboo, and no one except the elders of the district could enter them. The building was not a place for feasting or celebrations and was much smaller than the village or district *maneaba*, which was designed for community gatherings.

Magical and ceremonial activities – *te kauti* and *te tabunea* were carried out at special sites away from the hamlets and more populated areas, usually down on the coast near the terraces. By the time of Maude's arrival on Banaba in 1931, many of these *uma n anti* had already been destroyed. Maude's opinion regarding the purpose of these buildings is incorrect.

The only exception to this general practice occurred in Tabwewa district. The district had two separate divisions of Te Karia and Te Karieta, each of which had its own *uma n anti* buildings. Elders from Te Karia and Te Karieta took their decisions from their individual *uma n anti* to the main *maneaba* shared by the two divisions of the Tabwewa district.

33. Teitintakanoi *maneaba* relocated from Te Aka to Buakonikai (Williams Collection 1901–1931).

Names and locations of the *Uma n Anti*

Uma n Anti	Founding Elder's Name	Hamlet	District
Buntiritiri	Nan Teraro III	Karia (lowland)	Tabwewa
Karawaititi	Na Naning	Karieta (upland)	Tabwewa
Nei Karibaba	Kabonna	Rakin te Kawai	Uma
Tabera n nene	Nei Teborata	Toakira	Toakira
Tokia I-Matang	Na Makaina	te Maeka n anti	te Aonoanne
Tieraki n te bong	Na Bakanuea	Etani Banaba	Tabiang

Names and locations of the *Maneaba*

Maneaba	Founding Elder's Name	Hamlet	District
Teitintakanoi	Na Itirakabuta	te Aka	te Aonoanne
Teitinikauriri	Naning / Nan Teraro III	Aurakeia	Tabwewa
Tenikora	Bakanuea	Etani Banaba	Tabiang
te Kaotinengiran	Eri	te Tarine	Uma
te Toa	Nei Teborata	Toakira	Toakira

The Terraces of the Districts

Banaba has many ancient coral terraces around its coastline. In earlier times, the terraces on the eastern and northern coastlines were used for *te kauti* or worshipping the rising sun. The terraces on the southern and western sides were mainly used for snaring and keeping frigate birds. In the early 1900s, Banaban elders recorded a list of terraces. The European staff of the mining company leased these terraces for their weekend recreational camps. Today, many remain intact, but the fine coral shingles that covered them are gone, used by the Europeans as foundations for their buildings, and the terraces have been covered with cement.

Te Aonoanne (Te Aka) district

Terrace
Bareimwim
te Tarine

Toakira district

Terrace	Region
te Ngeamanganga	te Aonoanne district

Tabwewa district

Terrace	Region
Karia Makin	te Karia
Nei Arei	te Karieta
Neina	te Karieta
Nei Koun	te Karia
Tawanang	te Karieta and te Karia
te Ngea Bakeke	te Karia

Tabiang district

Terrace	Region
Nakatabuki	Tabiang district
Nam Natea	Toakira district
Nii	Tabiang district
Ta Bon te Rengerenge	Toakira district
te Kabeo	Tabiang district

Uma district

Terrace
Karia te Ang
te Meai
te Mwemweneitei

34. Aon te Tarine terrace (H. Maude Collection 1930-32).

15: CLAIMING THE RIGHTS

For non-Banabans, inherited clan roles and duties must seem complicated. Many of them were introduced as far back as the sixteenth century through a process of trading for land called 'the claiming of the rights.' Auriaria's arrival on Banaba is the beginning of a complex web of cultural evolution that eventually produced today's Banaban culture.

Certain Banaban clans are still recognised as the official holders of their rights, even though they live on Rabi. Until the time of the Banabans enforced resettlement on Rabi in December 1945, there were no recorded disputes over the 'claiming of the rights.' On Rabi, elders did everything they possibly could to duplicate Banaban society in a new environment, including attending to all aspects of inherited rights and duties within the community. Without their actions, society would not have such a rich culture that is still virtually intact despite being so far from their beloved homeland.

Disputes and Confusion – When a little bit of knowledge is dangerous

With so much emphasis on individual family clans, and their rights to hold and conduct certain significant social events, we might expect some confusion to occur over the generations. The first signs of division over 'the claiming of the rights' became evident in the 1960s, 20 years after the Banabans arrived on Rabi. Much of this conflict was spurred by the writing and publishing of Banaban history books by western historians. While earlier generations were raised on a rich culture of oral history and tradition passed on by elders, by this time, an increasing number of the young generation were receiving a western education. With access to libraries in high schools, young, educated Banabans began to learn from history books written by well-recognised Pacific historians and anthropologists of the time. They began to look up to these senior European scholars and to accept western books instead of their elders' teachings. Both sources need to withstand scrutiny.

Scrutinising the history books

In November 1997, Harry Maude was asked why he and Grimble had written Banaban history mainly from the perspective of Kiribati culture. As he explained, Te Aka were secretive, and he was more familiar with Tabwewa and Uma villages in 1932 while he worked as the British government's Land Commissioner. Maude stated that during Grimble's many years living on Banaba, Grimble had been adopted into the Nei Beteua clan from Tabiang village. Nei Beteua was an old lady at the time and was responsible for supplying him with a wealth of information on Banaban culture. She was a direct descendant of Nei Anginimaeao from Beru. As Maude explained, he thought preserving whatever knowledge they were given was essential, so it would not be lost in the way he believed the history of Te Aka people was lost. It was not until 1997 that he discovered Te Aka clan history had been secretly guarded and preserved over the generations. From as early as 1932, Ken's great-uncle, in cooperation with numerous Banaban elders, began to record this history in written form. Unfortunately, during the 1960s, Grimble and Maude's research, especially regarding genealogy charts, became increasingly accepted as a correct record. If only Grimble and Maude had gained the trust of Te Aka people and the Auriaria clan, their writings would have provided a more balanced and accurate account.

The Maude's tried to resolve the issue of conflict within the stories collected for *The Book of Banaba* (1994) by publishing two versions of various genealogy charts. Their good intentions only confused the young people; hence, the clan elders decided it was the right time in history to come forward and set the record straight for future generations. Families who, through their birthright, had inherited significant rights and roles within society suddenly found their rights disputed.

The following 'rights' are based on genealogy charts according to *Te Rii ni Banaba*, the simple three-point formula handed down by elders to ensure that Banabans always keep their records correctly. Some of these rights and duties have origins in Kiribati, having been introduced by the more recent settlers to Banaba.

Buakonikai rights

The Title of the Right	Came from	Given to	The Right Today
1. *Burita* (War Canoe)	Tekana	Itirakabuta te Aka hamlet	Robeia te Aka –te Aonoanne
2. Itimoa (Canoe of Protection)	Tekana	Itirakabuta te Aka hamlet	Na Moti te Aka –te Aonoanne
3. *Taeka* (Speaker) Teitintakanoi Maneaba	te Aka	Itirakabuta te Aka hamlet	Nei Kabuta te Aka – te Aonoanne

4. *Bukiniwae* (Forerunner)	te Karia	Namakaina Tabwewa	Kaintong Temaeka-n-anti hamlet te Aonoanne
5. Owning the *Kibena* (Fishing Scoop)	Nei Teborata Toakira	Namakaina Tabwewa	Kaintong Temaeka-n-anti hamlet te Aonoanne

Tabiang rights

The Title of the Right	Came from	Given to	The Right Today
1. Stranded Driftwoood On Tabiang coast	Nei Anginimaeao	Na Bakanuea Tabiang	Nei Beteua, Tabiang Nam Betai, te Karia, Tabwewa
2. Te Nati n Atei (Adopted Child) Karieta, Tabwewa	Na Borau Tabiang	Na Bakanuea Tabiang	Nei Beteua Tabiang

Uma rights

The Title of the Right	Came from	Given to	The Right Today
1. *Taeka* (Speaker) te Tarine hamlet	Maninimate	Na Kabakia te Tarine hamlet	Eri of te Tarine Uma District
2. *Bukiniwae* (Forerunner) Rarikin-te-Kawai	Maninimate	Nangkabonna Rarikin-te-kawai hamlet	Na Kura Rarikin te Kawai hamlet

Tabwewa rights

136

The Title of the Right	Came from	Given to	The Right Today
1. Uplands Karieta division	Auriaria	Naning Aurakeia hamlet	Nei Totintake II Karieta, Tabwewa
2. Lowlands Karia division	Auriaria	Nan Teraro III Aurakeia hamlet	Nei Meti Karia, Tabwewa
3. *Bunna* (Sacred Garlands)	Auriaria	Na Batiaua te Maeu hamlet	Na Itiniwa te Maeu hamlet Karia, Tabwewa
4. *Bukiniwae* (Forerunner) Karieta division	Na Borau	Nan Tabora Teinamoriki hamlet	Naitinibantabuariki Teinamoriki hamlet Karieta, Tabwewa
5. *Bukiniwae* (Forerunner) Karia division	Na Borau	Nan Tabora Aon-te-bonobono hamlet	Areanauriaria Aon-te-bonobono hamlet Karia, Tabwewa
6. *Te Wantieke I* Canoe which takes out the elder to board foreign vessels	Auriaria	Naning Aurakeia hamlet	Nei Totintake Karieta, Tabwewa
7. *Te Wantieke II* The other canoe which takes out the elder to board foreign vessels	Auriaria	Nan Teraro II Aurakeia hamlet	Nei Meti Karieta, Tabwewa
8. *Tewa-ni-Kaiowa* Canoe that accompanies the two boarding canoes	Auriaria	Na Batiaua te Maeu hamlet	Na Itiniwa te Maeu hamlet, Karia, Tabwewa

9. Killing of the Turtle	Nei Anginimaeao	Nan Tabora te Inamoriki hamlet	Kobunimatang te Inamoriki hamlet, Karieta, Tabwewa
10. Cooking of the turtle or fish that have been brought to Tabwewa village	Nei Anginimaeao	Nan Tabora te Inamoriki hamlet	Nei Teiaonikarawa te Inamoriki hamlet Karieta, Tabwewa
11. Sharing of the turtle and the stranded fish that have been brought to Tabwewa village	Nei Anginimaeao	Nan Tabora te Inamoriki and Aon-te-bonobono hamlets	Tounata of te Inamoriki hamlet, Karieta, Tabwewa and Anuantaeka of Aon-te-bonobono hamlet, Karia, Tabwewa
12. Fishbone collectors and magic powers to make the fish return to Banaban shores	Nei Anginimaeao	Nan Tabora	Nei Koriri Tekerau hamlet, Tabwewa
13. Calling the games of *katua* and *karemotu*	Na Borau Tabiang	Naning Aurakeia hamlet Karieta, Tabwewa	Nei Totintake Aurakeia hamlet Karieta, Tabwewa
14. Calling the games of *katua* and *karemotu*	Na Borau Tabiang	Nan TeraroIII Aurakeia hamlet Karia, Tabwewa	Nei Meti Aurakeia hamlet Karia, Tabwewa

Today on Rabi and Banaba, these customs have been absorbed into the culture. Nei Anginimaeao and her clan brought many skills with cultural links to the Kiribati culture, about which there is no dispute. It is easy to understand that, by the time of European settlement, these skills could have been confused with those already witnessed on other islands. It was then an easy step to mistakenly identify Banabans as an offshoot of the I-Kiribati. The rights listed here are very much part of community life on Rabi, although a few are currently under dispute. The authors hope that publishing the background to these rights will assist in resolving these matters.

A note on individual family clans

Each family member has an inherited role, which then interacts at hamlet and clan levels. From there, these groups interacted at district and village levels, which then impacted on the whole Banaban community. (For the relationship between a hamlet, district, and village, see Chapter 24, Figure 4.5). To do justice to the families involved and the background of each of these rights, the authors would need to write another book focusing on this topic alone.

35. Glimpse of Buakonikai village early 1900s (Postcard F & S Photos).

36. Uma village (Williams Collection 1901–1931).

16: MYTHS AND LEGENDS

From the time of the arrival of Nei Anginimaeao and her party, descendants have had disputes and misunderstandings regarding origins and rights. The following three legends are the most common among those retold in interviews with Arthur Grimble and published by Maude and Maude (1994). The authors hope to expose the contradictions in these stories and give a clearer perspective of history related to the eventual partitioning of Banaba into five separate land districts.

The story of the settling of Banaba by Nei Beteua from Tabiang district consists of three separate legends.

(A) The Arrival of Nei Anginimaeao and Her Party

This was the manner of the land in former days: it was not divided up among the people. It only began to be divided when the canoes came from Beru, bearing Nei Anginimaeao and her brother Kouteba, with Nei Teborata and Na Maninimate. Nei Anginimaeao and Kouteba were the dividers of the land. They stood on the foreshore and then separated. Kouteba paced the shoal water eastward to fetch a circle around the land, while Nei Anginimaeao paced the shoals to westward. So Nei Anginimaeao measured the foreshore westward, from Na Bitakini Kainnako to Te Ruarua [An Te Karuarua]. This first portion she gave to Na Maninimate. She said to him, *'Tiku, i aon te ora aei n amarake i maiu'* (lit. Stay on this foreshore and feed before me and continue to use this foreshore until I reclaim it from you). Again, Nei Anginimaeao measured the foreshore from the place called Te Ruarua [An Te Karuarua] to a place called Te Matabou. That portion she gave to Nei Te Borata, saying, 'Take this foreshore and use it until I claim it from you.' For herself, Nei Anginimaeao measured off the foreshore from Te Matabou to a place called Aon Te Maiango: that was her own portion. And behold, she returned to her *kaianga* [*kainga*] at Tabiang and remained there. She had two children, Na Borau and Nei Anginimaeao the Younger.

(B) The Giving Away of Tabiang Rights

Nei Anginimaeao the Younger had a child, Na Kataburi. Na Kataburi had a child, Na Borau the Younger. Na Borau the Younger had a child, Nei Anginimaeao, and she had five brothers. Then Na Borau the Younger arose to pace out his foreshore. He came to the northern boundary at a place called Aon Te Maiango. Then he went forward until he met a man who invited him to go home with him, but he refused and went forward again along the shore until he came to the place called Aibong [Aon-aibong], where he met another man whose name was Nan Teraro. This man invited him to come and stay at his home. So, Na Borau the Younger followed Nan Teraro home to live with him. However, when they came to Nan Teraro's house, it was not ready to be lived in, for it was being floored. Nan Teraro took the remnants of the material of the house of his brother, Na Ning, and began to finish his floor with that. However, while he was at work, his brother Na Ning called to him, saying, 'Send your guest to me, for my house is ready for him to live in.' Na Borau the Younger left Nan

Teraro and went to live with his brother Na Ning. There he remained until the arrival of his daughter Nei Anginimaeao, who had come out in search of him. When Nei Anginimaeao found her father, Na Borau, with the man Na Ning, she approached him and asked him to return home again. But he said to her, *'Tai kuri moa ni kairai ba N na iangoa arou nkai [ngkai] I mena i roun teuaei'* (lit. Do not be in a hurry to take me away for I must consider my conduct now that I am staying with this man, i.e. do not call me away until I have repaid the courtesy of having me to stay). His daughter said to him, 'I know nothing about it; the matter is in your hands.' Na Borau considered, and after a while, he said to his daughter, 'Woman, these things you shall give to this man:

Wa-m n tieke (your prior right to board strange vessels or canoes);
Ao kanam te amarake (your right to take the peace offering of food);
Ao kabiram te ba (of oil for your anointing);
Ao mwaem te kaue (your right of garlanding the stranger who arrives);
Ao kanam te ika te ke te kua (your right to take the turtle or the porpoise stranded on the foreshore);
Ao kanam te ika te urua (your right to the stranded urua).
Ba arom ni bane aikai a bon tiku iroun teuaei (for all these your customary rights indeed remain with this man) ba e uotia ba te mane (for he takes them, being a male).
Ao Ruoiam (your right to direct the rouia);
Ao taekan aon te aba (to decide on land matters);
Ao katikani koran aon ti aba (drawing the measuring cord across the land.),
and he concluded by saying: Ao boni bukia arei irom (indeed such matters are in your hands).'

143

And as Na Borau told her, so did Nei Anginimaeao, for these things, which Na Borau gave away to Na Ning, were not given away in very truth. For when Na Borau spoke to Na Ning and apportioned him his foreshore, he said to him, *'Tiku amarake I aon te ora anne I maiu'* (Remain, feed upon this foreshore before me, i.e. remain with your foreshore rights until I claim them back from you). Therefore, the foreshore rights were not given away in perpetuity. So Nei Anginimaeao returned to Tabiang, and she appointed to each of her (five) brothers a portion of the foreshore of the island. Then the brothers of Nei Anginimaeao arose in battle against the people of Tabwewa, for they disputed the Kingship of the people of Tabwewa. And behold, they won the Kingship; and the decision was that the brothers of Nei Anginimaeao should rule over the land. This they did, and they upheld all the judgements of their father Na Borau concerning the foreshore rights.

(C) The Battle of Taaira (Tairua)

Nei Anginimaeao had a child, Nang Konim; Nang Konim had a child Nan Tetae, and Nan Teat's brothers were Borirai and Boin te-Itei. These were the deeds of Nan Tetae. The man Kamtea came to him one day and told him that the people of Taaira had taken his land. The people of Taaira lived on the north side of Banaba and were eaters of men. So, Nan Tetae told Kamtea that he must not give way before them. Kamtea went back to his land, and he saw that his boundaries had been pushed back to a place called Te I-Namoriki. So, he told his people to move them again to their former place. They did so, but afterwards, the people of Taaira came and seized the land again. So, this was the judgement of Nan Tetae: he said to Kamtea, 'Prepare your torches of dried leaf, for we will fight with them on the sea,' and he also told the people of Uma and Buakonikai that there would be a fight at sea.

When night came, they fought with the people of Taaira from the sea, but there was no decision in that battle. So, the judgement went out again that there should be a fight on the summit of Banaba. First came Nan Tetae with his brothers; then came three or four of the people of Uma then came the people of Buakonikai and the people of Tabwewa, to fight the people of Taaira. Na Korobeing was the leader of the people of Taaira, and it was said of him, that he was skilled in the *wawi*
(death magic). The fight was fought; Nan Tetae and his people were victorious, and only two of their side were killed. This then was the word of the people of Taaira to Nan Tetae about the land of Kamtea: 'We have no share in it, for it is in your hands.' So, Nan Tetae took the land, together with the *bangabanga* (water cave) called Teba. Then Nan Tetae returned to Tabiang; there he had a child; whose name was Na Mbaia [Nam Baia].

Contentious Points

These myths raise some questions regarding the **partitioning of land**:

- Kouteba heads eastward to draw a circle around the land. There is no mention of his return or link to any new land division.

    Fact: Kouteba married into, and stayed with, Te Aka people from Te Aonoanne district (according to evidence in Te Aka genealogy charts).

- Nei Anginimaeao is said to have marked the other three land divisions.

    Fact: The original Te Aonoanne land borders remained intact after the second invasion.

- Nei Anginimaeao uses words that suggest she is already the owner of the land.

Fact: It is generally accepted today that the land in this region was owned by the descendants of Auriaria (the Tabwewans) at this stage.

- Nei Anginimaeao apportions land for herself between Te Matabou and Aon Te Maiango to form the Tabiang district.

Fact: Aon Te Maiango is not shown on the map (c.1600 onwards), and this marker is instead recognised as Te Kaoti-n aine (Chapter 13, Figure 3.1).

The myth also contains contentious points concerning the giving away of **Tabiang rights**:

- Nei Anginimaeao gives the right to board strange (foreign) vessels or canoes and to take the peace offering of food by her father.

Fact: The Tabwewans already had the right to board foreign vessels and perform the garlanding of the stranger. The only rights given to the Tabwewans were the rights to the *karemotu* and *katua* games and to claim stranded fish.

- Na Borau tells his daughter he wants to give away his rights, but he does not really give them away.

Fact: Welcoming the *nati n ataei* into the Karieta clan is still practised today whenever the games are played. This suggests this custom was given away.

- There is a fight over the Kingship of Tabwewa, which the Tabiang people win.

Fact: The same descendants still own Tabwewa land, and no takeover of Tabwewa land holdings has ever been recorded.

The **Battle of Taaira (Tairua)** raises the following issues:

- The people are named the people of Taaira.

  Fact: No family or hamlet is known by this name. Taaira, or Tairua as it is spelt in Banaban, means 'foreigners.' This word, in Banaban history, has always been associated with the Battle of Tairua.

- A man called Kamtea comes to Nan Tetae and says the people of Taaira who live on the north side of the island are known as man–eaters.

  Fact: The name Kamtea should be spelt Na Kamta, who was an elder from Mangati hamlet from Tabwewa district. The people of Te Aka who lived in the northern district were wrongly called the people of Taaira (Tairua) by Nei Beteua.

- Nei Beteua mentions that 'then came the people of Buakonikai and the people of Tabwewa, to fight the people of Taaira.'

  Fact: Buakonikai did not exist at the time of this battle. The first mention of the existence of Buakonikai was not until Albert Ellis arrived in 1900. Buakonikai was formed when the district of Toakira merged with the district of Te Aonoanne.

Auriaria Myths of the Second Invasion of Banaba

An Auriaria legend of the second invasion was retold by Nei Teotintake, who lived in Tabwewa, Banaba and was a direct descendant of Auriaria:

Auriaria was about to rest upon his land of Banaba, so he began to set it in order. He overturned it; he capsized it and cut off the southern end of it and threw it away to eastward; it fell into the sea, and lo, it became the island of Tamana. [A poetic way of saying that Tamana was originally colonised by

147

Banabans (Maude and Maude, 1994, pp. 22-8).] After
that, Auriaria set a fence around his land (i.e. the
fringing reef); he set a guard of canoes about it. Not a
strange canoe must come near the land; if one
appeared, it perished; if another appeared, it perished.
After a time, a canoe from Beru appeared, and the
people on it were Na Kouteba, Na Maninimate, Nei
Anginimaeao, and Nei Teborata. That canoe Auriaria
allowed to approach, he brought it to shore, for he
wished to make his land more populous. At the first
coming of the people of that canoe, they had no wives.
They were able to marry only when they met with the
people of Auriaria, even the *Bun Anti* (the breed of
spirits), on Banaba. And the man Na Kouteba got his
wife from Tabwewa, from among the people of
Auriaria, *'nke[ngke] e a nakonako n otobong iaoni
maraeia'* (lit. When he had gone to fix a date on their
marae, i.e. after he had fixed a date to meet them on
the *marae* of Tabwewa). This was what the canoe
from Beru did when first it came to Banaba from over
the sea; it came to shore, and its people hastened to
measure out the foreshore in a circle around the
island, and they divided it up and took every man his
share. Each man was a master of his portion. And,
while they were busy with measuring out the
foreshore, Auriaria watched them encircle the island.
Then he parted from them and went to his own place
of Tabwewa, and they came ashore, and they sought
their wives from among the inhabitants of Banaba.
And afterwards, they again met together with Auriaria
at the place called Aurakeia, and they made a council
with him. This was the judgement made in that
council. Each man who came from over the sea should
be master of his portion of the foreshore. But as for us
of Tabwewa, the first people of Banaba and the true
inhabitants of the land, we abided our time, and our

time arrived. Our time arrived for the things that came out of the sea. Ours was the right of the *'Wan Tieke'* (canoes that board strange vessels) when a voyaging canoe arrived. For if perhaps a strange craft came to Uma, we alone might go to board it, we of Tabwewa; and none had the right to prevent us in what we did. And if presents came from the stranger, they were ours. And so, it was until even later times; for if something fell from a ship, such as a water barrel, we could take it as our own if it stranded on the foreshore, and none could prevent us. Again, if the turtle or the *urua* or the porpoise or the whale were stranded on the shoal, it was brought to us, for it was our food, and none might prevent us. This was the custom before us, in an earlier generation, and has been so until now. That is the history of us, the people of Tabwewa.

Contentious points

- The myth of Auriaria has historical links with the Kiribati island of Tamana.

   Fact: Auriaria had a short stopover on the Kiribati island of Nikunau on his way to Banaba.

- Na Kouteba marries a Tabwewan woman.

   Fact: According to genealogical charts, Na Kouteba married Nei Teanibuti from Te Aka clan.

When Legends are Legends, and History is History

In an interview in 1997, Harry Maude admitted that the people of Te Aka upheld the tradition of secrecy and silence during his time on Banaba, and he gained no information from them. It was a time when Maude knew, in his role as

Land Commissioner for the British government, that the British Phosphate Commission was intent on mining all the land.

When the authors discussed this matter with clan elders involved in writing this book, they said that most of Grimble's interviews were made as early as 1914 and that elders from Te Aka clan were never given the opportunity to have their say. Elders raised questions about Grimble's motives in this matter, pointing out that at that time, Grimble was, first and foremost, a Resident Commissioner working for the British government.

Grimble was responsible for solving many of the land disputes that arose from the mining company's efforts to gain more and more leases over Banaban land. He became involved in the controversial compulsory acquisition of land in 1929. Elders believe that as Kiribati was already declared a Crown Colony in 1916, known as the Gilbert & Ellice Island Colony (GEIC), Grimble was solely concerned with linking Banabans with the people of Kiribati so that any problems in future could be easily handled by British law. Once phosphate mining began on Banaba, Banaban identity seems to have been lost as the British government and the BPC pushed to absorb the Banaban people into mainstream Kiribati culture.

It seems ironic that a man so embroiled in the Banaban struggle should also be the man recording traditional history. How can a man fight to take more land from the people and at the same time remain objective enough to record culture and traditional history? This is the question elders and the young generation ask today.

17: SPORTS

A number of games have come into Banaban culture from Kiribati. *Te katua* and *karemotu* are two games created by a descendant of Nei Anginimaeao called Na Naborau. The origins of these two games share the same background. The following legend tells the story of *te katua* and *karemotu*. It records an early part of history as well as the cultural influence of games in the interaction between villages. It also relates to changing the name of the central meeting house in Tabiang district.

The Legend of *Te Katua* and *Karemotu*

One day, the Nei Anginimaeao clan elders were meeting in the Tabiang district at their *maneaba*, Te Kiakia n Tabiang. Accordingly, each of the elders shared their skills with others – such as in navigation, healing, or cutting toddy. These meetings could go on all day. They would only stop and have a break when women brought them food. At one meeting, Naborau was waiting for his granddaughters to bring his food. By the time of the luncheon break, his granddaughters had not arrived. He felt ashamed that all the others were eating and his family had not come. The elders noticed his plight and invited him to join them. Naborau decided to make an excuse to leave and started to walk away. He left Tabiang and walked right along the coast towards Tabwewa district.

When he arrived at Tabwewa, he decided to rest and sat down at a terrace now known as Tawanang. Here he began to lament, feeling very depressed because his granddaughters had shamed him in front of his fellow elders. While he sat there, a man from Tabwewa district saw him. It was now late in the afternoon. His name was Naning, an elder of Tabwewa, and he went over and invited Naborau to come back to his house. At first, Naborau declined Naning's invitation. So Naning went back to the house of his brother, Nan Teraro, and told him that there was a visitor down at the passage, and he wanted him to come up to their hamlet. So, Nan Teraro sent a message to his younger brother called, Na Batiaua, who had the duty of welcoming strangers with the magic *bunna*.

Na Batiaua went down to the passage and placed a *bunna* around Naborau's neck. After this, Naborau agreed to come back to Naning's house, accompanied by Nan Teraro. When they arrived at Naning's house, he was welcomed with food, dancing, and all the customary privileges shown to a special guest. At the end of the celebration, it was time for the guest to give something in return for the hospitality, another essential part of the custom of 'welcoming the stranger.' Naborau had nothing with him to give, but he did possess the skill of the *katua* and *karemotu*. So, he showed them how to play these games and told them all the rules. After he had given the two brothers all the information about the games, he agreed with Naning that his eldest son, Na Bakanuea, who lived in his district of Tabiang, would be permitted to come across to Tabwewa. Here he would join them in the playing of the games and be recognised as *te Nati n ataei* (adopted son of the Karieta folks). Naning agreed. From that time forward, right up until today on Rabi, every time the *katua* or *karemotu* is played, the people of Tabiang are always there to attend the event as special guests of the Tabwewans. When Na Bakanuea heard that his father had given away their heritage and rights to the *katua* and *karemotu* games, he was very sorry. He built a small *maneaba* in honour of his father and named it Tenikora, which has two meanings: 'feeling unsettled' and 'one set of three.' After the disgrace that Na Bakanuea's daughters had brought upon the family, he gave them the following names: Nei Tokanikaiaki, 'to be won over, Nei Tongabiri, 'so far away' and Nei Tawa, 'barren'.

When Europeans came to Banaba, they saw that the people of Tabiang were using this *maneaba* called Tenikora. The old *maneaba* known as Te Kiakia n Tabiang was no more.

Initially, only the people of Karieta and Karia of Tabwewa district played the games, and as time passed, the games extended to other districts. The first people to play the games outside of Tabwewa were those of Te Aonoanne district, and from there, the games were taken to Uma district. In history, Toakira district was said to be playing games with Te Aonoanne district, even before the districts were merged around the late 1800s as Buakonikai village (Chapter 24). All the districts of Banaba were then involved in playing the games. The exception was Tabiang village, where only the descendants of Naborau's eldest son Na Bakanuea, known by the Tabwewans as te Nati n ataei, could join in the games, which is how the Tabwewans came to have the rights to these two games.

Preparation by elders and *bukiniwae* (forerunners)

It was the duty of the two elders from the Aurakeia hamlets in Te Karieta and Te Karia to get together and decide where and when to play the games of *katua* and *karemotu*.

It was the duty of Te Karia hamlet to convey the decision about the plans for the upcoming game to the people of Te Aonoanne. The people from Aon Te Bonobono then with the people of Te Maekananti, which was the *bukiniwae* hamlet for Te Aka clan. After this meeting, the elder from Te

Maekananti discussed the message with the elder from Te Aka. From there, he carried the message to the hamlet of Rarikin Te Kawai in Uma district, which was the *bukiniwae* hamlet for te Tarine clan.

Preparation by players

Once the date was set, each district chose their teams. The men's team was put under the care of male elders, while the women's team was placed under the care of female elders. Three days before the start of the games, *te kauti* began to invoke the powers of *tabunea*.

On the day of the games, people from all over the island assembled at the ground chosen to host the event. The games usually began at Tabwewa playground, then moved to Te Aonoanne playground before moving to the Uma playground. The players and spectators assembled around the specially prepared grounds, forming themselves into clan groups under the three districts. The Nati n Ataei clan from Tabiang played from Te Karieta side, while the rest of the villagers generally mingled with their relatives from other participating clans and villages and joined in the competition.

Before the games began, the individual players were anointed with coconut oil and garlanded with flowers on their heads. Each man or woman brought his or her *kai ni katua* (weight) or *kai ni karemotu* (tossing stick). Players were not permitted to borrow equipment, so if they did not have their own, the elders in charge of the event did not allow them to participate.

The game of *katua* (putting the weight)

Only men play *te katua*. The game's object is to throw a weight to hit the centre of a coconut trunk marked and partly buried in the ground. The marker is barely visible, making it difficult to hit the centre.

37. Men playing *katua*, putting the weight game (Miller Collection 1908-1939).

THE KATUA GAME
Played by Men

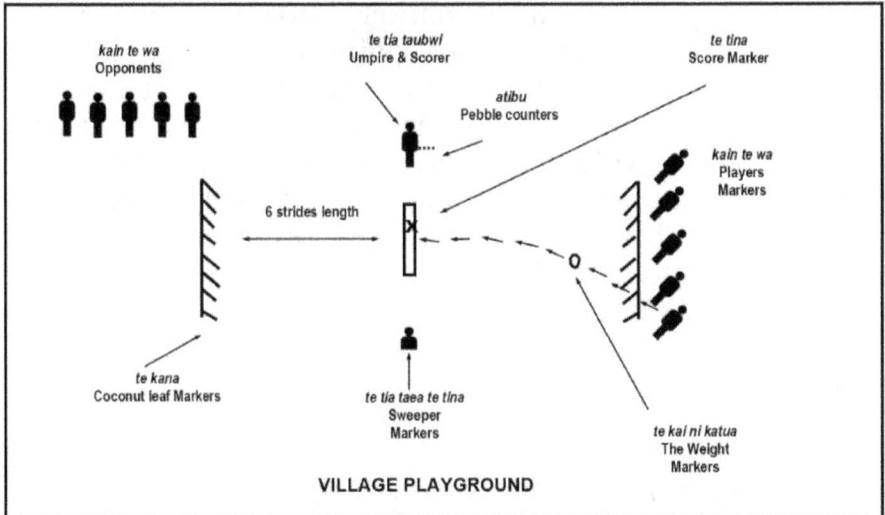

Figure: 3.7. *Katua* game played by men (by R.K. Sigrah).

155

Five men in each team stand at approximately six strides on either side of the marker. These two lines were marked by splitting the leaves taken from the coconut tree in half and placing them along the ground. The length of the trunk or marker is about one metre. An umpire sits at one end of the marker to see if the weight hits the spot. He uses stones to keep the score, and when the first team reaches ten, they are deemed the winners. At the other end of the marker sits a man known as the cleaner. His task is to sweep away the dirt from the top of the marker after each toss and ensure that the marker stays in the correct position (Figure 3.7).

The game of *karemotu* (tossing the stick)

Only women play *te karemotu*. The object of the game is to toss a throwing stick across a space to hit the *motu* (coconut markers). Each team comprises six players, and seven markers are positioned at either end of the oval at approximately nine metres away.

The markers are made from dried coconut shells, and the way they are arranged is significant. They are laid out in two straight rows, with the head marker, known as the *nei tere*, at the back in the centre. One point is awarded for each standard marker that is hit. If the *nei tere* is hit, two marks are awarded. The scorer's role is to keep a tally on a sand marker with twelve furrows, six on each side. The scorer moves a *nati* (marker) to the next furrow every time one of the markers is hit. The game is over when the first team completes a full circuit and all twelve holes on the marker have been filled (Figure 3.8).

Other Games

In 1932, the Maude's mention other games played on Banaba, such as *te kaunrabata* (men's wrestling), *te kakuri* (a game), *te oreano* (a ball game), *te kati* (bow and arrow shooting),

38. Women playing *karemotu*, tossing the stick game (Williams Collection 1901–1931).

THE KAREMOTU GAME
Played by Women

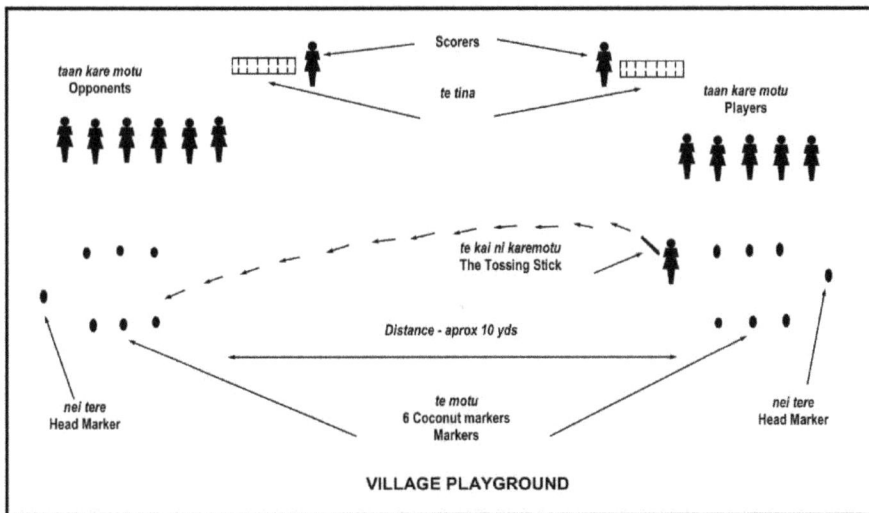

Figure: 3.8. *Karemotu* game played by women (diagram by R.K. Sigrah).

157

te tie (swinging), and *te karetika* (throwing of *babai* plant stems). These are Kiribati games and are not part of Banaban culture in terms of either origin or the trading of land for the claim of 'rights.' Instead, these games were played on Banaba by the Kiribati and Tuvaluan workers employed by the BPC from 1900 onwards. The Banaban community never adopted them.

As recently as the 1960s, some I-Kiribati who married into Banaban society on Rabi tried to introduce some of these games into the official cultural programme at the annual 15 December celebrations in Rabi, but the elders would not permit it. Since then, elders have banned the playing of all these games, especially *te oreano* and *te kaunrabata*, on Rabi. They argued that these games were never part of Banaban custom and should never be part of any cultural programmes.

18: CUSTOMS AND CULTURE

Growing up on Banaba

From the time of Nei Anginimaeao's arrival, the population of Banaba grew. With an increased population, new problems arose, such as the lack of water resources, especially during droughts, which brought on food shortages. During the nineteenth century, infanticide was practised as a last resort to restrict births to two or three per couple. Two girls for water gathering from the *bangabanga* and one boy for fishing. Rather than taking such drastic action as infanticide, however, families often arranged for babies to be adopted by childless couples or those with only one child. Adoption was and is a necessary part of Banaban custom. Every couple must have children to care for them in their old age. When parents can no longer carry out heavy work, the children take over the everyday tasks and care for their parents until death. The use of birth control was also prevalent in society. During hard times pregnant women could abort their babies. Certain women elders were experts at a particular type of massage or the use of herbal potions.

Birth

Families never completely released their hold over their daughters, who, as water gatherers, were the most valuable member of the family. This Banaban custom is still significant in modern society. Daughters are always needed for a family unit to be secure and well cared for, even though water supplies are not a concern on Rabi. Sons move away when they marry and live with their in-laws. From the moment the first child was born, the grandmother helped rear the newborn. All resources during this time were focused on the welfare of the baby. The grandmother and female relatives pampered and supported the lactating mother to ensure her milk was kept at a premium. In this way, the newborn was given every possible chance to survive what all Banabans consider the most crucial part of their lives, the first twelve months. The grandmother usually instructed the new father to move away from his wife. At her discretion, she permitted him to return to the marital bed between six and twelve months after childbirth. The family preserved the baby's umbilical cord and incorporated it into *tabunea*. Although Christianity has now come, the old beliefs still exist, and some families preserve their child's umbilical cord in the belief that, in some way, it will protect the child in the future. Banabans now celebrate the child's first birthday, mainly in keeping with tradition and new Christian values. A great family feast and celebration is held; other birthdays are not celebrated like the child's first year.

Precious water

Droughts occurred in cycles, roughly every seven years. As the need for water also increased with the growing population, water rationing became a daily part of life. Women and girls collected water from the family *bangabanga* in *binobino* (coconut shell containers). Each shell had a hole drilled in the top and a stopper placed in the hole so the water gatherers could carry out these containers in *te bwaene* (plaited coconut leaf baskets). Water was always precious and never wasted. People bathed in the sea. For small babies and children, mothers held the water in their mouths and spurted it over the child's body. All other water was reserved for drinking and food preparation, especially during droughts.

Puberty

From when a girl first began to menstruate, and each time her cycle occurred, she stayed in a special house within her hamlet known as *uma n teinako* (house for menstruating women). The purpose of these arrangements was to ensure that she had no contact with men, which was thought could significantly weaken the men's powers if they were performing *tabunea*. When boys reached puberty, they were usually sent to the terraces to begin their lessons in the ways of men. If they were to perform *te kauti* for the game of *katua*, they resided with other young men from their district in a house known as *te uma n roronga* (house of the young men). If a boy was to perform *te kauti* for boxing, he went to the *uma n roronga,* of his hamlet, where his male relatives had performed the same rites for generations before him.

Engagement and Marriage

Marriages were arranged to link families and gain land or crucial rights. Today, although issues over land and rights are less important, the linking of two families is still valued. Thus, as soon as a child could talk and walk, from approximately five years of age, he or she could be betrothed to marry. As the children grew older and began understanding life, they were encouraged to play with their chosen partner. When the girl's first period occurred, her parents and elders set a wedding date. By about ten years of age, both children knew that their playmate would become their spouse. Marriages were conducted at an early age to ensure that girls were virgins when they were married. This is still part of custom today. Marriage does not mean that the couple leads an independent life; on the contrary, family bonds are even stronger. So, if problems arise between the couple, the whole family is involved in resolving the issue quickly, and the family's elders will step in if required to settle the matter.

Engagement customs

After the arrival of Nei Anginimaeao, people began to practice *te kakoaki* (bleaching process). In this process, the engaged girl or boy spent two to three months in a heavily screened house, away from the sun's scorching rays. They were fed a special diet and permitted only outside at night. As a result, they were well prepared physically for their upcoming marriage, and their skin would lighten considerably. By the time of the wedding, the bride and groom stood out with fair skin and trim figures. Although the ceremony of *te kakoaki* had disappeared by the 1800s, the evidence suggests that some engagement customs were practised for several weeks in the lead-up to the wedding. When not working, the young couple wore a new *riri* (grass skirt), flowers in their ears, and flower garlands around their necks. They made chaperoned visits to their respective relatives, and the two families exchanged presents of coconuts and mats.

Wedding Ceremony

Thanks to Webster's visit to Banaba in 1851, we have a written account of a traditional Banaban wedding ceremony as it was before the arrival of the missionaries:

> "No man in Panapa [Banaba] has more than one wife. When a young man is paying his addresses to a girl, he affixed a band of leaves around his ankle. The children

are frequently betrothed as husband and wife when very young. On arriving at a certain age, they are united by a formal marriage ceremony. The age at which these nuptials take place is generally that of fourteen. The young people sleep together several nights before the marriage. The nuptials are consummated by extensive feasting, and a meeting of friends and relatives, as well as other ceremonies at which the old women officiate" (as cited in, Maude & Maude, 1994, p. 79).

In the ceremony of old, the actual ritual or marriage ceremony itself would go on for days. When Webster says that the young couple slept together a few days before the actual marriage, he refers to the arrangements for the couple who, being so young and virgins, do not know what is required to consummate their marriage physically. Here the old women within the families provide help through what he refers to as certain rites. This assistance can still be called on today when a young couple needs to prove the bride's virginity to their families and relatives. The question of the boy's virginity is less critical, but if he is a virgin and does not know what to do, the old women will be called upon to assist them on the wedding night. Once this part of the ceremony is over, the couple's families are anointed with oil. The groom's relations will anoint the bride's relations with specially scented oil as a symbol of their daughter's virginity. Then the wedding party rejoices, and the celebrations move into full swing again for a week or two of constant feasting and dancing and the coming together of the two families and all their relatives. The elders from both sides decide when the celebrations are over. Today on Rabi, red cloth is used by the *utu* (immediate family) to symbolise the bride's virginity. After the wedding night, relatives wear red coloured *te be* (sarongs) and fly red flags and banners to celebrate the event.

Today on Rabi, most weddings incorporate traditional

39. Banabans in ruoia, sitting dance costume and some wearing wigs (Postcard 1910).

customs and rituals, and are regarded as one of society's most important cultural events. The ceremony is similar to the one Webster described, reduced to one day, although celebrations can continue for one or two weeks.

Music and singing

After the arrival of Nei Anginimaeao, Kiribati culture began to influence traditional music. The words of songs especially reflect this influence more than traditional forms of dancing. In music, Banabans use the Kiribati language. Some songs came from Kiribati tunes but have been adapted to suit Banaban history and storytelling. In modern compositions, there is added influence from Fijian melodies and harmonies. Banaban music today reflects these cultural changes that have come through invasion and interaction, resulting in a unique form of Pacific music.

In traditional music, hand clapping is used with voices to provide the backing for dance performances. Although I-Kiribati and Tuvaluans pound wooden boxes with their hands to produce the beat, this is not part of Banaban music. Over the years, Banabans have added instruments found in European society, such as drum kits, guitars, ukuleles or mandolins. If no instruments are available, they resort to traditional hand clapping to supply the rhythm needed for the dancers. Children are taught from a very early age to sing in harmonic tonics. So, singing is available anytime during daily life without instrumental accompaniment. For example, women sing while washing their clothes. Men sing while *koro karewe* (cutting toddy) perched high up among the leaves of the coconut tree.

The evolution of dancing

The first well-known Kiribati dance, introduced by Nei Anginimaeao's party, was the *ruoia*, performed in a sitting position. Nei Anginimaeao's descendants were still performing this in the early 1900s. After the arrival of Kiribati and Tuvaluan labourers, other dances like *te buki* (swaying hip dance), *te kaimatoa* (set pattern dance) and the Tuvaluan *fatele* were adopted. None of these dances are performed on Rabi today during official Banaban traditional performances, but they can be seen occasionally during general entertainment programmes. The Kiribati word *te batere* means dance performance. The use of this term by Banabans has caused confusion for younger generations and outsiders who mistakenly view Banabans dancing as similar to Kiribati dancing. In Kiribati dances, set patterns of movements and harmonies are repeated over and over in slight variations, each song and dance telling a different story. Initially, men and women performed separately. In Banaban dancing, there is evidence from the early 1900s that women and men danced together, even during war dances. In

40. Dancing group on Rabi (King Collection 1993).

other dances, the women made soft flowing motions with swaying hips and intricate hand and head movements. The men made powerful movements and actions taken from the old war dances, adapted to complement their female counterparts in combined or separate performances. Banaban traditional dance performance highlights the softness of the females with their long flowing hair and the strength and power of the males.

Storytelling through dance

After arrival on Rabi, dancing groups began a new style of mime performance to re-enact the stories of the past. The miming dances trace society's most important aspects of culture and historical change. They help preserve oral history in dance form, which can be easily taught to the young generation and shown to the rest of the world. In recent times dancing groups have been honoured by invitations to perform in a cultural performance for Her Majesty's Royal Tour of Fiji in 1970, the opening celebrations of the Sydney Opera House in Australia in 1972, the South Pacific Forum conference held in Nauru 1992, and a dance tour of Japan in 1997. Dancing groups have also competed at various Pacific Festival of Arts contests.

Cultural programme

Here is a copy of a typical cultural dance programme held on Rabi during 15 December celebrations which commemorated the Banabans arrival on Rabi in 1945.

1.	*Kunean te ran*	Discovery of underground water on Ocean Island
2.	*Nangi Bibira*	Fetching of water from water holes by women
3.	*Te Tatae*	Traditional fishing for flying fish
4.	*Tebotebo te Aii*	Coconut crab bathing
5.	*Kunikun*	Collection and procession of *kunikun* almond fruit for food
6.	*Karanga Short Stick*	Traditional war dance using short sticks
7.	*Rokon te Aro*	Arrival of Christianity
8.	*Karanga II*	Traditional war dance with long sticks/spears
9.	*During the year*	Discovery of phosphate by Sir Albert Ellis
10.	*1900*	
11.	*Ai Kakubara WWII*	Invasions of Ocean Island by Japanese during World War II
12.	*15 December 1945*	Arrival on Rabi from Ocean Island

These traditional and modern dance performances are uniquely Banaban and reflect culture and history.

Te Tatae (Flying Fish) Fishing

One of the major fishing techniques that Nei Anginimaeao

brought from Kiribati was the skill to catch *te tatae* (flying fish). Mahaffy provided a vivid description of catching flying fish:

> The most picturesque method of fishing is that used against the flying fish which abound in the waters around the island and seen at night to be particularly fond of coming almost to the very edge of the reef. A large supply of torches, made from dried coconut leaves, is prepared and stowed on the outrigger of the canoe. Two of the crew are provided with long-handled nets made from native fibre, and a dark moonless night is chosen. The canoe cruises round the edge of the reef, often most alarmingly close to the breaking sea, and one of the crew lights the torch and stands up waving it. Immediately one sees the flying fish rush into the light, some lie half-dazed on the surface of the water and are easily scooped up, others fly across the canoe and are taken in the nets like butterflies, and a good night's sport will result in the capture of two or three hundred fish (Mahaffy, 1910, p. 8).

Nei Teborata gave away the rights of *te kibena* (long-handled net scoop designed to catch flying fish in mid-air) and *te ikabuti* (smaller version to scoop schools of sardines along the shore) in exchange for land.

Kiribati Customs That Have Not Continued

Grimble in 1989 and Maude and Maude in 1932 and 1994 have described Kiribati cultural practices that Nei Anginimaeao's party brought to Banaba but which did not become a part of society more generally after that.

Te boti in the village *maneaba*

When Nei Anginimaeao arrived on Banaba, she named her

district Tabiang after the village *maneaba* back in Beru. In Kiribati culture, *te boti* was where each family elder sat within the *maneaba*. The Banaban district *maneaba* has only two official *te inaki* (sitting places). First, *te Inaki ni Karimoa* means 'the sitting place of the eldest' and is always located on the eastern side of the *maneaba*. The second position is called *te Inaki ni Bukiniwae*, 'the sitting place of the forerunner or the right-hand man to the elder', on the western side of the *maneaba*. The forerunner only takes up this position during meetings to decide the calling of the games. During all other meetings within the *maneaba*, the eldest of the district will take his position to the east. Family members can sit at any position during general meetings. Thus, this practice differs from Kiribati's '*te boti*' described in detail in Grimble (1989), and as cited in, Maude & Maude (1932, 1991). Grimble admits that the Banaban *boti* were different:

> "On Ocean Island (Banaba), no detailed information about clan groups is available, but some of the old people can still remember that there were boti in the *maneaba*. The vagueness that exists cannot be the result of European influences alone, as this island was little visited before 1900. It is probable that the clan grouping had been in process of decay for some long period, probably as a result of the tendency towards purely local groupings" (Grimble, 1989, ed. H.E. Maude p. 217-218).

Grimble's assumption in this last statement is incorrect. When I-Kiribati refer to *te boti* in the *maneaba*, they talk about the whole island's social structure through the family's sitting place in the *maneaba*, from the *uea* (king or high chief) to *kaunga* (commoner). Banabans do not recognise *uea* or kingship within Banaban society. *Te boti* is a custom that Banabans have never recognised.

Taitai (tattooing)

Grimble, cited in Maude and Maude (1994), mentions that "by 1931, only three men on Banaba were tattooed. Te Baiti, Na Ewantabuariki and Kabunginteiti; while no women were tattooed" (p. 49). Nei Anginimaeao probably introduced the custom of tattooing. It is not recognised as part of the Banaban culture. Although European visitors witnessed a high number of tattoos in 1851, this practice died out shortly after due to missionary influence.

Te Ati ni Kana (hair cutting and offering ceremony)

Grimble also recorded the ceremony of cutting and making offerings of hair. Introduced by Nei Anginimaeao, some of her descendants practised it. However, this Kiribati ceremony was not in general practice on Banaba.

Te Butirake (asking for social standing or to inherit land)

Te butirake was the term used in olden times to offer personal favours to procure either land or certain important rights or clan duties within the community. This process usually began with the garlanding of the person receiving the offer with flowers and anointing him or her with scented oil. The receiver then replied, stating whether he or she accepted *te butirake* and thus became the new partner. When families used this custom to inherit land, it was called *te aba ni butirake* (land of the asking). This practice was introduced by the I-Kiribati newcomers who needed to gain land to ensure their survival on Banaba. After the missionaries arrived on Banaba in the 1880s, this practice was discouraged because they believed it was unfair and open to abuse. The colonial government eventually outlawed the practice when land disputes occurred in the mining years. By 1931, the Government Land Commission no longer legally recognised land inherited in this manner.

Right for gathering the first fruits

The right to take the first fruits, such as coconuts, pandanus and almond fruit was brought to Banaba by Na Maninimate from Beru and belonged to a particular family within Uma district. They would celebrate gathering the first wild almond fruit and dedicate the offering to Nei Tituabine, the stingray goddess who was part of Nei Anginimaeao's culture. This ritual was only part of Te Tarine hamlet from Uma district and not part of general Banaban society. It is not practised by Te Tarine descendants today.

Becoming Part of Banaban Culture

When Nei Anginimaeao arrived on Banaba and traded certain rights regarding fish and games in exchange for land from the Tabwewans, some aspects of her cultural influence became integrated into mainstream Banaban life, as did aspects of Auriaria's Gilolo heritage. Auriaria, the warriors, and Nei Anginimaeao, who came in peace, strengthened the foundations of the existing Te Aka society. Although missionaries, beachcombers, European administrators, and indentured phosphate workers came later, Banaba customs and traditions moulded from these three earliest cultures remained strong.

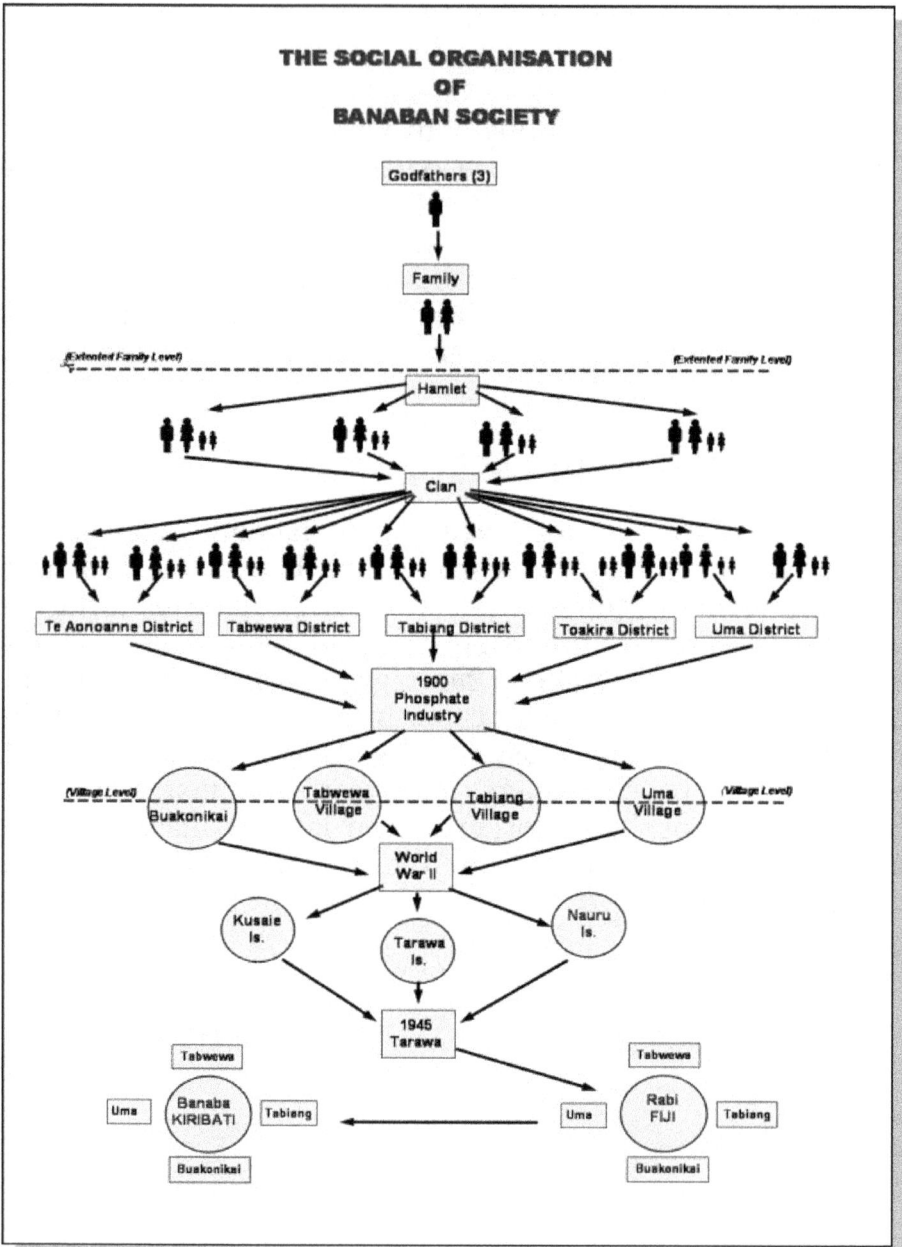

Figure: 3.9. The social organisation of Banaban society (by S.M. King).

PART FOUR:
TE I-MATANG

41. BPC facilities at Home Bay, Uma (Williams Collection 1901–1931).

19: EARLY CONTACT AND MISINTERPRETATION

Captain Jered Gardner made the first known European sighting of Banaba on 3 January 1801. He sailed the 219-tonne *Diana*, an American ship owned by Rodman and Company of New Bedford. At first, the captain mistook Banaba for nearby Byron Island (Nauru). Realising that he had discovered a new island, he named it Rodman's Island. Another European discovery of Banaba occurred in 1804, credited to Captain John Mertho. He named it after his ship *Ocean*. Amongst the many whaling, blackbirding and trading ships that called there, the island became known as Panapa or Paanopa. This last name was the phonetic spelling of the name used by Banabans: the 'p' spelling in English translates to the 'b' sound in the Kiribati language. There is no 'p' in the Kiribati vocabulary. Europeans increasingly affected the Banaban way of life.

European Misinterpretation of 'Chieftainship'

Webster, in 1851, provided the first recorded instance of European misunderstanding of chiefly status in Banaba society. In observing the Banaban ceremony of boarding foreign vessels, he described the rankings that he thought he saw:

> "In a few minutes, three canoes were seen paddling from the shore; the first canoe, being more ornamented than the others, we rightly concluded contained the monarch. We let down the side–ladder for his accommodation and welcomed his Royal Highness on board. He was accompanied by three Chiefs, apparently much older than himself, and richly tattooed. The King appeared in all his naked majesty, a fine stout jolly–looking fellow, but entirely devoid of the tattooing which was so profusely displayed on the bodies of his attendant chiefs" (as cited in, Maude & Maude, 1994, p. 73).

Traditionally, Banabans have not used the terms king, queen or chief. When these terms were used in European historical recordings about Banaban society, they caused great misunderstanding and confusion among the people. In Banaban culture, all men and women are equal, and elders are only respected more than anyone else for their knowledge and understanding in matters relating to culture and daily life.

Webster referred to an elderly woman who garlanded him on his arrival as a 'priestess.' He later recorded the names (spelt phonetically, according to the sounds he heard) of the 'kings' he met. One was Tapuranda, who governed the southwest end of the island with his son Tapu-ki Panapa. The other chief or king, he said, came from the northeast region and was named Tapati.

From Banaban genealogy charts, focusing on this period and the clans involved with the rights of welcoming the stranger, we find Nan Takabea. Nan means 'man', while Webster could have mistaken the sound of the name Takabea for what he recorded as Tapuranda. (There is no 'd' sound in the language.) Nan Takabea was a descendant of Auriaria and came from the Karieta region of Tabwewa district. His duties included welcoming newcomers or strangers to Banaba's shores. No other name in Banaban genealogy charts matches Tapuranda or Taburana (as Banabans would spell it more closely).

Temwate	Kamaria	Burarang	Eri
Elder Tabwewa	Elder Buakonikai	Elder Tabiang	Elder Uma
Descendant of Takabea Karieta Clan	Descendant of Raobeia Te Aka Clan	Descendant of Nei Beteua te Kaoti-n Aine Clan	Descendant of Na Butintoa Rarikintekawai Clan

42. Four of the elders who signed the contract with Ellis in 1900 (by S.M. King).

Webster recorded that the lead canoe was called, Te wa-n Tieke of the Karieta, the second canoe Te wa-n Tieke of the Karia, and the third canoe Te wa-ni Kaiowa from Te Maeu, from the Karia, all within Tabwewa district. The 'son' of Tapuranda, Tapu-ki Panapa (Tabukinbanaba, Banaban spelling), was the son of Banaban woman Nei Teienimakin, who was known in history as the woman who garlanded Tabwewa Karieta elder, Nan Takabea. Through this process of *te butirake* (favours from the asking), she and her son gained certain privileges, even though they were not related by marriage or birthright to Nan Takabea. He was not a king or chief, nor was Nei Teienimakin a queen. Finally, genealogy charts suggest that 'Tapati' was probably Tebaiti (in the Kiribati language, the spelling 'ti' corresponds to the pronunciation of 's'). Tebaiti came from Te Aonoanne district, the northeast region of the island, as Webster recorded.

The descendants of one of the hamlets from Te Aonoanne District were shocked to see Tebaiti named as the 'king' for this region. Perhaps when Tebaiti met Webster, he had been given a role as *kaekeko* (a young man permitted to speak on behalf of all the elders of that district for a particular time).

The misinterpretation in relation to signing contracts

The most glaring example of the incorrect use of European concepts of rank and title was after Ellis' first arrival on Banaba in 1900. He made a contract with certain Banabans, which gave the Europeans the right to mine for 999 years at £50 per annum. The man responsible for boarding foreign vessels, Temate, was wrongly described as the 'king' of all Banaba on the original contract dated 3 May 1900. Kariatabwewa signed as the chief witness to Temate's signature.

By 18 September 1900, the same contract carried the signatures of the following elders from each district: Kamaraia, Chief of Puakonikai; Eri, Chief of Ooma (Uma); and Pulalang, Chief of Tabiang. No doubt adding the title of 'chief' or 'king' to each of these signatures gave the contract an air of greater authority in British law. 'Chief' was written under their crosses representing their signatures, which were added to the original document and witnessed by Albert Ellis's brother George. (By the time of this historical document, Toakira District was no longer mentioned as part of Banaba).

The roles of these Banabans were very different from the ones that the Europeans recorded for them. Temate was the elder from Karieta of Aurakeia, hamlet, who represented all the Karieta region in Tabwewa district. Kariatabwewa was the elder from Karia of Aurakeia hamlet, representing all the Karia region in Tabwewa district. He held the role of *kaekeko*. Kamaraia was the elder from Te Aka clan, representing all of Te Aonoanne district. Eri was the elder from Te Tarine clan, representing all of Uma district. Burarang was the elder from Tabiang and represented all Tabiang district. One of Temate's official clan duties was to share the role of boarding foreign vessels with his counterpart from the Karia region. According to clan records, that counterpart was Na Mita, not Kariatabwewa, as mentioned on Ellis's contract. Maybe Kariatabwewa was included because he was a *kaekeko* (acting on behalf of) Na Mita, who might have been considered at the time too immature for this role.

Each of the 'chiefs' who signed the mining contract was an elder whose role was coordinating community activities within his district. He had no rights as an individual to make decisions on how his community was run. All elders within the district spoke for the community and were responsible for calling and chairing meetings in their district *maneaba*.

Webster and Ellis assumed that Nan Tekabea and Temate were 'kings' and had power over the rest of the community just because the Karieta elder from Tabwewa had the inherited right to board foreign vessels or welcome strangers to the island. This custom seems to have caused a misconception for all newcomers to Banaba, especially surrounding the discovery of phosphate.

At the time of the publication of Ellis's first book in 1936, *Ocean Island and Nauru*, he admitted that Temati [Temate] was not a king as he had initially documented. However, the damage of misinterpretation had already been done:

> "The principal native visitor was Temati [Temate], called "The King" by the steamer people, but it appeared afterwards that he was more a "Minister for Foreign Affairs." It was his province to establish communication with the few vessels that called at the island and come to an understanding with the captains regarding the object of their visit. Owing to his position; therefore, he took a prominent part in the proceedings which followed" (p. 56).

179

Elders today argue that this mistake gave credence to the British legal responses to the Banabans struggle over land issues and the document they believe was an unlawful contract signed by their unsuspecting and innocent ancestors.

Later Misinterpretations: Grimble's 'Chiefship'

By the time of Grimble's research, at least he had dropped the use of the terms 'king' and 'queen', but he gives detailed descriptions of inheritance regarding 'chiefship', which continues the myth that the concept is part of Banaban culture. He also mentions that men and women were equal in their rights to chiefship through inheritance, mainly determined by order of birth, although the parents could change it at their discretion. Again, with a confusion of terms, Grimble stated that if the eldest child was a woman, she was referred to as 'chiefess', and the nearest male relative would act in the role on her behalf until her son was old enough to take over the role of chief. The custom he refers to is the inherited role of clan speaker. The clan speaker does not hold any chiefly powers over the people but only acts on behalf of his elders to represent them during clan or district meetings. When all the clan's elders came together under one district, the oldest of the elders who had the capacity to do so was chosen to chair the meeting, while the clan speaker spoke on behalf of their particular group of elders from their clan. The chairman could not implement any actions unless the rest of his elders agreed, and the rest of the community always respected their decisions.

In clarifying Banaban social structure here, the authors hope the misinterpretations of the past will finally be put to rest, and future historians will acknowledge that Banabans have never had this form of royal lineage or inherited hierarchy within their society.

20: BEACHCOMBERS, BLACKBIRDERS AND WHALERS

Long-Term Visitors – Beachcombers

Not all the Europeans who came to Banaba arrived because of mining or colonial rule. Some of the earliest Europeans to live on the island, often for several years, were beachcombers, while shorter-term visitors were blackbirders and whalers. According to Maude and Maude (1994), in 1837, a European beachcomber and former Norfolk Island convict, Jack Jones, arrived on Nauru via Rotuma. It was later reported that, for some reason, he was transferred to neighbouring Ocean Island. By 1845, records show that 17 Europeans had settled on Banaba, and several were runaway convicts from New South Wales or Norfolk Island. Further evidence comes from the 'Notes and References' on the life of Louis Becke and an unsigned article in the Christmas issue of the *Bulletin* (XII, 24 December 1892), which reported the massacre of white vagabonds on Ocean Island in the 1850s. No other information regarding this event has been found, but it is apparent beachcombers were on Banaba in the early to mid-nineteenth century.

By the Great Drought in the 1870s (Chapter 21), the last of these Europeans had fled the island, apparently because of the Drought. There are no more reports of beachcombers arriving after this period. The observations of the HMS *Barrosa* when it called at Banaba on 3 June 1872, were published in an address to the House of Lords, 10 February 1873', regarding extracts of *'Communications of Importance respecting Outrages Committed upon Natives of the South Sea Islands'*, the captain stated:

> "Several canoes came alongside; one native spoke English very well; he had served in whalers and visited America. He informed me that there were no white men now on the island. Vessels had been at the island two or three years ago and had carried off a great many natives."

The life of a beachcomber

In Rolf Boldrewood's novel *A Modern Buccaneer* (1894), he describes the allegedly last known beachcomber on Banaba. The story is fiction, but it matches similar tales of beachcombers. Here is how Boldrewood describes the outlook of Banaba's last beachcomber just before he leaves the island:

> "Mister Robert Ridley, aged seventy, sitting on a case in his house, on the south-west point of Paanopa, as its people call Ocean Island, with a bottle of 'square' face" before him, from which he refreshes himself, without the intervention of a glass, is one of the few successful deserters from the convict army of New South Wales. ...For seven years he has been the boss white man of Paanopa, ever since he left the neighbouring Nauru or Pleasant Island, after seeing his comrades fall in the ranks one by one, slain by bullet or the scarce less deadly drink demon."

As the story continues, it reveals that Ridley must now leave for the Caroline Islands because 'a mysterious Providence has afflicted his island with a drought.' A second reason for going seems to be conflict over land: 'Blood had been shed over the ownership of certain cocoa-nut trees.' Boldrewood also mentions the beachcomber's family, who appear to be Banabans:

"From out the open door he sees the '*Josephine*', of New Bedford, and Captain Jos Long, awaiting the four whaleboats now on the little beach below his house, which are engaged in conveying on board his household goods and chattels, his wives and his children, with their children, and a dusky retinue of blood-relations and retainers; for the drought had made food scarce" (p. 122).

Albert Ellis recalled seeing several beachcomber's descendants on the island during his first visit in 1900, noting their fair skin and different features. He confirmed that no beachcombers were left on the island by that time.

In 1909, Arthur Mahaffy became Acting Resident Commissioner on Banaba for six months. He had visited the island in 1896, before the discovery of phosphate and found it occupied only by Banabans. His comprehensive report on Banaba discussed at length the beachcombers who had lived amongst the Banabans during the mid-nineteenth century. Regarding their origins, he says that they were,

"...sometimes deserters from whalers, sometimes convicts who had escaped from Norfolk Island or from New South Wales and had been picked up at sea by passing ships, from which they afterwards deserted or were expelled. Some of the grim annals of these villains may be found in the picturesque pages of Mr Louis Becke. They were usually bad, adopted the dress of the natives, and were tattooed like them."

He seems unimpressed by the character of beachcombers. Mahaffy goes on to describe the ills they brought to Banaban society. Beachcombers, he says, instructed Banabans:

> ... in all the vices of a 'superior' civilisation and communicated to them its most terrible diseases. They taught them to distil a spirit from coconut toddy through gun-barrels; they mended the dilapidated muskets which the natives possessed; they practised polygamy; they brawled among themselves, and not infrequently murdered and poisoned each other. Pleasant Island (Nauru), more fertile and abounding in food, however, attracted these men in greater numbers than the barren and forbidding Panapa (Banaba); but I have heard some stories from one of the oldest and most respected captains of a well-known line of mail steamers who visited Ocean Island in 1852 on a whaling ship, which prove that, in their general character, the white beachcombers of that place were no better than those on Pleasant Island.

In his report, Mahaffy also notes beachcombers involved in conflict, including among the Banabans themselves:

> "Wars were of frequent occurrence among the natives of the four villages on the island, and in these struggles, the white men took a leading part and were sometimes killed. They plotted and accomplished the cutting out of at least two ships and the massacre of their crews at Pleasant Island (Nauru) ..." (Mahaffy, 1910, p. 12).

However, he concluded that he found no lasting memory of the beachcombers among the Banabans, other than that 'they were bad men', and they left 'no abiding mark' on society. His information also ties in with other accounts and the snippets in the 1892 *Bulletin* about the massacre of white vagabonds in the 1850s.

Blackbirding and Recruiting of Banabans

As Banabans began interacting more with European ships, fit young Banaban men seized the opportunity to join the crews and later became labourers on foreign plantations. Although not all experiences were negative, they often found they had been 'blackbirded', which was close to a form of slavery (see David Chappell, *Double Ghosts: Oceanian Voyagers on Euromerican Ships*, 1997).

Webster describes a young Banaban who had been blackbirded in this way and later came home on the Australian *Wanderer*.

> "On the 12th August 1851, we left the island of Tapeutuwea [Tabiteuea] and sailed westward for Ocean Island, the native place of Timmararare. No sooner was Tim aware that we were now steering for his native island, that he was constantly aloft looking out for land. On the morning of the 15th Tim's sharp and anxious eye discerned his beloved island far on the horizon. No sooner did he see it, then he began shouting for joy exclaiming, 'that my land! – that my country"! (as cited in, Maude & Maude, 1994, p. 73).

From the rest of the information in Webster's article and genealogy charts, it appears that Timmararare could be Na Itinaumaere. Webster says Tim was terrified to meet with the elders of Tabwewa, who came out to greet their vessel. If 'Tim' was Na Itinaumaere, he was a descendant from Tabwewa who would later marry a woman from Uma district.

Another record is of an 1875 visit by the Queensland brig *Flora* to Banaba on a recruiting trip. In his diary, Mackay says that after they recruited 60 Banaban men to take to Queensland, he was approached by the elder from Tabwewa (perhaps Nan Takabea, who was in charge of boarding foreign vessels and was mentioned in the visit of the

Wanderer in 1851). With tears in his eyes, the elder said that most of their men had already been taken away and that they had no food left after the drought. If the captain took the last of their young men away, he asked who would be left there to fish for them (for more details on the Great Drought, see Chapter 21).

In the latter part of the nineteenth century, islanders from around the Pacific were reported to be working overseas, especially in plantations. The main destinations for these labourers were Fiji, Samoa, Tahiti, Hawaii, and towards the end of the century, Central America. Australian cotton farms and Queensland sugar plantations began seeing the arrival of some Banaban labourers during this period. In the 1860s, the Peruvian recruiters were considered virtual slave traders, and the Islanders later learned to fear the 'men-stealing ships', especially from Tahiti (see Harry Maude, *Slavers in Paradise*, 1981). Nevertheless, many of the young islander men were willing recruits, especially during the time of drought.

Passing Through – The Whalers

From the early 1800s, Banaba was well known to whaling ships, which came to buy meat (pigs) and to add fresh food to their sea rations while on their three-year-long journeys. From 1819, whaling ships discovered what they referred to as the 'on-the-line grounds'. The waters extending along the equator from the Line Islands in the east to Nauru in the west. This location became very popular with whalers, especially during the northern winter. Instead of seeing one ship, perhaps every three years, Banabans could expect to meet them much more frequently. With several hundred ships a year in this region, many no doubt stopped off at Banaba to obtain fresh provisions. In this period, the waters around Banaba were visited by many British and American whaling vessels seeking sperm whales. Seamen from some of these vessels occasionally deserted or were shipwrecked. Adventurous Islanders were taken aboard these visiting ships as crewmen. Even though these visits were numerous, they could not have been lengthy because Banaba does not have a proper anchorage. Even modern full-powered steamers had to keep their engines running so they could leave quickly should the weather suddenly change.

In Wilson's Journal dated 22 December 1841, he mentions the local population:

> "Light winds and agreeable weather: Ocean Island to the westward, steering W.N.W. & passed within a league of it: observed a reef running off the S.W. end, upon which was placed a flag or signal staff: saw smoke & huts, and likewise natives on the beach, but not a single canoe came off to us, which is unusual; as they are known to crowd on board ship, perhaps, some of them may have been caught in actu derelicto, as they are adroit thieves, and received punishment upon the champ de forfait (or, in modern terms,' caught in the act and punished at the scene of the crime.') We passed on, steering a zig-zag course, for Pleasant Island" (Wilson, 1991, p. 247).

Whalers also picked up beachcombers and carried them to other Pacific Islands such as Rotuma, Nauru and Pohnpei.

Trading or Bartering of Goods

As growing numbers of Europeans arrived for a long or short-term stay on Banaba in the nineteenth century, they influenced many aspects of Banaban life. The accounts mentioned some of these: loss of young men to overseas' plantations, the introduction of western products such as guns, and some among the new generations of Banabans had European blood. In this final section, the visitor's impact on the economy and health of Banabans is stated. With such an influx of visitors, the Banabans began to trade their food and crafts for clothing and other goods. From the late nineteenth century, their economy gradually began to change from self-sufficiency, where the island provided Banabans with their every need, to an economy based on barter and exchange, in which Banabans increasingly focused on making items of value for trade with the outside world. Recalling his first visit to Banaba in 1896, Mahaffy stated that communication with Banaba and the outside world had been restricted to the occasional visit of a Sydney steamer, which called in to buy shark fins and tails for export to China. He also made some interesting first-hand observations on the goods that Banabans sought in exchange:

> "I well remember the natives coming off in their canoe with bundles of shark fins, and their extreme anxiety to exchange their murderous looking spears and swords edged with shark's teeth for glass bottles, with which I suppose they shaved themselves and cut each other's hair."

Banabans had discovered that they could use glass to make crude swimming goggles which would greatly assist them when diving for fish off the island's surrounding reefs. Mahaffy also mentions that they traded beautifully crafted shark's teeth, swords, mats, hats and fans with visiting ships in exchange for European food such as rice, ships' biscuits and knives. Unlike several other Pacific Islands, Banaba never grew enough surplus coconuts to produce oil or copra to become a commercial proposition.

European Diseases

In the late nineteenth century, there was a drastic drop in the Banaban population. There has already been much conjecture on the cause, but it has now been identified as the Great Drought of the 1870s. Given the influx of ships to Banaba during this period, we must also consider the devastating effect of new diseases introduced to an unsuspecting population. Many first-hand accounts of visits to the island during the latter part of the nineteenth-century state that the Banabans were a fine healthy race who were well fed and physically fit. For example, the juice of a very young coconut was used for sore eyes. However, by the time of Ellis's first visit to Banaba in 1900, it was a very different story. In one unpublished document (in the private files of Harry Maude), simply titled, 'Ocean Island (1903),' the unknown author states the Island was once thickly populated, but drought and sickness were said to have been introduced by American whalers had decimated the inhabitants.

Before the discovery of phosphate in 1900, the Banabans had already come in contact with quite a few Europeans and some of the worst traits associated with western civilisation. Some of these Europeans assisted the community during the Great Drought in the early 1870s and prepared the Banabans for the first arrival of missionaries fifteen years later. Maude and Maude (1994) also reflects on the devastating effects of European diseases:

> "Intercourse with foreigners, furthermore, resulted in the introduction of a variety of exotic diseases, of which yaws was the worst. Hitherto they had been able to cope with their indigenous illness and mishaps by means of home-made remedies, mainly herbal but including many magic antidotes. But they were helpless in the face of yaws, leprosy, diabetes, measles and the gamut of imported ailments" (p. 117).

During the early mining era, diseases raged on the island, introduced inadvertently by Europeans, Asians and other Pacific Islanders.

Yaws, lupus, asthma, and syphilis affected the Banabans, and when ships came in, influenza and colds. When a dispensary was erected later on, and the Pacific Island

Company supplied the medicine, Banabans went to the dispensary. Rather than being treated immediately, they preferred to sit around, chat and watch others being bandaged and given medicine. Banabans and mine workers with recognised sores or illnesses were known among the European employees as 'the man with the rotten leg', 'the woman without a nose', 'the ulcerated boy' or 'the child with the lips.' Albert Ellis's wife, Florence, was known to be involved in assisting in the first dispensary set up on the island, but on 6 October 1909, at only thirty-four years of age, she succumbed to sickness and died. Her tombstone can still be found today on the island.

21: DROUGHT

Official Climate Records – Rainfall

It was only in the late nineteenth century that records of Banaban weather began to be kept. In terms of documented droughts, we have the following dates:

- 1871, 1872, and 1873 were the years that Maude and Maude suggested for the Great Drought.
- 1887 was a drought year recorded by the *Missionary Herald*, June 1887.
- 1901 as a drought year recorded by *The Friend*, Nov 1901.

The British Royal Naval Intelligence Division provided the first official records of Banaba's weather patterns. Except for the years 1920 to 1922, 1926 and 1927, when data were not available, there is a complete record of the rainfall patterns from 1909 to 1938. Even though this information begins nearly 40 years after the Great Drought, it is valuable evidence. Before these records, information could only be drawn from random documented encounters with the island between 1837 and 1909.

According to these naval records, the average rainfall on Banaba was approximately 70 inches (1,925 millimetres) per annum. The chart shows that yearly above and below average rainfall was about the same. Droughts are generally said to occur in a cycle of approximately seven years, but co–

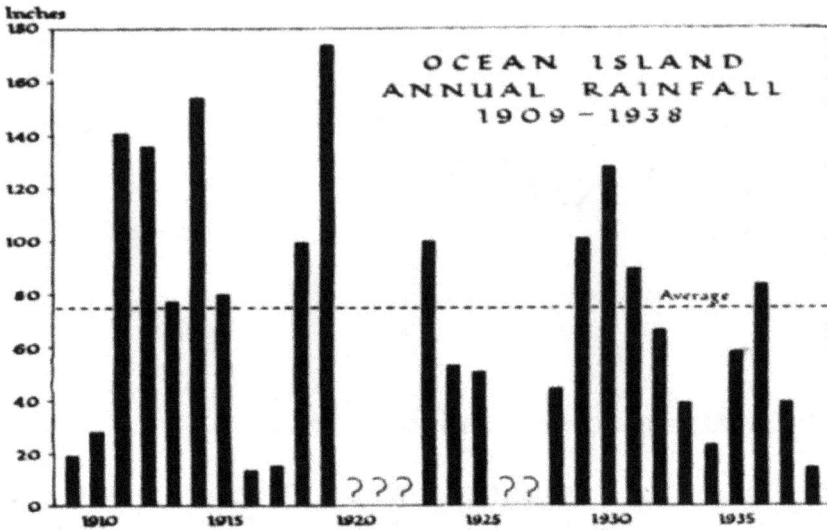

Figure: 4.1. Copy of original 'Ocean Island Rainfall Chart' taken from British Royal Naval Intelligence division records.

vering twenty-seven years, shows droughts occurring every four to five years. The drought between 1924 and 1928 was significant.

From 1930, when Banaba had a rainfall of 128 inches (3,251 millimetres), the rate declined to 90 inches (2,286 millimetres) in 1931, then slowly dropped until the drought of 1934, when the rainfall was 23.5 inches (597 millimetres). From 1931 to 1938, six of the seven years had below average rainfall. In most of the central and southern Kiribati Islands, to the east of Banaba, the rainfall variations are not as high even though the average rainfall is lower. Another interesting aspect of these official weather records and charts is that except for the five years when data was unavailable, some rain fell in each of these twenty-seven years. A complete lack of rain had been a feature of the Great Drought.

Impact on the Population

It was not until the nineteenth century when Banabans first started to encounter European ships, and the first population figures were discovered in written records. The list below shows documented population figures spanning more than one hundred years. There is a sharp drop in the estimated population size between early and later figures. Some Pacific historians argue that the earlier estimates (such as Webster's at 2,000 to 3,000) were exaggerated.

There are many reasons for the decrease in population, some related to the Great Drought and other droughts, and others related to introduced diseases and the tragic events of the twentieth century (to be discussed in the following chapters). The authors hope to shed more light on this period in future years by researching genealogy charts to deduce population figures. The genealogy charts show only recorded births, not age or date of deaths, but they indicate the continuation of family lineages of those who survived this tragic period.

Recorded Banaban Population Figures 1851–1945

Year	Population size	Recorded by
1851	2,000–3,000	Webster 1851 (Maude 1994:77)
1869 (approx.)	Over 1,000	Mahaffy (1910:11)
1875	500–600 (at general meeting held at Tabwewa *maneaba*	Mackay 1875 (Maude 1994:86)
1885 (4 Aug)	200 or more	Capt. Walkup 1885 (Maude 1994:90)
1900 (11 May)	451 Tabwewa 133 Uma 138 Tabiang 60 Buakonikai 120	Ellis (1900)
1909	475	Mahaffy (1910:2)
1914	Over 400	Maude and Maude (1932:263)
1931	729	Maude and Maude

		(1932:263)
Late 1941	500 approx.	Ratieta (1996:21)
1942	Over 600	Samuelu (1962:28)
1945	703 (arrived Rabi)	Kennedy (1946)

In 1945, 703 Banabans arrived on Rabi, Fiji (with 300 I-Kiribati). (H.E. Maude 1946, p. 13).

Surviving the Droughts

Droughts had a devastating effect on the plants that supplied Banabans with much of their food. The first plants to die were the pawpaws, pumpkins and fresh coconuts. The only tree that could usually withstand the worst of the droughts was the *Calophyllums* which were situated mostly on the island's crest and survived by sending down long twisting roots in search of water into the moist caverns far below. Great skills were needed to ensure that the Banaban communities survived. Ellis gives an account of how the Banaban women prepared special foods:

> Preparing pandanus for food was another important part of the women's duties. Outside each hut we would invariably see a number of 'pancakes' drying, each about a foot in diameter. These were made from the soft part of the pandanus drupe or fruit mashed up into a fibrous mass which was subsequently powdered laboriously and used in various ways. These pandanus food preparations were very wholesome and as the pancakes, or the sawdust as we termed it, could be kept for a considerable period, they constituted a reserve against the inevitable 'rainy day', which on Ocean Island meant a drought period. Other food reserves for such a time were the coconut kernel allowed to dry into a hard ball inside the nut, and capable of keeping indefinitely, also the nuts of the wild almond (Ellis, 1936, p. 76).

During Ellis's first visit to Banaba in 1900, during meetings he held with Banaban elders, he learnt how Banabans dealt with the problem of maintaining a supply of drinking water during a drought:

> It was the duty of the women to visit these caves [*bangabanga*] each morning with torches and baskets of coconut shells for the day's supply. But in drought times these pools were soon emptied, and the woman had to go deeper and deeper in search of others. On such occasions, so they informed me, mortality was caused by want of water, and one of the practices in their extremity was to go out catching flying fish at night merely to suck their eyes, which are exceptionally large and of a pronounced aqueous nature. It was not unusual they said for a piece of land to be exchanged for a single coconut shell of water (Ellis, 1936, p. 66).

The other source of food was, of course, the sea. The men used their seafaring skills to catch fish. They also paddled out with water containers made from coconut shells and tried to collect water from rain that fell offshore from the island. In this way, they tried to salvage what they could from a heart-breaking phenomenon witnessed by many people over the centuries. As rain clouds and squalls build up and move towards the island's land mass, the heat generated from the land causes an upward draft of hot air that divides the clouds. The clouds suddenly split and dropped their precious load into the sea on either side of the island. As a result of the devastation of the island's natural vegetation, the exposure of rock and limestone during droughts, and then mining, the drought phenomenon has become more frequent.

The Great Drought

Maude and Maude (1994) estimate that the Great Drought

occurred between 1871 and 1874. The most affected area was Buakonikai because it is away from the sea. John Mackay, Master of the *Flora*, described how the island was still suffering in 1875:

> "It is about 10 miles in circumference, rising in the centre to a height of 300 feet, covered with stunted breadfruit, coconut and pandanus which on this occasion presented a parched and dried up appearance, in consequence of no rain having fallen for three years. In approaching the island, the large number of houses to be observed would lead to the supposition that it is thickly populated, which, however, is not the case, as, on entering several of them when on shore, I found them mere receptacles for canoes, fishing gear and such."

During their first day on the island, Mackay and his crew recruited men to take back with them to Queensland. The following morning, they went ashore and were taken to what he describes as the Tabwewa *maneaba*. During the meeting, Mackay asked the Tabwewa elder if more people wanted to emigrate. The elder became very emotional; tears began to run down his face as he told Mackay and his party of their struggle with the drought and how the community was now wholly dependent on the ocean for subsistence. They did not have anything left to plant. He also told them that most of their young men had already gone, and if the European party recruited more, they would have no one left to fish for them. At the meeting, Mackay estimated five to six hundred Banabans were present. Maude and Maude suggest this estimate is unreliable because sixty men were said to have been recruited by Mackay on the *Flora,* and others had returned after the drought.

Ellis's census on Banaba on 11 May 1900 recorded the population as four hundred and fifty-one people. If we accept Mackay's earlier estimates, the loss across the following fifteen years was only about fifty to one hundred and fifty people. Mahaffy's official government census of the Banaban population in 1909 recorded a figure of four hundred and seventy-five, a growth of only twenty-four people in the nine years since the previous census.

Given Webster's 1851 estimate of two thousand to three thousand Banabans, the drop to an estimated five hundred to six hundred after the Great Drought in 1875 is drastic. Walkup's low population estimate of two hundred (Walkup, 1885, as cited in Maude & Maude, 1994, p. 91) was probably because he had not sighted all the hamlets and therefore underestimated the population. However, there is no evidence for rumours, noted by Maude and Maude, that catastrophic events had caused the population to fall to below fifty (Maude & Maude 1994, p. 85). Further study of Banaban genealogical charts could reveal more details of population movement and decline before Ellis's census of four hundred and fifty-one Banabans in 1900.

Other important aspects of Mackay's account

Relevant information can be learned about the Great Drought from Mackay's report of his 1875 visit. First, his **meeting in the Tabwewa** *maneaba* probably referred to a gathering of surviving Banabans who had come from every district to meet the new visitors. Maude and Maude believed that the Tabwewans were the least affected by the Great Drought. Although the meeting was held in the Tabwewa *maneaba*, it was not a meeting solely of the Tabwewa people. In Banaban tradition, Tabwewans had the right to board foreign vessels, meaning they also had the right to host meetings with strangers. Banabans would have been keen to meet with any visitors during these tragic times. Another significant aspect of Mackay's report is that he observes that there were parched and stunted trees but **does not mention dead trees**. Maude and Maude (1994) draw on this observation to suggest that the island had started to recover by the time of Mackay's visit. This could be true. During the author's visits to Banaba, it was amazing to see how quickly the island again becomes green when rain returns. However, Mackay clearly states 'stunted' trees, not a multitude of dead trees.

In contrast, other records of the Great Drought, which are usually by people much later, who were involved in the phosphate industry, stated that the trees died off completely, especially the coconut trees, with *Calophyllum* trees as the last survivors. In interpreting such accounts, the interests and origins of the observers must be considered. Someone from a wooded place in England would perhaps consider an island with few trees to be desolate; exaggeration after the event also makes a better story.

Note: The three-year drought broke on Banaba in 1897 while Mackay was visiting the island. The vegetation was very green, but the island had hundreds of dead trees silhouetted against the skyline. Coconut trees and the traditional *te itai* trees seemed to be still growing with no ill effect.

Eri's story

Some Banabans have given first-hand accounts of the Great Drought. Eri, an elder of Uma district, told his story to Grimble, Resident Commissioner, in 1957, and the story was retold by Maude and Maude in 1994. Here are some extracts from Eri's story:

> I was a young man then, and my parents, who lived in Uma village, had arranged for me to take a wife from Buakonikai. She was a girl named Marawa, very beautiful in my eyes, and we were to be married at the full of the fourth moon at the Season of the Pleiades. But when the third moon went out, and for three months no rain had fallen, her father said to mine, 'You will need your son to fish for you and we shall

need Marawa to fetch water for us now that a drought has set in', and my father answered, 'Even so, let there be no marriage until the rains return.' But it did not end; and even when the sun showed a full year gone, we knew that it would not break yet, for the rainclouds at sea, from which we had contrived to collect water up to then, ceased to come near us. Then our council of elders issued an edict: 'From now on, let no household take more than one coconut shell of water a day from the *bangabanga*.' So, the water was made to last for another whole year. But long before the next solstice in the south our food trees were gone; not one stood living in the land. We had nothing but fish to eat, and the fish often stayed so far from our shores, that for many days together there was none to be caught anywhere. We were already half starved when the drought sickness came, that white men call beriberi. People's gums rotted in their mouths; their teeth fell out; their bodies were covered in ulcers. They fell in the pathways and died there; and where they died their bodies remained, for who was strong enough to carry corpses home for burial rites? In the middle of the third year, when the waterholes were nearly dry, word came from Buakonikai that Marawa's parents had died. Things were a little better for us in Uma than in Buakonikai; Uma is by the sea; we had found seaweed to suck, and some said that this protected us against the sickness. But we were very weak. I was the only one of our house who could walk a hundred paces. So, my mother said, 'Go now to Buakonikai. Speak to the brother of Marawa's father and, if he will let her go, bring her to us here. So, from this drought you shall have a wife and I a daughter.'At her words, the strength came back to my legs. I made nothing of the long walk to Buakonikai. I came to the house of Marawa's father's brother. My heart said to me, 'Now you will see her.' But alas! When I lifted the screen to enter, she was not there. Only her father's brother was within, and he was dead. And the stink of corruption was everywhere around me as I walked through the village to her father's house. I found her with her parents. She had laid the bodies side by side and herself at their feet. The sickness was heavy upon her. Her lips were black, and her body eaten with ulcers. But she was still beautiful for me. I think she had been asleep before I entered; but when I lifted the screen she awoke and smiled at me, saying, 'I knew I should see you again,' and tried to sit up, but fell back looking into my eyes as I sat down beside her. Lying there, she smiled again and sighed very slow and deep. The smile stayed on her lips. She was dead. So, I brought no daughter to my mother.

Time went on. The waterholes were dry, but the rain clouds at sea had returned. Also, we of Uma village went down to the reef at low tide and lay covered with mats in shallow pools, so that our skins drank in the wetness. And on a day, I took my mother with me to a pool under the lee of certain rocks. We lay there, our heads resting on wooden pillows which I had brought, and soon we fell asleep. I did not wake until the rising tide floated the pillow from under me so that my head was spilled into the water. That nearly drowned me, but at last, I was able to kneel, and then I remembered my mother. She was not beside me. I looked out to sea; she was not there. I turned my eyes to the beach; she was floating there, on the edge of the tide. She had drowned beside me as I slept. How many times had she called me; I was deaf to her cries?

A ship arrived not long after ... a trading ship from New Zealand. The captain took my father and me, with most of the others who remained alive, to the island of Oahu, near Honolulu. There we lived until my father died, six years later, and then I returned to this place because I owned no land anywhere else.

This moving statement by Eri is a fascinating insight into Banaba's population decline and the exodus during the Great Drought. Eri referred to people within his family's hamlet of the Tarine in Uma district and the people of his fiancée from Buakonikai. Still, in those early times, it would have been a family hamlet within Te Aonoanne District. After Eri and his father fled Banaba, he did not return to the island for six years.

The story of the miraculous pool

According to Ellis (1936), an old lady informed her family that the last drop of water in their bangabanga was finished during the drought. The family decided they must leave the following day by canoe in the hope that some of their family would survive. In desperation, the old lady decided to make her last visit down to her *bangabanga* that night and went past the dried-up pool into an area she had never dared venture into. To her surprise, she came across a new pool of water that saved them from the drought. The family called the new miraculous pool Te Nei ni Borau in her honour.

The physical evidence of the Great Drought

On 21 August 1925, the *Sydney Morning Herald* published an article, 'Ocean Island - Remarkable Droughts', written by "Arthur Trimble MA FRIA". The name seems strangely close to Arthur Grimble – possibly he used it as a pseudonym while he held a government position on Banaba, or it was a typographical error by the newspaper). The author makes some interesting observations regarding drought conditions on Banaba and how the Banabans coped with these events. In a section headed, 'Vegetable Record', he refers to the effects of drought and the physical evidence for the history of the Great Drought:

> Droughts would come to Ocean Island in cycles of about seven years. How regular is their incidence can be judged by looking at any full-grown coconut tree. From the roots upwards at intervals of six to eight feet the trunk is seen to dwindle to girth, as if it had been compressed in a vice. Each of these 'corseting's' shown in the strangle hold of a drought, and the degree of each constriction will tell you just how near death came then to that tree. Moreover, if the vegetable record takes you back more than four seven-year periods, you will have some measure of the people's past hardships also, for the next portion as the trees suffered so did, they in the days when neither Government nor Phosphate Company was near to help them.
>
> Under normal conditions a coconut tree lives easily 60 years yet there is no tree on the island that records more than six droughts. That carries one back not more than 45 years. The reason is as simple as death, the seventh drought back, from the present left not a single coconut palm alive. It left very few people, too; to survey the abominable desolation that remained.

The author concludes that the minimum time that the drought could have lasted was three years. Much has been written about Banaban droughts generally. During the early years of the phosphate industry, it was promoted that the industry helped to reduce the effects of drought on the population. The mining company's contribution to the Banaban water supply, especially in the early 1900s, was to distil seawater and build many water cisterns on the island. However, they also made the Banaban population pay dearly as the loss of water holes, clearing of the vegetation and damage to reefs worsened drought conditions.

22: THE BANABAN EXODUS AND ARRIVAL OF MISSIONARIES

In the twelve years from the Great Drought in 1875 to the drought of 1887, Banabans suffered, and the community's general health declined dramatically. Vitamin deficiencies heightened their susceptibility. A later Resident Commissioner for Gilbert and Ellice Island Colony, H.W. McClure, reported, "The absence of any green food brought on scurvy and other ills." The elder Eri reported another debilitating disease: "We were already half starved when the drought sickness came, that white men call beriberi."

As ships passed through Banaba, some decided to leave, if only for a short time to improve their families' chances of survival. Banabans ended up in several different destinations. Eri left Banaba with his father aboard a New Zealand trading ship and was dropped off on the Hawaiian island of Oahu. *The Friend* (1 December 1873) carried a report from G.F. Bauldry, Master of the barque *Arnelda,* which reports taking some Banabans to Kosrae, then known as Strong's Island:

> "Left Honolulu December 1872 and cruised on the line between seasons; saw no whales. Touched at

43. Christian converts on Banaba led by Missionary Pastor Solomon (Ellis 1900).

Ocean Island, where the natives were in a starving condition. Took off 24 and carried them to Strong's Island, then proceeded North."

Two years later, the people who had been on this voyage were desperate to return, as documented by Wood when he found them living on Kosrae:

"I found on shore here [Kosrae, then called Strong's Island] about twenty natives of Ocean Island; their country had been stricken with a famine, and some trading vessel had carried them on here out of kindness. They now wanted me to take them home again; but I declined out of respect to the laws of my country. It is a pity they should be left here" (Wood 1875, pp. 188-9, as cited in, Maude & Maude, 1994, p. 86).

In Boldrewood's fictional work *A Modern Buccaneer*, the departure of many Banabans to Kosrae also features:

"Two whale ships had arrived, bringing half a dozen white men, which had a retinue of nearly a hundred natives from Ocean and Pleasant Islands.

The other men from Ocean Island, a famine having set in from drought in that lovely isle. They had also taken passage with their native following, to seek a more temporarily favoured spot. The fertility of Kusaie (Strong's Island) had decided them to remain" (Boldrewood 1894: Chapter 10).

Blackbirders also visited Banaba periodically, seeking to recruit the fittest young men. According to Binder (1977), five blackbirding vessels called into Banaba during the Great Drought and found desperate islanders only too willing to escape. A Tabwewa elder had also told Mackay, during his recruiting visit on the *Flora* in 1875, that young men had been taken away.

The First Missionaries

The first missionary to land on Banaba was Captain W. Walkup, who arrived aboard the Hawaiian Board of Missions' *Morning Star* on 4 August 1885. The reason for his visit was that a European in charge of the ABCFM (American Board of Commissioners for Foreign Missions) in Hawaii had claimed that nearly all the

44. Banaban girls in traditional *riri* dress (Williams Collection 1901-31).

205

Banabans had died in a drought or left the island. The Mission decided to visit Banaba and invite Banabans to move to Kosrae Island, where it would provide them with land.

To Walkup's surprise, he reported sighting over 200 people on the island. With the help of an old Banaban fisherman acting as his interpreter, who had picked up a limited knowledge of English during his time aboard American whaling vessels, he presented himself to a Banaban elder. The elder demanded to know the reasons for Walkup's visit and did not seem impressed with the stranger's talk of salvation and the introduction of a mission teacher to the island. He asked what good this business would be to his people. Following custom, the elder called a meeting with all the people and the other elders to let them decide for themselves. The good captain urged the people to confess their sins. After much discussion and from a list of sins he had suggested, the Banabans selected in order of gravity:

1. Stealing, which they considered the worst of all sins.
2. Quarrelling, which was frowned upon as bad manners, was not part of the usual social behaviour, so it was frowned upon.
3. Drunkenness, meaning the drinking of distilled coconut toddy or spirit and the behaviour it brought on, was considered very shameful.
4. Fornication, which, depending on the circumstances, was the least of all sins.

Walkup convinced the Banabans that they could learn much from a mission teacher and from the word and stories from the Bible *(Baibara)* that had already been translated into the Kiribati language. Onboard Walkup's ship was a teacher by the name of Isaac, who had come from Tabiteuea on his way to a mission posting in Nauru. Walkup was taken with the fact that the language spoken on Banaba was more like that spoken in Kiribati than the Nauruan language and instructed Isaac to encourage the people to learn the word of God as quickly as possible. Walkup mentioned, "The natives invited us to take a run down to New Caledonia (sic) and bring some friends home." These were probably Banabans who had fled during the droughts.

45. Early mission building on Banaba (F. Doutch Collection Circa 1915).

On his arrival, Walkup observed a heathen nakedness among the Banabans: 'The men and children were destitute of clothing, but like every other place we ever visited the women were covered with the *malo* (a short skirt of leaves strung around the hips) this observation was confirmed by comments by Webster (1851) and Mackay (1875). Walkup noted the contrast with a Banaban who had travelled abroad:

> "One native had been to Nantucket and Boston. He was, of course dressed and could speak some English."

46. Banabans marching to celebrate the arrival of Christianity early 1900s (L. Broadbent Collection 1923).

From the time of Walkup's arrival, mission influence over the Banabans affected at least half of the community. These converts embraced Christian philosophy, if not always the practices, and became known as tani Kiritian (Christians). The Missionaries soon recruited some Banabans to be admitted into their Mission school on Kosrae. They made it clear they, "did not favour intellectuals but accepted men and women who were morally faithful Christians to work for the church" (Benaia, 1991).

By 1908, a new ABCFM Mission school, called the Bingham Institute, was opened on Banaba after the mission on Kosrae was severely affected by a hurricane. Maude and Maude summarised the changes in this period as follows:

"The next fifteen years passed peacefully with the Banabans gradually turning to the Christian faith, building their village churches and schools and

208

learning to read and write with the Gilbertese Bible and other mission-produced literature to help them. Trousers for men and neck to knee (or ankle) Mother Hubbard's for women became the preferred dress for church when they could be obtained, and they now had two ships calling more or less regularly: The *Archer* and the *Hiram Bingham*" (Maude & Maude, 1994, p. 118).

The other half of the community apparently could not be swayed away from their traditional spiritual beliefs and became known as the *tani Bekan* (Pagans). These Banabans refused to destroy their sacred cairns and ancestral shrines, abandon their frigate birds, and purchase Mother Hubbard's and cotton trousers.

The cost of Christianity

The missionaries financially benefited from the punishments they imposed on backsliders. They would impose fines for sins, such as talking in church on a Sunday, walking outside the village boundary on a Sunday and, in one case, rescuing a drowning man on a Sunday who had broken the Sabbath law by fishing. Banabans faced a fine of thirty dollars or six months in jail for the sin of adultery and reportedly one week's jail or fifty cents for the sin of fornication. All fines were paid in coconuts.

In the early period of phosphate mining, it was calculated that more than one-third of the Banabans' modest incomes from royalties found its way back to the Missions, as Resident Commissioner Eliot observed:

"Banabans learned to cover their naked male children in the presence of white people, and to hide breasts and thighs of their women from judgmental western eyes.

Yet such a practice was also very profitable for traders and brought benefits for missionaries. The missionaries, too, I suppose all unwittingly, work hand in glove with the traders by telling the natives they should 'cover their nakedness.' It was Adam and Eve and the serpent all over again. I found for example an absurd missionary law in force in some of the islands. A child, as soon as it could stand, must be clad in a loincloth. In return all the missionaries received their goods at cost price" (Eliot, 1938, p. 156).

By the end of the nineteenth century, Christianity's influence on the community had expanded. Then Albert Ellis arrived. He had once considered a career for himself as a 'man of the cloth' and still had high regard for God's ways. The Banaban elders were impressed with Ellis's demeanour and Christian values. They signed his contract granting mining rights for 999 years in the belief that they were dealing with a Christian gentleman, a man whose word they could trust. Even as things began to go wrong, the elders often still held Ellis in high personal regard, in contrast to other European roughnecks, riffraff and non-Christian behaviour.

47. Banaban congregation at a church service (L. Broadbent Collection 1923).

"By 1925, the ABCFM had merged with the London Mission Society ... By 1935, the Golden Jubilee of the landing of Christianity and the progressive integration of the Banaban community into the Christian world was celebrated. The Banabans were asked to wear white instead of the black lava-lava to symbolise the transition from living in darkness to living in the light" (Benaia, 1991 pp. 36-7).

Rev. George Eastman, who attended the occasion, typically praised the conversion of the Banabans:

"From being a benighted poverty stricken herd of pagans they had been raised by the Gospel to a self-respecting and generous Christian community, and by the development of the Phosphate industry they had become comparatively speaking a well to do community not unmindful of their duty to help their needy brethrens" (cited in, Silverman, 1971, p. 138).

Traditional Banaban spiritual worship remained entrenched in the psyche, and on Rabi today, the blend of mainstream Christianity and other introduced religions play an important part in society.

48. Banaban girls wearing Mother Hubbard dresses early 1900s (Source: unknown).

49. Banaban girls wearing Mother Hubbard dresses (Williams Collection 1901-31).

50. Fatima Catholic grotto (Williams Collection 1901-31).

23: BANABAN LANGUAGE AND ITS DECLINE

One of the saddest western influences on culture was the decline of the Banaban language through the introduction of Christianity. The first Bible was written in the Kiribati language, and the Banabans were encouraged to speak I-Kiribati so they could more easily understand the word of God. In the process, and over the years that followed, Banabans used their language less frequently until only a few words remain today. The younger generations chant the words of the *te karanga,* which now is a blend of the old Banaban language and I-Kiribati. While they understand the Kiribati words, they do not know the meaning of the Banaban words in the dance. There are several records of words from the Banaban language. Some elders remember a few words, while other words remain in place names. (Appendix 9 gives the words used in *te karanga* war spear dance).

Banaban Elder's list

Banaban word	English translation
Kau!	Go!
Kauriri	Let us go!

Barebare	Hurry
Tingaro	Dawn
M'aro	Come in
Tia Buanna (an exclamation)	We are fed up with the nonsense
Kiroro (Gilolo)	Far away or as far as the deep ocean
Titimea	To break and splatter

Banaban place names

Banaban word   Taken from

Banaban word	Taken from
Taekarau	Hamlet, Karia, Tabwewa
Marata	Kabini marata Hamlet, Karia, Tabwewa
Mangati	Hamlet, Karieta, Tabwewa
Aurakeia	Hamlet, Karia and Karieta, Tabwewa
Tarakabu	Hamlet, Tabiang
Oraka	Hamlet, Tabiang
Bare bongawa	Hamlet, Tabiang
Nakieba	Hamlet, Tabiang
Kambo	Neingkambo Hamlet, Tabiang
Taiki	Hamlet, Tabiang
natiabouri	Ao n natiabouri Hamlet, te Aonoanne
Terike	Hamlet, te Aonoanne
te Aka	Hamlet, te Aonoanne
Niniki	Hamlet, Toakira
Tarine	te Tarine Hamlet, Uma
Koun	Nei Koun Terrace, Tabwewa
Tawanang	Terrace, Tabwewa
te rengerenge	Tabo n te rengerenge Terrace, Tabiang
Natea	Nam Natea Terrace, Tabiang
Bareimwim	Terrace, te Aonoanne
Meai	te Meai Terrace, Uma

214

Comparing Banaban and Kiribati Languages

Much has been said about the Banaban identity and its differences from the Kiribati culture. Language is a key element of this discussion. Harry Maude supplied significant evidence in his sworn statement for the UK court case in 1975 regarding 'The Linguistic Evidence of the Banabans and their Identity.' Here is Maude's argument to the Court:

> It is sometimes asserted that the Banabans must be Gilbertese because they speak Gilbertese. Apart from the fact that linguistic affinity is a shaky foundation on which to base racial relationship, that this was not always the case is not only affirmed by the Banabans themselves but was obvious to me when I was living among them in 1931–32. During the Lands Commission proceedings, which were conducted throughout in the vernacular, I soon became aware that part of the vocabulary and a number of idioms, being used by the witnesses and assessors were not, in fact, Gilbertese at all. As a matter of interest, therefore, the Land Commission Clerk was instructed to enter in a notebook words and expressions recognised to be distinctively Banaban. Though they amounted to a significant quantity, even then, due to the use of the Gilbertese Bible, of Gilbertese as the language of instruction in the mission schools, the influence of the many hundreds of Gilbertese phosphate workers brought to the island under indenture, and other factors, the original Banaban speech had long been swamped by introduced Gilbertese, just as Cornish and Manx have been swamped by English, and it is doubtful if any of it still survives today. Nevertheless, its former existence is an indication of separate identity while its extinction is attributable to pressures emanating from European contact.

215

The words Maude's court clerk recorded and their Kiribati and English equivalents are below.

51. Banaban words from H.E. Maude's Notebook, 1932.

Banaban words from Maude's List 1931–32

Lands Commission Court
Kaokoron taekani Banabama Kiribati
'The Difference Between Banaban and Kiribati Language'

Banaban word	Kiribati translation	English translation
Itingaro	Karangaina	Early in the morning (Dawn)
Aua!	(mane) ao ake a ngaira!	Oh!
*Barebare	Kawaetata	Hurry
Nanta	Antai	Who
*Kau	Tia nako	Let us go
Taboni kaneati	Bukini waiwai	At the edge of the reef
Karawa	Tanrake	Eastern side

216

| *Tia buanna* | *Tia buara* | We are fed up of the nonsense |
| *Maro* | *Rin* | Come in |

(*The same words are found in Banaban Elders' List in Maude papers, Barr Smith Library, University of Adelaide, MSS 0003 Part II Source materials: Gilbert and Ellice Islands notebook no. 9).

Banaban and Kiribati languages in the following two examples when compared:

Example 1

English: Oh! Be quick while it is still dawn so that we can be at the edge of the reef on the eastern side.

Kiribati: *Mane! Ani kukuri ngkami ngkai e karangaina bwa ti aonga n roko ibukin waiwai i tanrake.*

Banaban: *Aua! Ani barebare ngkai tingaro ba ti na kauriria taboni kaneati i karawa.*

Example 2

English: Who is it?

Kiribati: *Antai anne?*

Banaban: *Anta nae?*

A Linguistic Opinion on the Banaban Language

A copy of the notations from Harry Maude's notebook and Banaban Elders' list was sent to Dr Alun Hughes in Wales, who specialises in the Kiribati language, and to Avi Gold in Israel, a scholar of ancient languages, to see if they could shed more light on the origins of Banaban. Dr Hughes has supplied the following information regarding the Banaban words:

> In all cultures and in all languages, change is inevitable. Institutions die, and words change their meaning or vanish all together. Who in England, other than a select band of professors, fully understands words used by Geoffrey Chaucer in his 'Canterbury

Tales'? How much more rapid is change in languages orally transmitted until the nineteenth century.

In Abaiang, Tarawa, Funafuti, Nauru, Ponape and Majuro, village elders have told me traditional tales and sung ancient songs for me, unable to explain the meaning of some of the words used. The meaning has been lost in the telling through long generations. In some islands, the elders speak of a 'lost language' from which these unknown words stem.

For one to believe in such 'lost languages', a very considerable corpus of traditional texts would be needed, for expert linguistic analysis and comparison with cognate languages. A score or so of isolated words is wholly insufficient for such examination.

Welshman once sincerely believed that their language, Cymraeg, was akin to Hebrew – on the basis of a handful of words similar in form and meaning. They wanted to differentiate themselves from the usurpers of their land, in every way. I have great sympathy with the desire of the Banaban people to preserve all that is fine and distinctive in their ancient culture. Mr Raobeia Ken Sigrah and his colleagues deserve praise and support in their work of scholarship.

Future generations will be truly in their debt.

In matters of language, caution is essential. Dialect, local usage, desuetude – all need to be considered before one poses the possibility of a 'lost language.' The distinctiveness of such nearby languages as Nauruan or Ponapean points to a complex history of language evolution and dissemination. Serious research is long overdue in this respect.

Far be it for me to dogmatise, as to the existence or otherwise of a distinctive Banaban language now lost and supplanted by Gilbertese. So far, I have not seen more than a score of 30 words or phrases supposedly surviving from an 'Original Language' (Ursprache) of Banaba.

Close examination of the short lists of words sent to me by Stacey M. King has convinced me that the 'Banaban' words therein are, in fact, Gilbertese words, some admittedly seldom heard today. Most of them appear in the early dictionaries of Gilbertese by Hiram Bingham Jr (1908) and Father Ernest Sabatier (1954; 1971). *Itingaro and karangaina*, to cite but one instance are near synonyms and both indubitably Gilbertese. *Kau* is another interesting example that is listed in Sabatier's dictionary and has the word 'Rabi' in brackets beside the listing. The other difference with the words were what I believe were phonetic style spellings which are not found in Gilbertese dictionaries.

The urgent task for Banaban scholars is to assemble a corpus of the oral literature of their homeland while memories are keen.

The authors want to raise the following points regarding Dr Hughes' comparisons of Banaban language. Dr Hughes bases his argument on Banaban words being Kiribati from evidence taken from the early Gilbertese dictionaries by Hiram Bingham Jr (1908) and Father Ernest Sabatier (1954, 1971). It must be remembered that the first missionary, Captain W. Walkup, arrived on Banaba in August 1885, (see Chapter 22). He was the man responsible for translating the Bible into the Kiribati language. He encouraged the Banabans to take up the language so they could understand God's words. So, when Bingham and Sabatier recorded vocabularies, twenty to thirty years had passed, and Banaban and I-Kiribati terms had become misspelt, merged or corrupted.

Hiram Bingham, from the American Board, wrote the first Gilbertese-English dictionary. One thousand copies were printed and first published in 1908, and fifteen hundred copies were reprinted and published again in 1953. Bingham provides valuable insight into the language and status of the region in the 'Preface' of his dictionary:

> The people number about 30,000 and dwell in a group of islands now under the protectorate of the British Government. They have been nominally Christianized, but they still need much help. Their group lies in the mid–Pacific on the Equator in longitude about 175 E. It consists of eighteen islands, all coral. The people speak one language, but local or provincial words are in use at the north and south and extreme west. It was the privilege of the compiler of this dictionary to be among the first who went to carry the Gospel of Christ to that race of savages in 1857. As he resided, while in the group, in its northern central portion, it is natural that many provincial words may not be found in the dictionary. No claim is made that it is exhaustive, but it is hoped that it is sufficiently full to be of service in the line for which it has been compiled.
>
> This Dictionary contains over 12,000 words, including derivatives and 500 Gilbertized foreign words, which occur in Gilbertese books printed since 1857, principally in the Bible, the Geography, and the Arithmetic. The definitions of many of the less common words are such as the writer has understood his assistant, Mr Moses Kaure, to give.
>
> Mr Kaure assisted him for four years in the translation of the Old Testament into Gilbertese in 1886–1890.

Bingham's statement that "it consists of eighteen islands, all coral" was confusing because there were only 16 atolls. The traditional word for the Kiribati Group is a contentious point, and language plays a major part in this issue. Grimble's *Tungaru Traditions, Writings on the Atoll Culture of the Gilbert Islands* stated,

"The Republic of Kiribati now consists of the sixteen Gilbert Islands, Banaba, the eight Phoenix Islands, and eight of the ten Line Islands ...
The Gilbertese formerly called themselves I-Tungaru but are now usually known as I-Kiribati (Kiribati being a transliteration of Gilbert). (Grimble, edited by Maude, 1989: xvii)."

David Stanley gives another interesting definition of these words:

"The name pronounced 'kir-EE-bas,' is an indigenous corruption of the name 'Gilberts.' To further confuse you, the Kiribati name of the Gilbert Islands group is Tungaru. Originally the Gilbertese wanted to call their country Tungaru, but the Ellice Islanders had already chosen Tuvalu; Tungaru sounded too similar. In this book, we use Tungaru to refer to the group of 16 atolls forming the Gilbert Islands and apply Kiribati to the country as a whole" (Stanley, 1992, p. 273).

The word Tuvalu, given to the Ellice Group at independence, means 'a cluster of eight islands.' The word's very meaning indicates that Banaba was not an island within their group.

So why did Bingham refer to eighteen islands in his dictionary? Even if Banaba was included, one of the islands is still missing. Could Bingham refer to Nauru, which also had historical links via the American Mission? Nauruans have a very different language. Walkup stated when he first arrived on Banaba that "their language is more like that of the Gilbert Is., than that spoken on Pleasant Is. [Nauru]." If Bingham is referring to Nauru in his preface, then he and the American Mission were optimistically hoping their missionary publications could be universally understood across Nauru, Banaba and the Gilberts (Kiribati), regardless of their separate vernacular languages.

221

Other influences of Banaban language

Until the discovery of phosphate in 1900, Banaba was never considered part of the Kiribati group. Still, Banaba had already experienced fifteen years of influence from the introduction of Captain Walkup's Bible and the American Missionary Board. By the time of the publication of Bingham's first dictionary, the influence of the phosphate company on Banaba had been well established, along with the introduction of Kiribati labourers to the island. During the same year of this dictionary's publication, the Resident Commissioner of the Gilbert and Ellice Island Group transferred his office from Tarawa to Banaba. Albert Ellis, in a chapter titled "Full Speed Ahead, 1908-13", stated:

"About the middle of this period changes were made in the mission arrangements, the American Mission which had been the pioneer on both Ocean Island and Nauru, handing over the work on the former island to the London Missionary Society. Several years prior to this the Americans had shifted their central station at Kusaie to Ocean Island where the Rev I. Channon remained in charge" (Ellis, 1936, p. 148).

Banaban	English translation	Bingham's 1908 Gilbertese dictionary
Aua!	Oh!	Not recorded in dictionary
Barebere	Hurry	Slowly (in use in Banaba)
Tia Buanna	An exclamation	Not recorded in dictionary
Karawa	Eastern side	Not recorded in dictionary
Kau	Go	Leather or shoe
Kauriri	Let us go!	Hasten
Kiroro	Far away	Ocean near the horizon as seen from land
M'aro	Come in!	To founder
Nanta	Who!	Not recorded in dictionary
Tingaro	Dawn	Not recorded in dictionary

[Itingaro]
Titimea   To splatter   Not recorded in dictionary

Comparisons with Banaban elders list and 1908 dictionary

By 1908, the small, insular, Banaban population of "475 aboriginal inhabitants," as stated by Mahaffy (1910, p. 2), would have been overshadowed by the expatriate population;

> "the white staff was increased to about seventy at each island [also referring to Nauru], and the labour force reached its maximum at Ocean Island which had just over 1,000 kanakas together with nearly 400 Japanese coolies and mechanics" (Ellis, 1936, p. 145).

The headquarters of the Gilbert and Ellice Island Colony (GEIC) had been moved to Banaba during this period. The 1908 dictionary would have been one of the significant learning guides for the European staff, so they could understand the language of the workers who, by this time, were mainly I–Kiribati.

The claim that the language of Banaba is Gilbertese can be found in various Gilbertese dictionaries. However, comparisons between words from the lists provided by Banaban Elders and Harry Maude, with Bingham's 1908 dictionary suggest the vocabularies were corrupted by misrepresentations of earlier culture and language, making it difficult to say definitely the original words were old Banaban words.

One of the words of interest in the above list is the word *Kau*, which means 'go' in the Banaban language. In Bingham's version, the word's meaning is 'leather and shoe', which is a prime example of the authors' argument of European influence over language. Shoes and especially leather, have never been part of any island culture. A word to explain the unusual foot coverings worn by Europeans was introduced through the Kiribati language.

Hughes compares the words stating, *Itingaro and karangaina*, to cite but one instance, are near synonyms and both indubitably I-Kiribati. *Tinagaro* or *Itingaro* sounds nothing like the I-Kiribati word he mentions, *karangaina*, which means 'the break of day.' The two words, 'dawn' and 'break of day', may be similar, but the words themselves are of entirely different origins. In Bingham's dictionary, *barebere* is listed as 'slowly'; however, in Banaban, it is the opposite, meaning 'hurry.' It has become apparent during research on the Banaban language, especially place names, that they are a mix of I-Kiribati and Banaban words with unknown meanings. Here we list one typical example:

Banaban Word   **Taken from**
Marata   Kabini marata Hamlet, Karia, Tabwewa

The meaning of *marata* remains unknown. *Kabini* is the Kiribati word for 'bottom.' This hamlet is in the Karia (lowlands) region of Tabwewa district. We know it has something to do with the 'bottom of ...' or 'towards the bottom of ...' in modern times.

In Bingham's 'Preface', he stated that in the Gilberts (Kiribati), "The people speak one language, but local or provincial words are in use at the north and south and extreme west." Is Bingham referring to Banaba when he quotes, 'extreme west'? On the topic of the lost Banaban language, Maude and Banaban elders seem in agreement:

> We know, for instance, that the importance, function and size of their *maneaba* and *uman anti* had deviated markedly, for they remained different until recent times when the *uman anti* fell into disuse with the advent of Christianity. Even in their physical characteristics and skin colour, we know from later writings that they were different enough to be noticed. Their land tenure system was different, as were their customs of inheritance; their fishing techniques, canoe

types, dances and games differed in many respects, as did the status of their women. There is no point in listing further deviations unless we detail the nature of the differences, which would require another paper, but we can sum up by saying that the Banabans had deviated substantially from the people of the Gilbert Group in their social and material culture by the time of the arrival of the fleet from Beru. But, in language, always a tricky matter, we cannot be sure, for though there were several dialectical differences even in later years, the Gilbertese who came with Nei Anginimaeao seem to have had no difficulty in understanding the Tabwewans. When I was supervising the lands settlement of Banaba in 1930, we recorded a dozen words in use which were unknown in the Gilberts, but only a competent linguistic specialist can estimate the extent of probable deviation in the past (Maude & Maude, 1994, p. 112).

Banaban elders remain adamant that there was a distinct language used by older generations, especially those descended from Te Aonoanne. Historians agree that language is a critical marker of identity, so the information provided in this chapter supports evidence regarding the existence of a unique Banaban language.

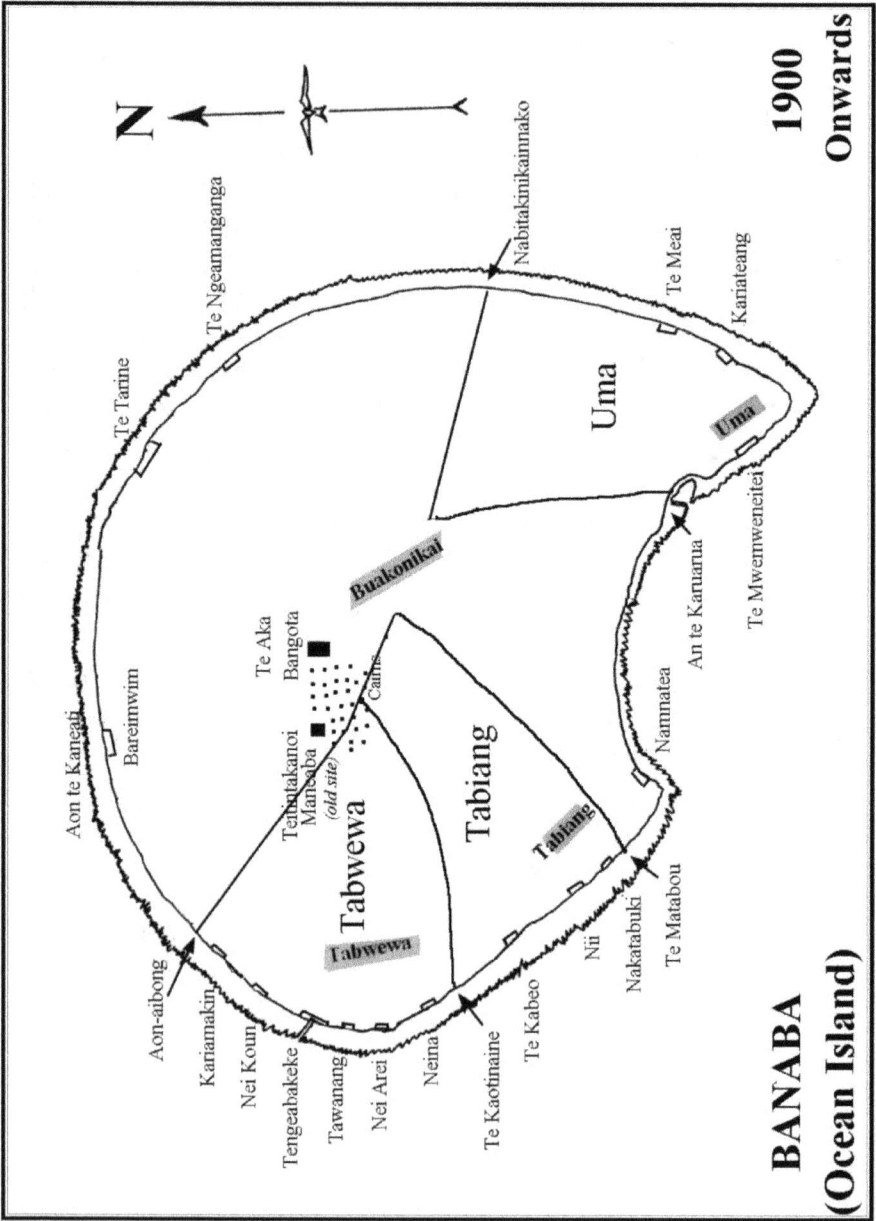

Figure: 4.2. Banaba 1900 onwards forming of Banaban villages (by R.K. Sigrah).

24: BANABAN VILLAGES AND INDIVIDUAL LAND HOLDINGS

The Creation of Buakonikai Village

Te Aonoanne and Toakira districts were amalgamated into what became known as Buakonikai village in a process that is a mystery to most Banabans. There were five known districts on the island. No story or legend explains why the two districts were merged into Buakonikai, which means, in the Kiribati language, 'amongst the trees.' One of the many changes Banabans experienced after the arrival of the I–Matang was concerning land. Boundaries changed, new villages were established, and individual landholding began to be recognised, but many unanswered questions remain concerning many of these events.

What happened to the Toakira clan?

Banaban elders cannot explain why Toakira district merged with Te Aonoanne district. The Toakira clan's *maneaba* and certain associated clan rights have vanished without a trace. The gap leaves many uncertainties.

For example, the Toakira clan initially had the right to bring stranded fish to the Tabwewans. So, who now can fulfil that duty? Genealogy charts show that many Banabans are descended from this clan. Today there is a dispute over land holdings within the Toakira district. Descendants need to back up their claim through *Te Rii ni Banaba* to prove their original land holdings. We know that the Toakira people were established (originally as the Teborata clan) by Nei Teborata, a woman in Nei Anginimaeao's original party. The descendants later married into families in the other four Banaban districts.

In seeking an explanation for the disappearance of the Toakira clan, Maude and Maude date it back to the second half of the nineteenth century and the time of Great Drought and famine in the 1870s:

> "... when the hamlets in the interior of Banaba lost almost all of their inhabitants, and the few people who remained alive came to live in Buakonikai village. As a consequence, there were two chiefs in Buakonikai, the chief descended from the former chief of Te Aonoanne having the greater traditional authority and speaking first in the council and assembly, see Maude and Maude (1932:275) ... where we state it was the Te Aonoanne *maneaba* Takamoi that was removed from its former site in the hamlet of Te Maekan Anti (by the old Wireless Station) and placed in Buakonikai Village, while the Toakira *maneaba* Te Toa was abandoned" (Maude & Maude, 1994, p. 53).

There are three errors in the extract above:

1. The correct name of Te Aonoanne *maneaba* is Takanoi, not Takamori, which is wrongly identified by Maude

and Maude as being situated in the hamlet known as Te Maekan Anti. Takanoi *maneaba* was in Te Aka hamlet, the actual site of Professor Lampert's dig, in 1965 (Chapter 9, Figure 2.3).

2. No maneaba was situated in Te Maekan Anti's hamlet. There was only an *uma n anti* (a spirit house) called Tokia I–Matang.

3. There were no chiefs in these districts. The correct term is elders.

52. A view overlooking the old Toakira district towards Uma (A.J. Hobbs Collection 1932).

Questions raised

The statement by Maude and Maude raises interesting questions. If the population of Buakonikai dropped as dramatically as he claims, why do genealogy charts continue a strong lineage for the Toakira descendants back to this era? Why is there now missing knowledge of oral history, legends, individual rights and hamlets within Toakira district? If the two elders came together within the newly formed Buakonikai maneaba, why did the elder

53. Te Itintakanoi – the new maneaba built at Buakonikai Village (Maude Collection 1932).

from history, legends, individual rights and hamlets within Toakira district? If the two elders came together within the newly formed Buakonikai maneaba, why did the elder from Te Aonoanne hold the greater traditional authority? According to custom, an elder from one district has no right to speak in another district's maneaba. Could the Toakira elder's lesser role be evidence that the Toakira population loss had been unusually high in his district, leading to a merger, as Maude suggests?

The BPC company's plant and equipment were mainly situated in this area. How did the mining company acquire what must surely have been large parcels of land within this area? By the time of the mining, there was no reference to Toakira district at all; only the two villages situated on either side of their operations around Home Bay, Uma and Tabiang. How did the whole district of Toakira disappear and be replaced by a massive power station, cableways,

54. Scene in Buakonikai village (Maude Collection 1932).

crushing plant and conveyor belts for the mining company that traversed the hillside down to the shoreline?

Putting the facts together

Due to the Great Drought and famine in the 1870s, people fled Banaba to settle in Kosrae and other Pacific islands. Many returned to Banaba, but there is a lack of evidence for Maude and Maude's claim of a sharp drop in population. Banaban genealogy records indicate the population remained high. Other evidence was provided in an early census by Ellis in 1900, Webster (1851) and Mackay (1875).

There is little in the population statistics on which Maude and Maude can base their lengthy explanation for the merger of Toakira and Te Aonoanne districts. In a small footnote by Maude and Maude in 1932, they stated, "The districts of Te Aonoanne and Toakira have been in recent years joined together by the Government, forming the single village district of Buakonikai" (p. 266). The keywords in this simple statement are 'recent' and 'Government.'

Missing Descendants of Toakira

On 8 May 1992, the Rabi Council of Leaders in Fiji were contacted by a family from Hawaii claiming to be descendants of 'the landowners of Puakonikai'. The family controversially claimed to be Banaba's rightful owners, which they called 'Puakonikai'. However, they had used wrong terms, confused facts and wrongfully claimed their family had been forcefully removed from the island in the 1890s by the British government and never allowed to return. Other evidence indicates that the British had no official influence or governance over Banaba before 1900 and the discovery of phosphate. Still, the family's story in Hawaii provides a fascinating link to earlier events. It is well documented that Banaba suffered from droughts during this period, especially the Great Drought between 1871 and 1874, and this caused some Banabans to move to Kosrae. There is also evidence from Bauldry, the Master of *Arnelda* in 1872, that he "took off 24 starving natives to Strong's Island" (Kosrae). Two years later, in 1875, there was a report of about 20 Banabans on Kosrae being rejected by a ship's Master (Wood) who refused to return them to their homeland. There is also evidence in 1885 that a missionary Captain Walkup invited Banabans to migrate to Kosrae, where a Mission had been set up in 1871. This information probably explains the presence of former landowners who moved from Banaba to Kosrae and then later descendants to Hawaii. The Hawaiian family's history fits into this timeframe.

Their story also provides valuable information on the missing clans from Toakira District. They have provided their family records, and in part, they claim their descendant and head of their family is a man called, Tutuk

PUAKAONAKAI BEAUX! OCEAN ISLAND

55. Buakonikai village (Postcard 1910).

(1780-1870), who arrived on Banaba and married a Banaban woman, Nei Kamoa. There is no mention of where Tutuk came from. They further claim:

> "Tutuk and Nei Kamoa had two children, ITisinirak (Tisiniriak 1820-1915) and Nei Bubure. They stated that Tutuk died in Ooma Village in 1870, and his daughter Nei Bubure then left the island to marry William Harris in Nauru.
> Tutuk son, ITisinirak (Tisiniriak) married Nei Kariana from Tapewa village (Tabwewa), and they had three children: Itinterunga, Tekoniti and KarianaII. The family, along with many others, were removed from Banapa (Banaba) in the late 1890s by the British Government orders."

The family's belief of their link to 'Puakonikai' (Buakonikai) and the mention of their ancestor dying in

TOAKIRA DISTRICT
The Missing Link

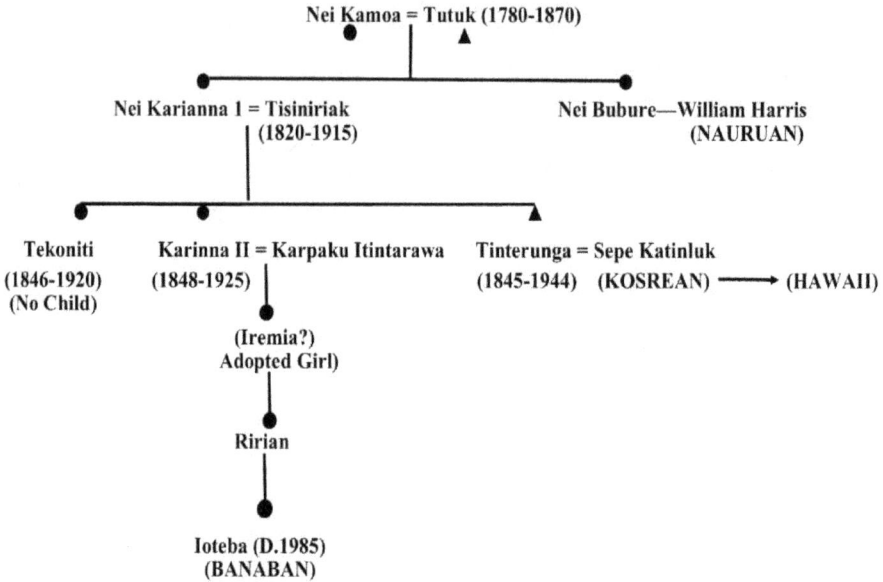

Nei Kamoa = Tutuk (1780-1870)

Nei Karianna 1 = Tisiniriak
(1820-1915)

Nei Bubure—William Harris
(NAURUAN)

Tekoniti
(1846-1920)
(No Child)

Karinna II = Karpaku Itintarawa
(1848-1925)

Tinterunga = Sepe Katinluk
(1845-1944)   (KOSREAN) ——→ (HAWAII)

(Iremia?)
Adopted Girl)

Ririan

Ioteba (D.1985)
(BANABAN)

Provided by Tonna Tinteruna Penrose (B. 1954)

Figure: 4.3. Toakira genealogy (provided by T.T Penrose).

'Ooma Village' (Uma) in 1870 shows a connection to the two areas on Banaba that were known as the Toakira District. However, the arrival of Tutuk seems to be well after Nei Anginimaeao, nearly a century later, according to the family's records. The mention of the '*Honu*' (turtle totem) also aligns with the Tabakea turtle totem from Nei Anginimaeao party and their descendants. The term 'warrior' could refer to the belief that Nei Anginimaeao and her party were fleeing conflicts on Beru. The family's belief that Tutuk was around ninety years of age suggests that at the time of his death, he would have been revered as *tibu taratara* (which was the most sacred stage of an elder's life in Banaban tradition). His death also is just before the beginning of the Great Drought on the island. In another extract from the family's records, they state:

"After the death of Tisiniriak on Kosrae in 1915, his son, Itinterunga, married a Kosraean girl Sepe Katinluk and inherited land on Kosrae, while two of his aunties, Tekoniti and KarinnaII, together with Banabans from the original [Toakira] party returned to Banaba. The aunties, by this time, were 55 and 53 years of age; they could not bear children. In time, Kariana II married a man named Karpaku Initarwa (Itintarawa) and adopted a baby girl (Iremia?), whose name we do not have and her sister Tekoniti never married or had children."

This statement provides information on the family's connection to the Toakira clan and genealogy. The correct name of the adopted daughter in Toakira genealogy charts is Taberanangiti. Their descendants live on Rabi today. The Hawaiian descendants are the missing link with Toakira.

Formation of the Village System

Historians have ignored one of the most interesting questions that have been raised by Banabans. Elders state that the island had no set concentration of dwellings or villages until after the phosphate mining began. So how and why were they formed? Ellis recorded the first accurate census of the Banaban population in 1900 and referred to four 'villages.' His terminology indicates that each district, except for Toakira and Te Aonoanne, had a village system. On 11 November 1900, the following entry appeared in his diary: "Population of villages on Ocean Island – Tapewa (King's Village) – 133, Ooma (South Village) – 138, Tabiang (village situated between the other two) – 60; Puakonikai (Interior Village) – 120. Being a total of 451 Banabans." The two districts of Te Aonoanne and Toakira had already been merged to form Buakonikai. Banaban elders argue that a village system was not yet in place at that time. Rather than 'villages', Ellis should have referred to the *kainga* (hamlets) within these regions. All had a central *maneaba*. A *kainga* comprises several families who occupy an area of land bearing a common ancestral name. Each *kainga* usually consists of several *mwenga* (houses), together with various ancillary buildings such as *te uma ni kanaiai* (cooking house), *te bata* (sleeping house) and *uma n teinako* (menstruating house). A group of *kainga* represents various families living within a district. The grouping has one central *maneaba* and numerous te *bareaka* (canoe sheds) with individual owners (Figure 4.5). Each *kainga* has individual rights to clan roles and land ownership, which are not shared amongst the community (see Chapter 9, Figure 2.3). They were not 'villages' as used in European terminology.

The Colonial administration and the phosphate company introduced a new system whereby Banabans from various *kainga* within a district were brought into one common land boundary, known as the village. Introducing a church to each village was another significant influence in bringing the people together under one community body and moving them away from their *kainga* system. The individual families still retained the legal right to their *kainga* land holdings. This introduced village system created new disputes within Banaban society over original land boundaries and inherited rights and duties.

The development of the village system brought about significant changes. It was only through the introduction of this system that Colonial control of the people and their land holdings became possible. The mining company recognised the need for such an approach when it realised that there was no overlord or ruler of the Banaban people and that it would have to deal with landowners individually. Even Ellis, in his diary, agrees that signing the contract

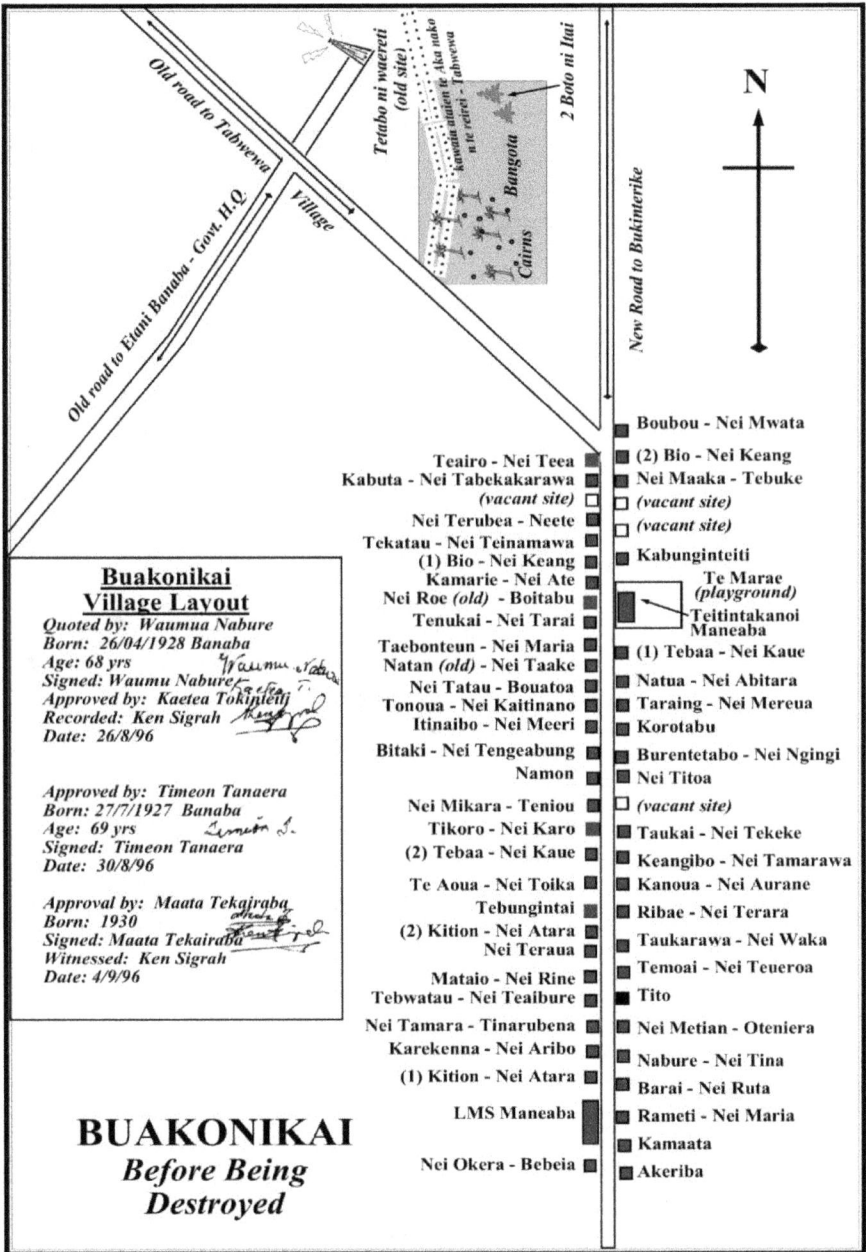

Figure: 4.4. Buakonikai village before being destroyed (by R.K. Sigrah).

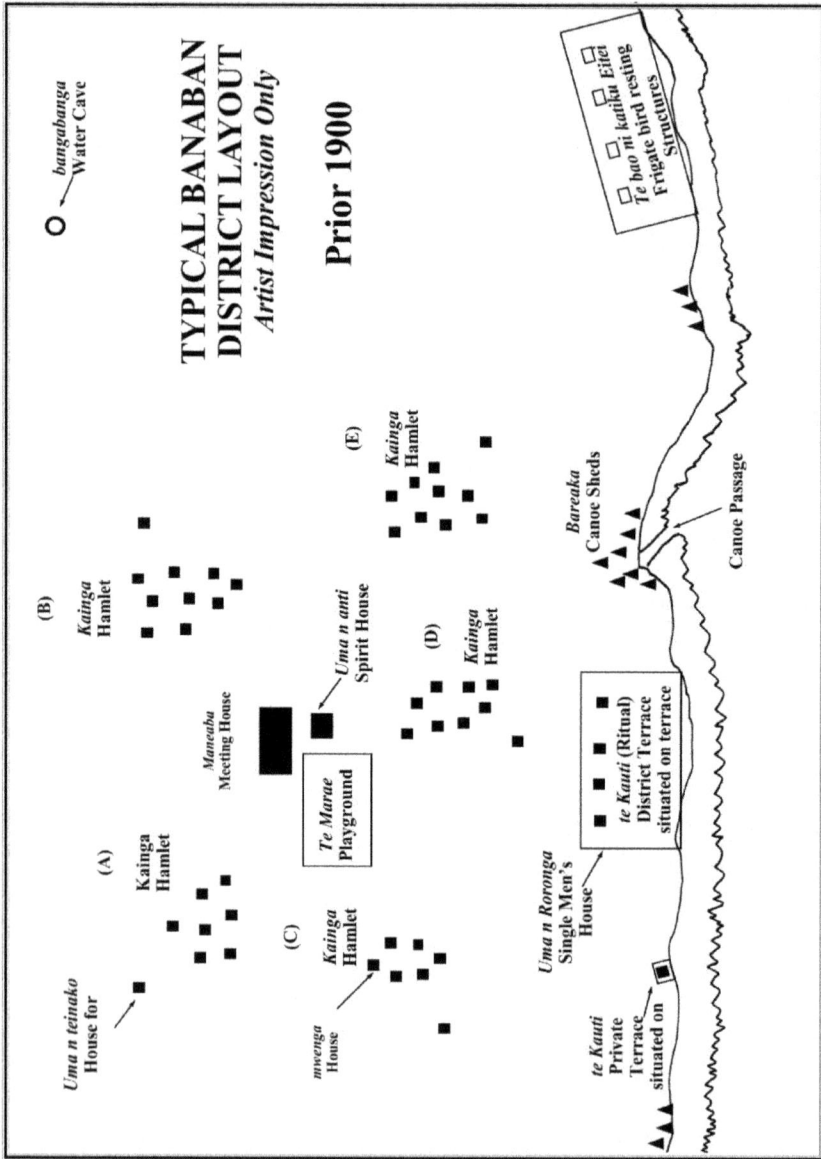

TYPICAL BANABAN DISTRICT LAYOUT
Artist Impression Only

Prior 1900

bangabanga
Water Cave

Te bao ni kariki Eitei
Te bao ni kariki Eitei
Frigate bird resting
Structures

(E)
Kainga
Hamlet

(B)
Kainga
Hamlet

Uma n anti
Spirit House

Maneaba
Meeting House

(D)
Kainga
Hamlet

Te Marae
Playground

Bareaka
Canoe Sheds

Canoe Passage

(A)
Kainga
Hamlet

(C)
Kainga
Hamlet

Uma n teinako
House for

mwenga
House

Uma n Roronga
Single Men's
House

te Kauti (Ritual)
District Terrace
situated on terrace

te Kauti
Private
Terrace
situated on

Figure: 4.5. Hypothetical Banaban "district" layout with five
hamlets (drawn R.K. Sigrah).

with the so-called king and chiefs was illegal. Within days of his arrival on Banaba, he signed up and negotiated land purchases or leases with individual landowners. As the Pacific Islands Company took more and more land, it foundthat access to proposed mining areas at Tabwewa and Uma was more accessible if it merged the hamlets into a central village.   Banaban elders say that the company allotted an area within a district and recorded those sites as Banaban villages.

Original buildings and landmarks within a District

The following buildings and landmarks were part of the original layout within each district. Banabans lived in districts, not villages (see Figure 4.5):

- Numerous individual *mwenga* (houses)
- A number of *kainga* (hamlets)
- One *maneaba* (district meeting house)
- One *uma n anti* (spirit house)
- A number of *uma n teinako* (houses for menstruating women)
- One *uma n roronga* (young men's house situated near district terraces)
- A number of *bareaka* (canoe sheds)
- A number of terraces for practising *te kauti*
- One playground for district games
- A number of *bangabanga* (water caves) owned by certain clans

After the villages were formed, some of these structures disappeared, and some new buildings were added. For example, Tabiang had a church building belonging to the London Mission Society (originally American Mission Board) and the Banaban School. Tabwewa had the Sacred Heart Catholic Mission, and other villages had churches with separate church *maneaba*.

Acquisition of Banaban Land

In his diary, Ellis refers to his arrangements for purchasing Banaban land and making leases initially around the island coastline starting at Tabwewa. The extract from the diary of his first acquisitions. The correct names of Banaban landowners (in brackets) have been identified from genealogy records:

> *10th May 1900 - Arranged to purchase 3 lots adjoining each other but without any sea frontage. The lots are as follows:*
> *1 piece from Manaeea (Maraeea)about 40 yds square @ 12 pounds;*
> *1 piece from Terakaputa (Tirakabuta) about 43 yds x 18 yds @ 6 pounds;*
> *1 piece from Tenaurwa (Ten Arawa) about 43 yds x 13 yds @ 5 pounds.*
> *Arranged to lease three plots with sea frontage from Kariatapewa (Kariatabwewa), Papaiment (Nei Bwebweniman) and Manaeea (Maraeea) at a yearly rental of 1 pound. We do have the right to build houses, make shipping places, lay tramlines etc. Papaiment (Nei Bwebweniman] reserves the right to take coconuts from his trees whenever he wants them, we do likewise. There are over 50 bearing trees on this piece. Measured off the land and, in the evening made a plan of it.*
> *14th May 1900 - Arranged leasehold at 1 pound per annum;*
> *Ebu ebue (Nei Bwebwe) extending about 1.5 chains along the bay.*
> *Tepurita (Teburita) extending about 1.5 chains along the bay, both with sea frontage.*
> *Site for Manager's House - Arranged to purchase a well-situated piece of land from 'Esaia' (Itaia) at Nor' West end of village and with sea frontage. Price 18 pounds. It would do particularly well for the site of Manager's house and store, has about 3 chain sea frontage.*

Ellis's diary refers to land in Tabwewa and Te Aonoanne districts in the northwest of the island. A year later, the following land titles were registered in the Government Land Registry as sold to the Pacific Islands Company.

Date	Banaban land owner (Recorded 1901)	Correct Name (According to Genealogy Charts)	District
6/05/1901	Na Weatoun	(correct)	Tapiwa [Tabwewa]
25/05/1901	Tea Benimatan	Teibianimatang	Tapiwa [Tabwewa]
5/06/1901	Nei Teteni	Nei Tetene	Tapiwa [Tabwewa]
10/09/1901	Tenemakin	Nei Teienimakin	Ooma [Uma]
10/09/1901	Tenemakin	Nei Teienimakin	Tapiwa [Tabwewa]
12/09/1901	Tetebaki	Nan Teribaki	Ooma [Uma]
16/09/1901	Teburitai	Tebungintai	Puakonikai [Buakonikai]
17/09/1901	Amerake	Na Maraki	Tapiwa [Tabwewa]
19/09/1901	Jobi	Iobi	Ooma [Uma]
20/09/1901	Burenimata	Burenimatang	Tapiwa [Tabwewa]
20/09/1901	Temitinaemaran	*Tematemaimarawa	Tapiwa [Tabwewa]
21/09/1901	Tiati	Nei Toaiti	Ooma [Uma]
21/09/1901	Tione	(correct)	Ooma [Uma]
23/09/1901	Korereman	Nei Korereniman	Ooma [Uma]
23/09/1901	Nei Tebuari	(correct)	Puakonikai [Buakonikai]
25/09/1901	Batiara	(correct)	Puakonikai [Buakonikai]
26/09/1901	Tebeaniburi	Teibianibure	Tapiwa [Tabwewa]
27/09/1901	Terina	Te Rina	Ooma [Uma]

Mahaffy gives details of Banaban land ownership and their knowledge of 'exact' boundaries in his 1910 article and identifies Temitinaemaran as Nei Temitinaemaran:

"...the pieces of land on Ocean Island held by 200 natives, men and women. The pieces number 2500, and this, too, in an island only 1500 acres in extent, of which some 300 acres are covered with mere pointed rocks. Some of these landowners have as many as thirty-six pieces of land, the exact boundaries of which are most accurately known, even when, as is often the case, some of the pieces only a few feet square. The names of the owners are curious... one name seem to be very significant. It is that of a woman, Nei Temitinaemaran or Miss the Corpse from the Sea. The importance of a native among his fellows depends largely upon the number of pieces of land which he possesses;" (Mahaffy, 1910, p. 10).

Payment and boundaries

In April 1902, the Pacific Phosphate Company Limited (PPC) was registered as a subsidiary of the Pacific Island Company. The leases, licences and all other rights related to mining on Banaba and Nauru islands were transferred to the PPC by a further licence dated 31 December 1902. This new company would include some powerful international businessmen, including German financial interests, with the provisions that Germans would be allowed to sit on the board. However, two-thirds of the directors had to be British.

The details of this newly restructured company can be found in the personal papers and documents. The 'J.T. Arundel Papers' held at the Pacific Manuscript Bureau, Canberra, Australia:

"This company has £125,000 in preferred stock, bearing interest at 7% and £125,000 pounds in regular stock, divided into shares of 1 pound each. Directors are: Lord Stanmore as Chairman, further Messrs. J.T. Arundel, G.W.H. Bowen, J. Ewart, E.A. Levy, W.H. Lever, all of London (the last named of the well-known 'Sunlight Soap Factory' – Lever Brothers), then Mr. A.O. Thiemer in Hamburg and the Director of the 'Union' Factory of Chemical Products in Stettin, A. Kaesemacher" (Arundel Papers – P.M.B. 480-492, 493, 495).

From 1900 to 1913, all land purchased for mining was from individual Banaban landowners under the so-called 'Phosphate and Tree Purchase' deeds. Compensation was reported to be:

"... a fixed sum, apparently averaging about £20 pounds an acre, which together with the payment of £50 pounds a year under the Agreement and compensation for any food-producing trees destroyed, was the sole consideration received by the natives" (H.E. Maude, 1946, p. 4).

By the time of the 1913 Land Agreement, the Banabans were arguing that they should receive "compensation for food-producing trees destroyed, as under the previous Phosphate and Trees Purchase Deeds" (H.E. Maude, 1946, p. 4). They also believed the phosphate company had inaccurate land features and measurement records, and approximate measurements were no longer acceptable to them. They made other objections too:

"There were objections to the switching of leases from outside to inside the mining area. In some cases, the original lease agreements had lapsed, and in others the accuracy of early surveys was uncertain. The replanting of food-bearing trees was impracticable, especially in dry times when the island was short of water" (Williams & Macdonald, 1985, p. 101).

Not until 1931, when Harry Maude became the Native Lands Commissioner, was the first and only attempt conducted with Banabans to define boundary marks.

Further efforts at land acquisition

By 1909, the PPC was already in conflict with the various Resident Commissioners sent by the Colonial Office.

Unaware of these internal conflicts, the Banaban community were becoming increasingly hostile to any more land dealings. Questions were also being raised in the British Parliament about the ill-treatment the Banabans. In 1909, during a brief period as Resident Commissioner, Mahaffy pinpointed the concerns clearly when he,

"... laid the issue squarely on the table where it could not be ignored, saying in effect that if the Company continued to get its own way in the development of its mining programme the island must inevitably become uninhabitable. It had become evident, then, that the British Government must sooner or later decide either to restrict the activities of the Company or to find the Banabans another island."

Lord Stanmore, the London-based Chairman of the PPC, was less than enthusiastic:

"Stanmore did not think highly of the idea, having in mind that mining could continue for a century by which time the indigenous population might have vanished by the mere effluxion of time. However, he thought that the Company might be able to donate £250 a year to such fund by way of an inducement for the natives to sell more land to the Company and remove themselves to some more fertile place" (as cited in, Williams & Macdonald, 1985, p. 89).

Mahaffy also published an article in 1910 with facts that Banabans were completely unaware of:

"There are at present 475 aboriginal inhabitants, the remains of a population which only forty years ago numbered over 1,000; and they are the owners of an island which, although only 1,500 acres in extent, had a total trade with the Commonwealth of Australia alone valued in 1908 at £314,000, and which in that year exported one-twentieth of the whole world's

244

supply of phosphate. Probably no richer island of the same size exists" (Mahaffy, 1910, p. 2).

Mahaffy's writings suggest he was distancing himself from the Company. He said:

"I am however, not so much concerned with this interesting but commercial phase [phosphate mining] of the history of Ocean Island as with the appearance and formation of and the life upon this wonderful place" (p. 4).

The Pacific Phosphate Company (PPC) and the colonial government tried to use the church's influence to acquire more land. A blatant example is evident in Ellis's correspondence to the company's Head Office in Melbourne, Australia. He describes an episode of collaboration with a missionary which backfired and then worked to the advantage of the rival (Catholic) mission:

56. Early Banaban *mwenga* central (Williams Collection 1901-31).

"The difficulty between Mr. Channon [American Missionary Board Pastor] and the Banabans is, that Captain Dickson [Resident Commissioner for the Gilbert and Ellice Island Colony] apparently asked the former to use his influence on the Ooma natives with a view of getting them to shift to Puakonikai. Mr. Channon agreed with the wisdom of Captain Dickson's reasons for the removal of the village, and had one or two talks with the natives, which they greatly resented. They blame him now for working against them, and of course this is playing into Father Quoirier's hands [a Catholic priest from Sacred Heart order]" (Ellis as cited in, PPC Confidential Correspondence, BPC Archive held Australia Archives (Melbourne) No. 63, 25 February 1911, p. 3).

It is evident that the company knew that the island's central plateau held the highest and deepest phosphate deposits. By 1910, PPC realised that the area around Uma, Home Bay had high phosphate grades and had already transferred all the main plant and administration buildings to this area. It was prepared to move its operations to Tabwewa if the Banabans could be talked into selling their land. The PPC noted that:

"... a report from Ocean Island showed that there were also richer areas on the island than those being mined, and that if Resident Commissioner Dickson pursued his express intention of limiting the Company's activities to particular areas it was imperative that the proposed areas should contain the highest quality phosphate available" (as cited in, Williams & Macdonald, 1985, p. 92).

On 9 Dec 1909, Confidential Notes made by Ellis from his meeting held in Suva between the newly appointed

Gilbert Islands Protectorate Resident Commissioner Dickson and the High Commissioner for the Western Pacific, Sir Everard im Thurn, shows the PPC had high expectations for Dickson's appointment to replace Mahaffy and resolve these issues:

> "Item 2: Employment of Kanaka Labour - Dickson is favourable towards more Gilbert & Ellice Islanders but adverse to Japanese.
> Item 6: Discussed future of Captain Dickson's inexperience and felt he is level-headed and will be better than Mr Mahaffy.
> Item 7: His Excellency concluded that Mr Mahaffy's want of discretion was not confined to Ocean Island.
> Item 9: His Excellency said he would look into the matter and assured Ellis that Mahaffy would not be going to Ocean Island and upsetting arrangements.
> Item 15: Conclusion - Captain Dickson is not tied to Mr Mahaffy's methods and holds that the natives respect the man who keeps them in their place".

Dickson was posted to the Gilbert and Ellice Islands as resident commissioner in September 1909. Dickson mirrored Mahaffy, by raising concerns over PPC's handling of Banaban land negotiations. His involvement would contribute to a deadlock for over three years. By 1912, the Colonial Office was becoming uneasy and made plans to send E.C. Eliot to the island to replace him. Eliot wrote:

> "... there was a definite feeling of unrest on the island so the Company agreed that I should be sent out in 1913 with a mission of far better terms. The landowners had flatly refused to part with another square yard of their land unless it was taken by force. This was their ultimatum. Captain Quayle Dickson my predecessor had already made the strongest representations to the Colonial Office in favour of the oppressed landowners. The Company brought

pressure to bear for his removal from office" (Eliot, 1938, pp 144-5).

Dickson's fate was settled:

"He was not a success in this post: administrative incompetence, financial ineptitude and the embarrassment caused when he supported the native Banabans against the Pacific Phosphate Company, led the Secretary of State to express his grave displeasure. Dickson was next sent to the Falkland Islands as colonial secretary in 1913 ..." (David Tatham, 2012-18).

Eliot wrote that Dickson's support for the Banabans was the end of his career:

"A more junior appointment was found for Captain Dickson in another Colony and shortly afterwards he was retired from the service. He wrote that his heart was broken" (Eliot, 1938, p 145).

It was not until 28 November 1913 that Banaban landowners finally signed the Land Agreement. For the first time, the Pacific Phosphate Company, the British Government, and the Banaban landowners agreed that some type of rehabilitation on Banaba was needed. The intentions in the Agreement were that the Company shall return all worked-out lands to the original owners. That they shall replant such lands – wherever possible – with coconuts and other food-bearing trees, both in the lands already worked out and in those to be worked out," was abundantly clear. The Banaban people expected the land to be returned to them in much the same condition as before mining, replanted with coconut and other food-bearing trees. This obligation has never been fulfilled. By 1920, the Pacific Phosphate Company Ltd had been brought out by three Governments (Great Britain, Australia and New Zealand) conjointly for the sum of 3.5 million pounds and renamed the British Phosphate Commission. Still, the issue over Banaban land holdings and rehabilitation continued.

In Harry Maude's Land Commission hearing in 1931, 2,479 pieces of land were listed, so there was now a shortfall of twenty-one pieces of land from Mahaffy's 1910 estimate of 2,500:

> "A further basis of comparison ... is furnished by the number of lands owned by the inhabitants of each district, obtained by the Native Lands Commission which recently sat on the island. This shows that 695 pieces of land are owned by people living in the Tabwewa village district, 291 by Tabiang, 650 by Uma, and 843 by the village of Buakonikai formed by the recent fusion of Te Aonoanne and Toakira" (as cited in, Maude & Maude, 1932).

Twenty-one pieces of land did not disappear between 1910 and 1931. Perhaps Mahaffy had over-estimated when he listed 2,500 pieces of land. It is more likely that the company blatantly and deliberately encroached over traditional boundaries, ignoring the dimensions listed on leases and documents. The issue of the missing lands was raised forty years later in the Banaban court case against the British Phosphate Commission in 1975.

In another issue over land, in a letter to the British government dated 15 April 1933, elders stated the Banaban position in a dispute with the mining company over a 150-acre (61 hectares) mining area. This area was taken away from the Banabans in the '1931 Resumption' (to use the term of the British government, under the Mining Ordinance No. 4 of 1928, which allowed compulsory land acquisition. The following is a copy of that original letter:

ARA TANGITANG IBUKIN ABARA MA KAOTAN ARA TOUTIA N EBERI 15TH, 1933

Ngaira aika tan ababa ni koaua inanon te eka ae 150, abon aki rau nanora ibukin te bo are ti anganaki ba boon abara. Ao te British Phosphate commissioners e a tia n teirake n urua abara imwin motikan ana boo nakoria.

Ao ngkai a tia ni mauna aba tabeua man aki reke tiaia ni koaua. Mangaia ae ti a riki iai n teirake ni kaoti tian abara ibukin tangiran abara, ba a na aki bua abakia ma maitia ao kain aoia. Ba ti bon ataia raoi ba ngkana ti aki kaoti tian abara ao a na boni bane ni bua, n ai aron abaia Nei Tina ma Nei Mimi, ngkai a tia ni bane ni kenaki ma ni bua tiaia ni koaua imain ara teirake aei n toutia.

Ngaira ibukia tan aba,

	(Signed)	Rotan Tito
		Abetenoko
		Tanaera
		Kabuta
		Naewantabuariki

Tani kaoaua:

Charles A. Swinbourne, Acting Resident Commissioner;
H.E. Maude, Acting Secretary to the Government;
Kureta, Tia Moti i Banaba.

OUR GRIEVANCES FOR OUR LANDS AND LAND SURVEY ON APRIL 15, 1933

We the true landowners within the 150-acre mining area are not happy or satisfied with the price for our land that was given to us. The British Phosphate Commissioners have destroyed our lands after imposing the price upon us.

And now some of our lands are being destroyed without the boundaries being disclosed. Therefore, we have decided to disclose the boundaries of lands because of our love for our land, so that their sizes and numbers will not be forgotten nor the trees thereon. For we well know that the failing disclosure of our boundaries would be finally lost, as have been those of Nei Tina and Nei Mimi, which have been dug before this survey.

We for the land owners,
(Signed) Rotan Tito
Abetenoko
Tanaera
Kabuta
Naewantabuariki

Witnessed:

Charles A. Swinbourne, Acting Resident Commissioner;
H.E. Maude, Acting Secretary to the Government;
Kureta, The Magistrate Banaba.

The above letter is one of many that would be written year after year in a desperate attempt to gain the British, Australian and New Zealand governments' assistance to stop more land sales.

What happened to the missing lands?

The elders' letter in 1933 names two Banaban women who had already lost their land. The two women, Nei Tina (Ken Sigrah's grandmother) and Nei Mimi were from Buakonikai, so the missing land would have been within this region. Were the missing twenty-one blocks of land absorbed into the mining operations between 1909 and 1931? Is there a connection between the missing twenty-one pieces of land and the merging of the two districts into Buakonikai village district? Was there a conflict between Banaban landowners that allowed these land holdings to be transferred or absorbed into other land titles? For example, during the drought, we know that land was traded for water or taken by others when whole families fled the island. These matters should have been resolved well before 1933. It might be argued that Mahaffy's figure of two thousand five hundred pieces of land was just an approximation; however, as Acting Resident Commissioner, his official duty was to make accurate reports for his superiors back in England.

This chapter has raised several questions, many of which still have no definite answers. Did European influence and the mining industry contribute to forming a village system that has no link to Banaban tradition? Were two districts merged into Buakonikai village solely because of a government plan to access more land for mining? What happened to the twenty-one pieces of land that went missing between 1909 and 1931? Will Toakira genealogy reveal their original landholding? The authors hope that by raising these issues, they will move forward in finding solutions and that future historians will consider these matters in their research.

57. Early phosphate mining on Banaba (Williams Collection 1901–31).

25: BANABAN ARCHITECTURE

Banaban architecture can be divided into two broad categories: traditional housing built before 1900 and more recent housing based on the Kiribati style. Both styles have proved highly durable, as Peter Anderson observes:

"This is the building that will defy the elements for many years, keep out torrential rains and burning sun, admit the cooling breeze, stand fast under the howling fury of the westerly gales. A house built of coconut fibre, string, leaves and branches will, with normal maintenance, last a generation" (Anderson, 1963, p. 19).

The original style of Banaban *mwenga* (see Photo 59) is different from the majority of houses seen in 1900. The main feature distinguishing the older from the modern style is that the floor was built on the ground. Lampert found this kind of housing in his archaeological dig at Te Aka village site He reported, 'floors were retained by low walls of partly buried, vertical slabs of water-worn coral rock' (Figure 4.6). The modern style of house has elevated floors. These suspended floors are the main style in Kiribati, where tides sometimes flood low coral atolls. Although flooding has never been a problem on Banaba, this housing style with raised floors was

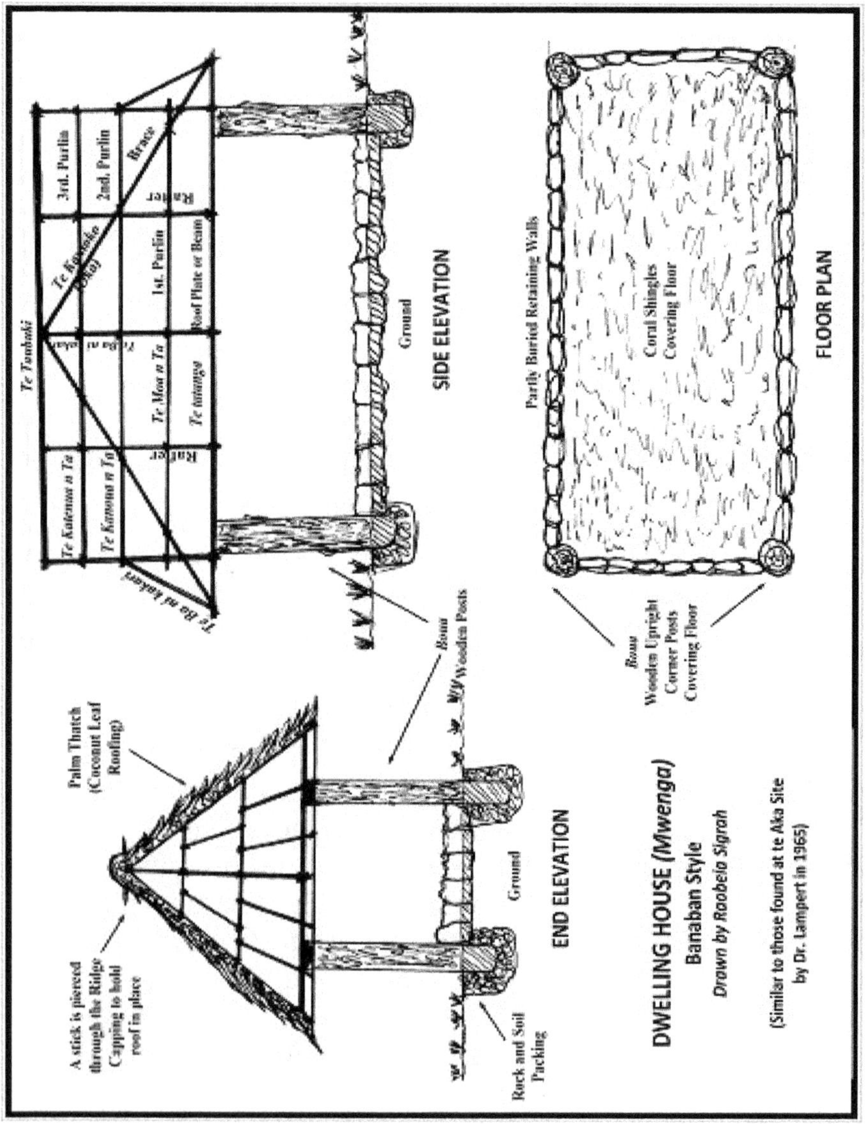

Figure: 4.6. *Mwenga*, traditional Banaban dwelling (drawn by R.K Sigrah).

built mainly after 1900 (figure 4.7).

The following discussion is based on the work of retired BPC Civil Engineer and Surveyor Peter Anderson, who published *Tropical Architecture* in 1963. Generally, all structural items were prepared from limited materials: coconut palm, pandanus, and a few species of timbers such as *Calophuyllum inophyllum, Cordia subcordata, Inocarpus edulis* and odd branches of driftwood. *Terminalia catappa* is common throughout the islands but useless as a structural timber due to its susceptibility to rot and borers. Even provided that all bark is removed from timbers and the core removed from pandanus logs, longevity varies significantly according to conditions.

Pandanus thatch is the common material for major dwellings throughout the islands. A smooth, dried pandanus leaf is woven by passing it around a vertical stake in the ground. This serves to remove most of the thorns along the edges. The leaves are rolled into neat bundles ready for use. Pieces of coconut leaf mid–rib are trimmed and cut to lengths of about 1.2 metres. This serves as a base upon which the thatch is to be fixed. Leaves are laid out on the ground, and a batten is placed on top about 46 centimetres from the broad end, which is bent over and pinned in place with long needles of coconut leaf. As each batten is covered, the thatching pieces are stacked in piles, with hundreds required to complete a roof.

On Banaba, pandanus roofing was not the standard material used for house construction. The Banabans preferred **coconut palm thatch roofing** because coconut palm leaves were abundant on the island. In Kiribati, palm leaf thatch is only used for minor structures, as it is quick and easy to make but lacks pandanus's durability and waterproofing qualities. This type of roofing differs as the palm leaves are plaited, and the fronds are laid one upon the other to add strength and protection from the weather.

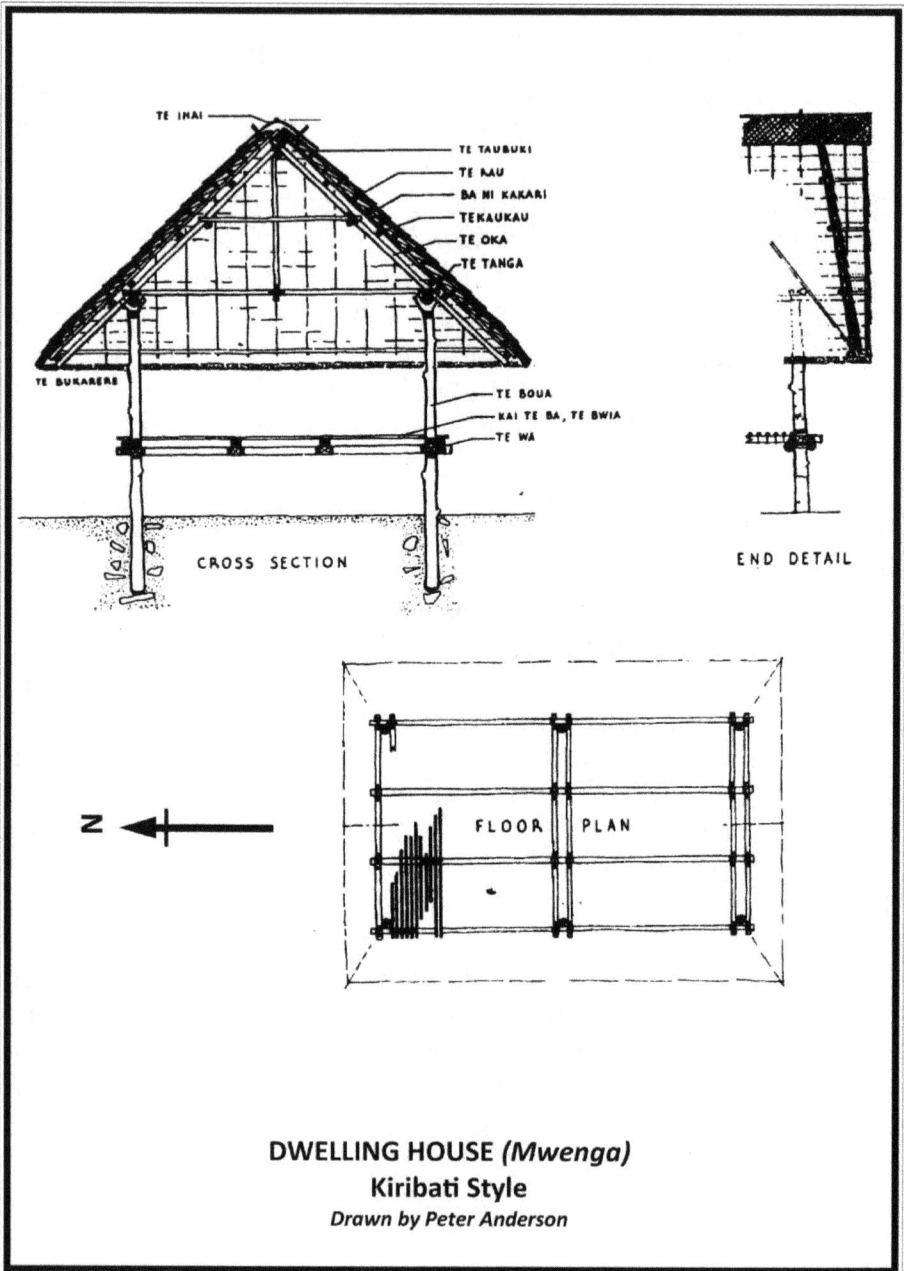

DWELLING HOUSE (Mwenga)
Kiribati Style
Drawn by Peter Anderson

Figure: 4.7. Kiribati *mwenga* (drawn by P. Anderson).

Women prepared lashings from **dried coconut husks,** the short fibres being twisted and rolled into cords of varying diameters on the side of their thighs. The women used strands of their hair to colour the lashings. Lengths of 15 to 18 meters were commonly made in one operation, larger ropes formed by twisting together smaller diameter cords, which are two-stranded. This material is durable, strong, and resilient and provides ideal 'springs' for vessels. Side weather screens and roof ridge capping are plaited from **green coconut palm fronds**. Trimmed coconut leaves from mid-ribs are the usual material for walls and floors.

Tools

For centuries people made efficient adzes in varying sizes to suit specific tasks. With hard coral obtained from a great depth, they shaped and sharpened giant clam shells into adzes. Wooden hafts were carved and lashed and fitted to the adze. Bowstring drills with shell points were used to make small holes (particularly in canoe construction). These are similar in design to drills used in China today. Banabans used sticks, reef shells and half-coconut shells for digging and excavation. They used their strong teeth as an efficient cutting tool, biting through the toughest cord with remarkable ease. They scraped and polished with shark skin, coconut oil and sharp shells.

Construction details

As women prepared thatch for the houses, men prepared the frame. All materials were roughly cut to size and stacked vertically to dry. The core was removed from pandanus logs, and all timbers had the bark removed to prevent rot and damage by borers and other pests. Usually, two or three men worked on the building. The roof was always constructed on the ground, then raised. The main roof plates were fitted

58. Construction of *mwenga* (Williams Collection 1901–31).

together and lashed, forming a rectangle upon which the roof was to be framed. The two pairs of end rafters were lashed in a position allowing about 15 centimetres to overlap at the top, which formed a V to receive the ridge pieces. The overhang at the roof plates was left untrimmed.

Single bracing timbers, from the centre of the end plates to the centre of the ridge, were then lashed to both upper and lower ridge pieces. Roofing purlins were then laid across the rafters at about 90 centimetres spacing. The rafters were trimmed at the lower purlin, and then thatching battens spaced about 23 to 27 centimetres apart were laid and lashed over the purlins. The end frames were constructed similarly, set at the bottom to line up with the existing overhang. Thatch was sewn onto the battens from the inside using a wooden needle like that employed by net makers. Lengths of coconut twine were knotted to each thatching batten, ready for use. Commencing at the lower end of the roof, the thatch was placed over the battens and pierced with the needle close to the stick on which it is folded, leaving the barb protruding.

A lower ridge piece was lashed below the apex of the rafters, and then the remaining rafters, at about 1.2 metres, were lashed in position and tie beams attached at the centre of the truss. At this stage, the central ridge timber was laid on top of the 'V' formed by the rafter and fixed. The free end of the twine was passed over the batten, looped over the barb and drawn back through the thatch. After disengaging the needle, the free end formed into a half hitch and was pulled tight. The free end was left hanging, and the operation repeated at the next batten until the whole thatch was firmly thatched.

Coconut midrib or slender timber poles were lashed to the joists. Spacing varied from 2.5 to 7.5 centimetres.

Four to eight men lifted the roof to the supporting posts and secured it into position by heavy lashings.

Overhanging thatch ends were bundled and trimmed; loose lashing ends were cut off, and neat coral paths were laid to access the building.

59. Banaban *mwenga,* house (Doutch Collection 1914).

259

Species of Trees on Banaba

The following species of trees and plants are found on Banaba. While many are used in buildings, many are also useful sources of food or medicine.

Local Name	Scientific classification	Common name/use	Other details
te ni	Cocos nucifera	coconut	
te kaina	Pandanus tecarious etc.	pandanus	
te kunikun	Terminalia catappa	almond	
itai	Calophyllum inophyllum	known as the Ship Tree by Te Aka	linking this tree to te Aka legend Chapter 3
te uri	Guettarda speciosa	a fragrant tree	
te ren	Tournefortia argentea	coastal tree	
te kanawa	Cordia subcordata	used for local medicine	
Te kiaiai wild	Hibiscus tilcaeus	hibiscus	
te kiriaua	Ficus benghalensis	banyan tree	
te ipi	Inocarpus edulis	hardwood tree	useful for building
te ngea	Pemphis acifula	coastal bloodwood	useful for tool and weapon making
te mao used	Scaevola kownigi	for local medicine for women and children	
te bero	Ficus tihctoria	edible plant	also used for local medicine
te baireati	Barringtonia asiatica	night flowering tree	the seeds stun fish
te obu	(unclassified)	a rare tree	the roots stun fish
te ukin	Coccolobis uvifera	with poisonous red berries	leaves used for medicinal purposes

26: TURNING POINT – WORLD WAR II

The Decision to Move the Banabans

The Banabans were determined to limit the mining operations of the British Phosphate Commission. The British had already decided that, eventually, the Banabans would have to be moved. A policy that had been mooted as early as 1927. Australian Commonwealth records reveal an official copy of a decoded telegram despatched by the Australian Governor-General to the British Secretary of State for Dominion Affairs, on behalf of the Australian Prime Minister, Dated 22 October 1927. This letter was written while the following people were in office and who probably were aware of the telegram's content:

> Lord Stonehaven, Australian Governor-General
> S.M. Bruce, Australian Prime Minister
> Arthur Grimble, Resident Commissioner for Gilbert and Ellice Islands Colony
> Sir Alwin Dickinson, KCMG, UK British Phosphate Commissioner
> Sir Clive McPherson, CBE, Australian British Phosphate Commissioner
> Sir Albert Ellis, CMG, New Zealand British Phosphate

Commissioner

In this letter, the Governor-General (see Appendix 6 for the full version) stated the intentions of the Australian government:

"As all the phosphate on Ocean Island will eventually be required, it appears to Commissioners advisable that steps should be taken to secure another island or islands for the use of the Banabans when Ocean Island is no longer suitable for their habitation, and the Commissioners have expressed their willingness to co-operate in this matter. The question of immediate removal to another island can be avoided if the land now required is made available without restrictive terms and conditions."

Twenty years later, H.E. Maude later described the Banabans' uncertain future in a Colonial Government Memorandum dated 1946:

"As long ago as 1914 the Authorities were worried about the fate of the Banabans when the phosphate industry on Ocean Island came to an end, and in 1927 the creation of a Provident Fund was proposed, which should be used for the purchase of a future home for the community. The Resident Commissioner pointed out that if the phosphate industry were to fail 'the race would literally be blotted out of existence: five hundred and fifty denaturalised natives could not possibly live on the interest yielded by the Banaban Fund.'"

It was intended that the Banaban Provident Fund, begun in 1931, be used to purchase a new home for the Banabans once that home was found. These discussions coincided with the outbreak of the Pacific War 1941-1945.

In 1940, six years before Maude published his Memorandum, the Banabans had been offered Wakaya Island or Rabi Island in the Fiji Group. In his memorandum, Maude had commented on the Banabans' concern over the future of their identity and culture:

> "They felt that the younger generation was growing up in too Europeanised an atmosphere and that, if they were to preserve their racial identity and culture, it was necessary to continue that culture elsewhere. At the same time, they were insistent that their rights to land on Ocean Island should continue undiminished. A survey of Wakaya was accordingly undertaken, which showed it to be unsuitable for the support of a large population owing to the shallow depth of most of the fertile soils and the poor water supply."

Banabans thought that compared to Rabi, Wakaya was "the better island of the two for their purposes." However, the British decided that Lever's Pacific Plantation offer for Rabi, off the coast of Vanua Levu, for the sum of £25,000 (Australian currency) was the preferred solution. The Colonial Office report was very favourable. It stated that Rabi was suitable for colonisation covering 70 square kilometres in area, with several deep indentations off the coast providing good anchorages and excellent fishing grounds. Three coconut plantations flourished, and the soil in most parts of the island was suitable for gardening. The south and east coast of the island was damp and mentioned as being somewhat 'gloomy.' The north shore, with Nuku in the centre, enjoyed a drier climate to which the Banabans would become accustomed. It also had broad sandy beaches and excellent areas where the Banabans could build villages.

The Banabans were unwilling to accept it because they considered Wakaya the better of the two islands. The High Commissioner advised them that he would not consent to their purchase of Wakaya unless they bought it in conjunction with Rabi. Maude states the Banabans intended to purchase Wakaya as a second home and use Rabi as an investment. The Banabans consented to buy Rabi, considering it an excellent investment, at a low price in the depressed copra market. However, the purchase of Wakaya never eventuated as the offering price of £12,500 (Fiji currency) was considered too high, and the High Commissioner's counteroffer of £5,000 was not accepted.

The freehold purchase of Rabi was made with the Banabans' funds in March 1942. Ownership of the entire island, except a 20-hectare Fiji government reserve, was transferred to His Britannic Majesty's High Commissioner for the Western Pacific. At the same time, an agreement was reached with the original owners, Levers, to lease the island back to them at a rate of £1,000 (Australian currency) until the Banabans wanted to move there. (The Banabans were unaware of the Lever Brothers' connections with the British Phosphate Commission (see Chapter 24).

War in the Pacific

On Sunday, 7 December 1941, the Japanese attacked the USA

60. Evacuation from Banaba by the Free French Destroyer *Le Triomphant* 28th Feb 1942 (Australian War Museum).

naval base at Pearl Harbour in Hawaii, with news of it reaching Banaba the next day via the regular shortwave broadcast. Then, in the afternoon of that same day, a flying boat appeared over the island, dropping bombs and firing machine guns at the government station, apparently to sever radio communications. By the end of the week, the government residency was destroyed. On 10 December, the BPC manager was instructed to destroy the company's equipment. Demolition gangs of BPC staff met secretly at midnight. Before dawn, they destroyed the jetties, mooring buoys, span chains, launches, boats, and company records. A Banaban, Karuoteiti (Keith) Christopher, remembers this event vividly. As a sixteen-year-old boy working in the BPC office, he was asked to burn sensitive documents behind the island's water tank under the darkness of night. He can still recall his fear that marauding enemy ships might see his fire, and he expected the Japanese to arrive at any moment. He

61. BPC staff and Chinese labourers aboard *Le Triomphant* 28th Feb 1942 (Australian War Museum).

also recounts how he wheeled the heavy old BPC safe down the steep jetty and, with some company men, watched it sink into the depths of the harbour. These may have been routine security measures for the company and government staff to avoid papers falling into the wrong hands. However, for this young Banaban, his fears went much deeper, especially when he was left behind to face the wrath of the invading Japanese. He prayed they would never find out he was involved in the sabotage, which he was sure would implicate him as a spy in Japanese eyes.

Evacuation of Banaba

Early in 1942, American intelligence predicted that the Japanese were about to push southwards in the Pacific. It was not until late in January that the evacuation of BPC staff on Banaba was authorised with the backing of the British War Cabinet and the Australian Navy. Brought in for the evacuation operation was the Free French destroyer, *Le Triomphant*, which was considered one of the speediest ships afloat. *Le Triomphant* arrived on Banaba on 28 February at dusk to find BPC boats already waiting with passengers as arranged. By eight o'clock that night, the ship had already set sail with two hundred and thirty-two BPC staff and eight hundred and twenty-three Chinese labourers aboard. Back on Banaba, the acting Resident Commissioner, Cartwright, and Ron Third, a radio operator, maintained British administration. Lindsay Cole, a BPC labour inspector, who oversaw seven hundred and thirteen I-Kiribati and Tuvaluan workers and their families, also remained. Father Pujabet from the Sacred Heart Mission and Brother Brummel refused to leave. A young BPC employee, Arthur Mercer, mysteriously 'jumped ship' at the last moment as he had fallen in love with a young Banaban girl and could not bear to leave her behind.

The food rations left behind by the BPC were limited, so the Banabans had to look to their food trees and the sea to provide them with their daily needs. Labourers from other Pacific islands, who owned no lands on Banaba, had to rely on the sea and the generosity of the Banabans for their food supplies once the rations were depleted.

Later in the year, Commander Green, a naval intelligence officer in the South Pacific area for the US Navy, received a request from the BPC Commissioners to evacuate the remainder of the BPC and government staff who were still on Banaba and Nauru. Green replied that an attack was being planned against the Japanese in the Solomon Islands and that it would be at least six to ten weeks before anything could be done. Further evacuation plans were also put in doubt when the new High Commissioner in Fiji believed that it would be wrong to bring out the British officials from Banaba without taking the native population as well. He expressed this view clearly in a telegram to his superiors back in London: "I need not enlarge to you on the figure we would cut ... if we cleared out in the face of danger. [If we stay] we may lose some officers, but that cannot be helped" (as cited in, Williams & Macdonald, 1985, p. 322).

All these matters were quickly laid to rest on the weekend of 22-23 August when Japanese aircraft and warships attacked Banaba and Nauru. Two days later, all communications with Banaba stopped. It was assumed by naval intelligence that both islands had been invaded. The relatives of the European men on those islands were notified. A garrison of 500 Japanese troops and 50 labourers had taken possession of Banaba. They set up anti-landing-craft barriers and electric fences at likely landing places along the reef, dug fox-hole defences and built bunkers. Meantime, the BPC was already planning for the future rehabilitation of Banaba and Nauru. This term 'rehabilitation' did not mean replanting mined-out areas; far from it, it meant rebuilding mining operations on both islands as soon as the war was over. On

December 1942, BPC General Manager A.H. Gaze issued a statement reviewing the effect of the war on the Commission's activities. He stated, "Chief Engineer Thompson was drafting a comprehensive report on headway being made for the rehabilitation of the islands, with plans in detail already on the drawing board" (as cited in, Williams & Macdonald, 1985, p. 323).

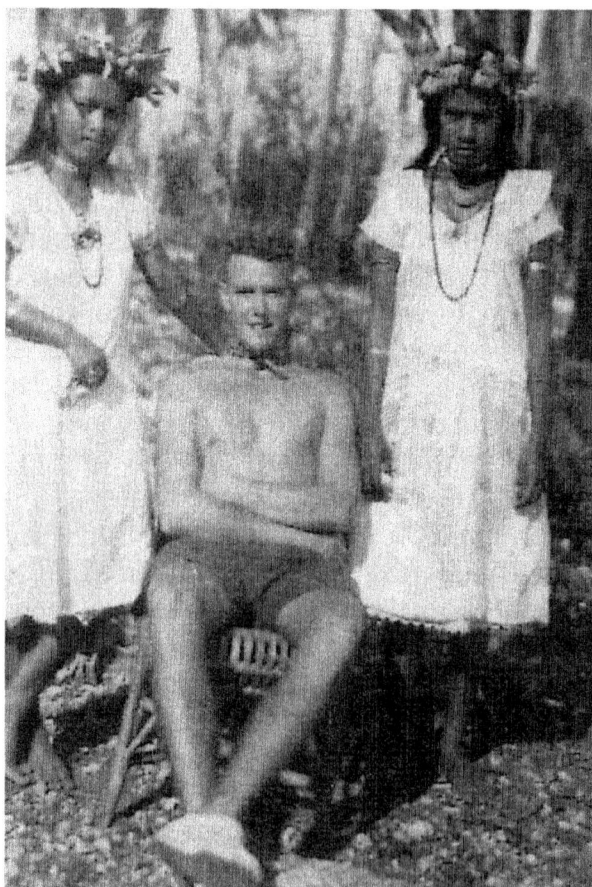

62. Arthur Mercer (centre) with Nei Kaitiro (left) and his Banaban girlfriend, Nei Terenga Aneri (right). Photo taken at Catholic Compound, Tabwewa prior to WWII evacuation (White Collection 1930-51).

27: JAPANESE OCCUPATION

The following information about the Japanese occupation comes from the detailed report of the committee appointed by the Kiribati government to investigate the death, injury, damage and other atrocities which happened in Kiribati during World War II. Through first-hand accounts from survivors, the committee uncovered information that had never been brought to public attention. The report was tabled in the Kiribati Maneaba Ni Maungatabu (House of Assembly) in November 1996. The report covers all aspects of the effects of war on Kiribati and its citizens. Details included the names and ages of people killed and injured and where and how it happened (Appendix 11). The report also describes injuries received, war damages, loss of property and personal possessions, and incidents of ill-treatment. For the first time, these survivors tell their story of what happened to the Banabans during the invasion by the Japanese. These English translations, which are as close to the original transcripts as possible, convey first-hand experiences of these events accurately (translations by Raobeia Ken Sigrah).

Samuelu Kaipati's Story

The following information comes from Samuelu Kaipati, a

Banaban interviewed by committee chair Titan Itetau, MP for Marakei. At the time of the interview, Samuelu was more than sixty-nine years of age. When Samuelu was asked how many Banabans were left behind at the outbreak of war, he answered, 'more than six hundred plus.' (Government records state over five hundred). Australian army intelligence, referring to the *Pacific Island Year Book* 1942, used a figure of 700 Banabans. This latter figure is more accurate, considering the number of Banabans who died during the Japanese occupation and the number of survivors who arrived on Rabi in December 1945. Samuelu's evidence is as follows:

When the Japanese landed, they destroyed the store, and they were looking for the wireless house. They destroyed it, and they captured the Europeans with the Father. So, Mr Cartwright who was here and one of the wireless men by the name of Mr Sei [Ron Third], and one of the BPC men by the name of Mr Goal [Cole] and the Father [Father Pujabet]. So, they gathered all these people to one of the BPC buildings. When they were in that house, they were guarded by a Japanese and put on rations... They were not given cigarettes. They would have a chance to smoke when people went past and dropped cigarettes next to their cells, hiding them from the soldiers ... While they were staying in the prison for about three months, the Father became sick. He was taken in a side car on a Japanese motorbike to the hospital for the purpose of treatment, but later on, the truth came out that the Japanese had been cutting up his stomach, so he died. Once the Father was taken away, he was never to be seen again. Three weeks later the Europeans were taken by the Japanese, and none of them ever returned. Nobody knows where they were killed.

Samuelu was asked, did people get injured when the Japanese took away their possessions?

Yes, one victim did not give any of his stuff to these people. He was taken to the northern side of Banaba to the place name of Bareimwim; he was killed. Another person who did not want to give his stuff was slapped by the butt of a rifle; his name was Tebuke; he was an old man.

He was a Banaban ... that is why they treated him this way. This old man wanted to fight, but they stopped him. But he did not want to stop, and when they got what they wanted they left him ... A few months later other people came along as workers, and these people came from a company known as Nangok, te Nangko Company [Nanyo Kohatu Kabushiki Kaisa] ... The workers came to help in retaining the power plant which the BPC left and other things ... The Japanese could not work the church generator, but they kept on trying until they got the power on ... people who came with the Japanese were the Okinawans and Koreans. They stayed amongst the Banabans until the food ran short ... some other problems happened because the Banabans had already run out of food. They had nothing left over from the BPC cargoes ... so the soldiers began to ration the people on a very low portion.

... the Japanese began to make other plans on how to survive. They sent 60 young people from Banaba who were Gilbertese and the tall ones to Kusaie ... So, these people could send back bwabwai and coconuts. So, when the food arrived, they split it up amongst the people as a ration ... It is not good, and when you eat the coconut it bites back on your tongue ... It has gone mouldy. There is nothing we can do about it; we will have to take it in order to survive ... And besides that, we look for our own food. We eat all sorts of leaves, even the leaves of the creeping plants, the leaves of the trees that grow beside the sea waters, the leaves of the grass known as the 'boy.' The soft inner part of the coconut tree, the inner stem of the pawpaw tree; which we peeled the skin off and started to mash up the inner part and mix it with fresh toddy and start to boil it. ... we eat it the best

way we can, so we do not go hungry, because there was no more food left. We have some other source of food from the sea, such as fish, but the problem when we go out fishing, and when we come back the Japanese will force us and take away our fish. If you do not want to give, you were beaten up, and they took away your fish. So, a father will go back home after fishing the whole day under the sun, to his crying wife and children because they were hungry. Even though the father will be as tired as can be there is one thing he can share with his family on his return, is his tears. That is what they used to do to us every day ... we will have to share our fish with the soldiers in the hope that we will have some to take home.

What was the difference living under the Japanese?

63. Banaba while under Japanese occupation. Official RAAF photo (Australian War Museum).

All the good things were put aside for the Japanese and what is enough for them cannot be shared with the people. So, the solution came that people will have to be dispersed to other islands. But before we were split up, the Japanese were organising things and setting the rules and giving orders on the island. They set the punishment for the offences committed by the people. Some people were beaten with the local timber known as te ngea, one of the hardwoods on Banaba. The people will be given the number of strokes according to their offences. Starting from five strokes, ten strokes, 20 strokes up to how big the offence is. Some people will have broken backbones ... some have back muscle infections ... most of these people were being beaten by their own people who have been selected by the Japanese to look after law and order.

They were Gilbertese, Tuvaluans and Banabans ... if they did not perform well, they too would receive beatings from the Japanese. Some of our Banabans pretended to execute their duties well, but they take pity on us, and when the Japanese found out these men were forced to beat up their people so badly that in the end, their victims suffer even more. This was the punishment for light offences. For heavy offences there were only two things that would be done, either shot or beheaded. So, the first beheading was done to two Gilbertese who were found stealing green coconuts. To the Japanese, stealing is the worst offence, so the price of death.

Do you have memories of people who were executed?

One of them came from Tabiteuea and one from Nonouti. One called Toanikarawa and the other Kamoaa. They stole green coconuts, and that is why they were beheaded ... One of the Banabans called Robert Corrie was also beheaded for stealing rice. I was watching those beheadings ... Kamooa was taken first. Before he [Japanese soldier] chopped

273

64. Nei Makin Corrie (she was 17 years old when she was made to watch her father's execution) (Maynard Collection 1945).

Kamooa, he tested the sharpness of his sword first. He was trying it on one of the tall trees called te kiebu. After wiping the blade, he came back and pressed Kamooa's neck forward. At this time, he was ready to cut his neck. He lifted the sword up and moved the sword to one side, and moved it back to the other side, and then he lifted it up and said, 'Uu tie!' and there it goes. The neck was chopped with only one blow, and the sword did not stop there and went as far down as hitting his knees. The head fell inside the grave with all the blood shooting in every direction; and then his body was kicked into the grave.

Then they called Toanikarawa, and another Japanese came to behead him. The same happened, except his head did not fall. They heard him moaning. When the people heard him moaning, they imitated the sound. We called out, 'his head did not drop!' That is why he [Japanese soldier] started to cut him up - in order to kill him fast. So, the head was dropped, and the blood was just shooting out in every direction, and he was asleep in his grave. So, we left. The job was completed, and they were starting to bury them. And so, we returned. And that Robert ... [Corrie] he is a brave man. He was so calm; he started to smile, he then said his goodbyes to his friends and his wife. They tied up his eyes, and they positioned him in the same way as those before him. With one stroke his head came off. So, they pulled him to his grave and there he was buried.

Two Banabans, one called Kauaba and the other Tabuia were prisoners. They were taken to test the power of the electricity and were electrified on the other side of the island ... When the first one went to test the electricity, Kauaba, the electricity was not turned on, and he got through alive, so the Japanese shot him dead. The other man, Tabuia met the power of the electricity and was electrocuted and burnt instantly. Until they saw that the whole of his body had been burnt, they turned off the power. No one knows where these people were buried.

Can you tell us about other people who were casualties of the Japanese?

One of the ladies who was from the Gilberts was ill-treated by the Japanese. This woman was caught committing adultery with another man, and this woman was called by the Japanese to face charges. She was tied to a mango tree at Tabiang Village near the Government office that was occupied by Japanese. She was tied naked to the tree. It was made a law that everybody who goes past this woman had to put a finger in her private parts. He will poke her, and after poking her, he will be sent on his way; ... if you did not want to, you were beaten. Until the people found out something was going on there, they stopped going on that road, and the women protested by starting to do what the other woman had done until this woman was released. This was about two weeks. They guarded her day and night and gave her some little drink and fed her a little bit. I do not know if she was released or killed. I did not know the true story about what happened to her, but I proved the fact because I walked that road and saw what happened to her. We ran away and tried to get as far away from her. Her body Was never found, and she was never seen again.

Can you tell us what happened to the lepers and their families?

The lepers and their families were taken by the Japanese, and they were all killed. The Japanese loaded them on trucks … somewhere like Lilian Point, that was one of the places they were shot at and thrown into the sea, the women, the men and all who were within the family. Like the person, I knew from Buakonikai called Abitenoko with his children and grandchildren. Abitenoko had only one granddaughter who got this sickness, and it was detected on the tip of her finger. When the Japanese found out, they were all taken … the other family was Ribaai, the same was done to these people … So, most of them were not lepers. The Japanese considered that they should be all killed because they just hate the family of lepers and believe none of them should live. Another man from Buakonikai, Nabeteko with his children and grandchildren, and Itinnaibo and all his children.

There is one of Itinnaibo's daughters who married somewhere else and who was not killed. All her children are now at Canton. All her brothers, cousins, uncles, the whole family were killed—a family from Tabwewa from Nei Kaebaa and the name of her husband, Nawine. Nawine was from Tuvalu. He was a school teacher in the government here, but he was the family of a leper. They were all taken. There was one who was a missionary in the LMS Church, and he was from the island of Tamana, and his name is Notua. The Japanese instructed that these people were to be taken away on a boat, out into the ocean to be shot and thrown into the sea, where the current is strong so that their bodies may never ever be recovered.

Can you tell us how long after Banaba was invaded, the Japanese dispersed the people?

The Japanese came in late 1942. It was in 1943 when the people were dispersed because we were on Tarawa for more the two to three months when the Americans arrived at Tarawa sometime in November or December. That's it! Because we were staying at Tarawa and saw what happened there.

Can you remember what people told you about ill-treatment on Kusaie (Kosrae) and Nauru?

Those on Kusaie were all ill-treated. The men were sent to work on plantations, and after that, they were told to dig a big pit, with the intention they were supposed to be killed at that spot by a machine gun that was already in position above them. As they prepared to be executed, another instruction came from the Japanese they were not to be killed. This went on until the end of the war, so the idea was to kill the men and leave the women to be the wives of the Japanese. I heard about three or four whole Banaban families were killed on Nauru by the bombing.

Information about Japanese abuses against women comes from the official transcripts of interviews by the 31/51 Australian Infantry Battalion (AIF), Nauru–Ocean Force, which was used as evidence in the war crime trials after the war. The name of people and places mentioned by witnesses have been reproduced in the same way as in the original documents, in capital letters.

Do you know any girls who were raped by Japanese soldiers?

Kiatara (19 October 1945): Yes. An interpreter named Taninta who was a Japanese civilian brought over from the Carolines used to go around the native villages and gather native girls and forcing them to go and be violated by Japanese officers. I know the name of one girl. Her name was Bakauer, daughter of a constable.

On three separate occasions between August 1942 and July 1943, ships took away Banabans. The first to Tarawa, the second to Nauru, and the last to Kosrae. One hundred forty-three of the youngest and fittest workers were left behind to supply fish for the Japanese forces.

65. Japanese Commander Suzuki Naoomi. Surrendered on Banaba 1945 (Australian War Museum).

Kabunare Koura, an I-Kiribati man, is one of only two who survived the horrors of this period, which concluded this tragic episode in Banaban history. His evidence helped convict the Japanese Commander Suzuki for war crimes committed on Banaba. Kabunare continues the tale with excerpts from his meeting with the Commission in the Kiribati Maneaba Ni Maungatabu on 23 September 1996.

Can you tell me what happened after the Japanese arrived?

... we will have to work for the Japanese without rations, we were forced to work, and we were not fed, so we looked for our own food. So, from there the deaths started. There was no more Number One [the phosphate company BPC], most

of the boys were thrown into the pits which were made by phosphate digging. It was the Gilbertese and Ellice who suffered most because they have to share the fruit and the rice among eight people each day, so how can you survive. Our elders began to die. From Nikunau to Tarawa, Taniera's father died, Iote also died, so there were only some of us left. Titanre and some others were still alive at that time. They stayed and faced the work. You were beaten if you were too slow; the leadership was so harsh.

We had to stand up and work with a stick behind us. If you stretched your back a while, they hit your head with a stick. Anywhere. Our work was to raise the stone for gun placements after we do the job, we come back to get about a pint of rain water. I survived by diving for octopus, and then exchanged them for coconuts. That's how we lived until the people were dispersed to Tarawa, Kusaie, Nauru and Ponape. There were people who died of hunger. But we were left behind because we were the only ones who could do the work.

How did they execute your people?

We stayed and worked and fished on and on and on. We heard that there was a big pit that had been dug to bury us in. So, my cousin called us together to stand up and attack Uma; my duty was to kill a certain Japanese. This motion was not approved. But they went ahead with the plan, and that is a trip they made without return. So, nobody knows our plan, but obviously someone did ... That is why our court case by the Japanese was delayed for another five or six months, concerning our death sentence. So, we were there until the day we were supposed to be killed. The commencement for our execution had started.

Yes, the way they kill us. We came back from fishing. We were so unsettled, and that night had nightmares. We asked each other what was happening. We prayed. Who can face this problem but only God? Early the next morning went out fishing, and we caught almost 100 bonitos. When we came back, we were told to wash ourselves *and to drink with the Gilbertese who were working on the farm. When we finished, we went down, but I did not drink because of feeling disturbed the night before.*

I was with one from Tabiteauea, Ueaititi, Taeka, Irome, Terara from Abaiang and some others. We were seated on the sand and asked, where do you come from, how old are you, but they lied. They were preparing the people they were going to kill. ... the Japanese started to tie our hands, one time, two times and I gave my hands.

We were taken to the seashore, and they put up very high barb wire. We felt homesick, but what can we do, the time is up. I was trying to concentrate on getting to the other life if there is another life. They will have to shoot their own targets, so I slid down facing the sea and in the middle of the rock. There is nothing I can see, and the other

66. Kabunare, the survivor of the mass executions. He is standing outside a cave after the surrender of Banaba 1945.

guy fell down, and I moved up, and I was poked by the bayonet. I stood up facing the sea and Tarawa with the rock underneath and one who is bigger and taller than me, and the shooting stopped. My ears exploded, and it was after 5 pm, and I pulled away thinking that I was shot, and I thought that I was going to die later.

The wave started to break on me, and I was surprised because my eyes were tied. My companions never talked because they were dead, and the Japanese were talking.

'Leave them for the sea will kill them and we will come back for them tomorrow morning.' I was going to lay down for a while longer not knowing if there was a Japanese guard, and for a while, I twisted my body and tried to free my hand. Then I climbed up the cliff to see if anybody was there.

I went back to check and see my friends, but they were

67. Nabetari survived by escaping on an outrigger at sea for seven months (Australian War Museum).

*all dead. About midnight I went to one of the caves, and I
was is where sorrow came in. The next morning, I heard the
surprised to see some of their bodies inside the cave. And
that Japanese yell, 'Here!' I waited awhile and then came a
boat. It was filled up with the people from Tabwewa, and the
big canoes were put into the water. So, they took the dead
bodies from off the shore and loaded them onto the Japanese
boat. While they were doing this, I left and went away. I
tried to get away, but the barbed wire blocked my way, so I
tried to break my way through. I injured my hands ... on
reaching the third wire, I was fortunate not to touch it, for if
I had touched it, I could have died.*

After Kabunare's miraculous escape, he hid for almost
two months in the pinnacles and caves until he finally
realised that the island was safely under the control of the
Australian occupation force. One other man called Nabetari,
a Tuvaluan was discovered alive after being adrift at sea for
seven months. He was from a party of seven fishermen who
risked a daring escape in their frail outriggers, choosing to
take their chances at sea. All the bodies of the Europeans
who had remained on the island were recovered, except for
that of Arthur Mercer.

War Comes to an End on Banaba

In a letter to the Commander of the Nauru Garrison, dated 13
December 1945, R. F. Wakefield, District Officer for Ocean
Island, urged that the evidence submitted was enough to
secure a general indictment against Lieutenant-Commander
Suzuki Naoomi, Commander of Japanese forces on Ocean
Island and his fellow officers. He lists the dates and sequence
of events on Banaba as the war concluded as follows:

(i)   Capitulation by Japanese
(ii) 19/8/45 – Natives told the war is over
(iii) 20/8/45 – Natives massacred

(iv) 21/8/45 - B25 Mitchell flew in low over OCEAN IS and dropped leaflets
(v) 21/8/45-Victims 'bodies dragged out to sea and sunk
(vi) 30/9/45-First Allied Soldiers landed at OCEAN IS.

Questions remain about what happened to Arthur Mercer. The Banabans, who knew Mercer before the war, knew he stayed behind because of his love for a Banaban girl. The rumour was that during the time of the European's internment by the Japanese, Mercer was hidden by his Banaban friends in a cave. Stories of what happened after that vary. One version is that someone reported his whereabouts to the Japanese, and he was taken into custody.

Another is that one of his Banaban friends was followed to his hiding place, and he was discovered. Another version claims that the Banabans were told to give him up or people from their village would be killed. In interviews with the Australian army over the deaths of the Europeans, some witnesses

68. Kaintong, Arthur Mercer's male friend with his relatives on Rabi after the war. (F. Christopher Collection 1946).

69. Japanese surrender to Australian Army on Banaba October 1945 (Australian War Museum).

state that he was one of those killed.

The last and most interesting rumour was that his Banaban friends put him out to sea in one of the island's largest outriggers.

Whatever the truth is concerning his death, his body was never found. Retired BPC engineer Peter Anderson was instrumental in recovering the remains and searched 'every square inch of Banaba.' He is confident that Mercer's body is not buried anywhere on the island. Supporting evidence for Anderson's opinion is found in secret intelligence documents of the 31/45 Australian Infantry Battalion (AIF) Nauru – Ocean Force, titled, 'Investigation of Atrocities on Ocean Island', dated 19 October 1945:

1.   ... Mr. Mercer evaded arrest for some days but eventually gave himself up due to lack of food.

5.   Mr. Cartwright died on Good Friday 1943, as a result, according to natives of malnutrition and indignities suffered. Mr. Mercer followed in June 1943 of similar symptoms. Natives buried Mr. Cartwright's body in the European Cemetery; of Mr. Mercer, there are no details of interment.

12.   Personalities that stand out for special mention are the Japanese commanders DASNURA and DOYAMA, the number two doctor, Japanese officers ICHI, OTUKA and MIJASUKA, Corporal NISHIJIMA, and the Japanese interpreter TANINTA. Of DASNURA, witness states he was transferred to TARAWA after Mr. Mercer died and was succeeded by DOYAMA.

If Mercer did escape Banaba, his escape would never have been made general knowledge; for fear that others would try and follow. A Japanese officer was transferred to Tarawa around Mercer's death. This suggests that Mercer probably had escaped. In 2000, Mercer's Banaban lover was alive and

70. Lt. Commander Suzuki Naoomi signs the surrender aboard the HMAS Diamantina, Banaba, Oct 1945 (Australian War Museum).

living on Rabi. Maybe the answers regarding his fate will remain in her heart and depart this world with her.

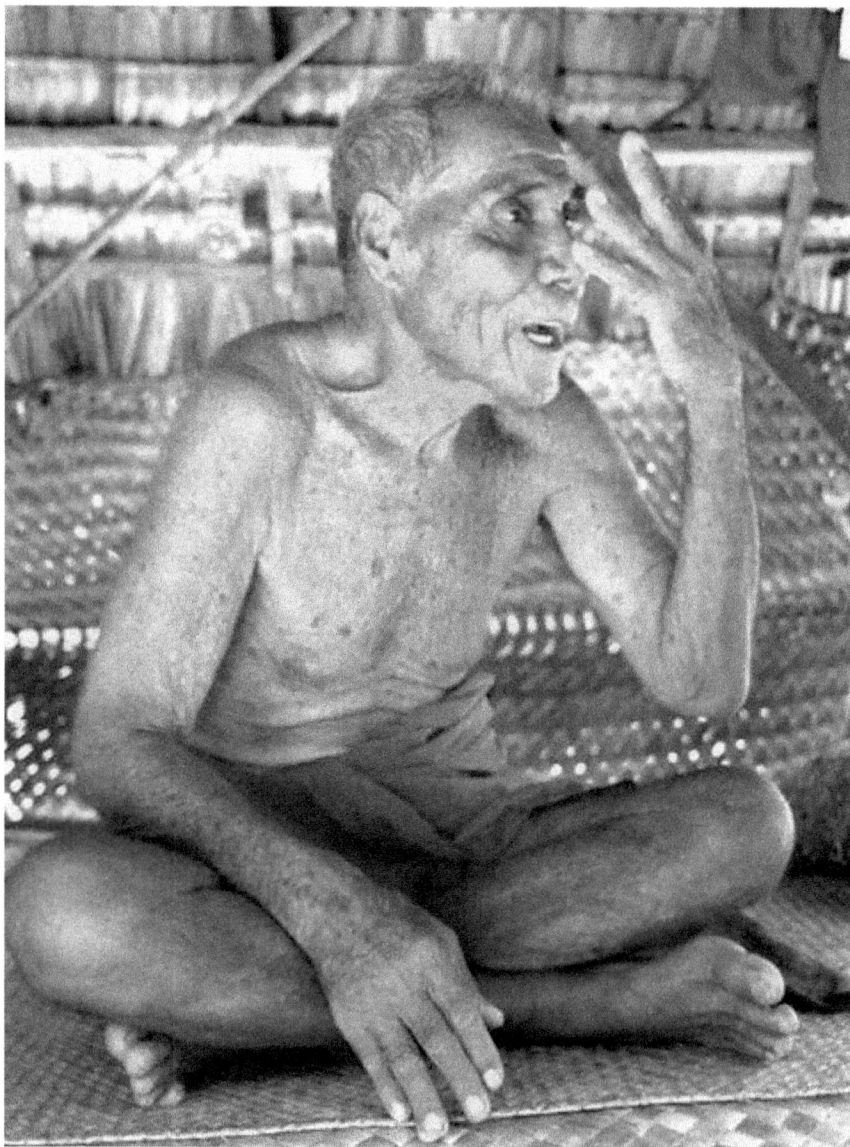

71. Interview with Kabunare Koura 83 years of age, Tarawa, Kiribati (M. Field 1999).

Banaban war dead

A Parliamentary Report tabled in Kiribati in 1996 lists eighty-seven Banaban, I-Kiribati and Tuvaluan workers who had died of hunger or malnutrition during the Japanese occupation. Starvation during the war has never been something Banabans like to talk about. In their eyes, dying of hunger is very humiliating for their family. A man cannot be considered a man if he cannot feed his family. This sad event in history is something that should not be looked upon with shame. The people who died from hunger during the war should be honoured and remembered. Seven others perished at sea, three were executed by beheading, and five were electrocuted. Twenty were killed for being lepers (Hanson's Disease), and one hundred and forty-two men were killed two days after the war was over. A further eighty-four died (see Appendix 11), and a further eighty-two were reported injured in some way, from beatings, breaking of backs and limbs, stabbing by bayonet, and two reported cases of rape.

The Banabans know of other ill-treatment that will never be openly spoken about because of the shame it brings upon the families. A total of three hundred and forty-nine people died on Banaba during the Japanese occupation. This chapter is dedicated to their memories.

72. First settlers on Rabi Island, 1945 (Maynard Collection).

28: EXILE FROM THE HOMELAND

After World War II, surviving Banabans were brought together on Tarawa, where their future would be decided. Harry Maude was there to meet them and was struck with the change he witnessed in the health and attitude of the people:

> "It will take some years for the Banaban community to recover from their treatment during the Japanese occupation: they were only a shadow of their former selves when discovered by the allied occupation forces. It appears, furthermore, that their attitude towards the Government, and Europeans in general, may have undergone a change. While for years they have distrusted the Government's good faith, they are now said to be more openly critical than before, which is ascribed to their having seen the European beaten, if only for a time, by a brown-skinned race such as themselves" (H.E. Maude, 1946, p. 12, no. 34).

The Banabans were told that the Japanese occupation force had destroyed and burned all four of Banaba's villages on the island before surrendering to Australian forces on 1 October 1945. Albert Ellis was on Banaba and Nauru to represent the British Phosphate Commissioners at the official Japanese surrender. He decided to call into the Colonial

Offices in Suva on his way home to discuss what should be done with the Banabans now that, as he notes, 'that their villages no longer existed.' Ellis also believed that the current situated could be advantageous as far as solving the BPC's constant problem over land dealings with the Banabans:

> "...while there is obviously a great advantage in the Banabans being transferred direct to Rabi ... the matter will require careful handling. His opinion was shared by the New High Commissioner, Sir Alexander Grantham, who noted in a memorandum, 'If we can persuade them not to go back to Ocean Island, we shall be spared many headaches'" (as cited in, Williams & Macdonald, 1985, p. 338).

The BPC's commissioned history, *The Phosphateers*, contains another interesting statement by Ellis:

> "From the point of view of the Commissioners and the Civil Administration, there was only one solution. Until the phosphate operation was well underway again there would be no money for such social and cultural luxuries as a great communal rehabilitation scheme: the Banabans owned Rabi, it was vacant, and the old plantation housing, though perhaps sub-standard, was available for immediate occupation. They could be collected and taken there in the Commissioner's ship, given foodstuffs sufficient for a month and the necessary equipment and assistance to start gardens. Furthermore, they each had four years arrears of annuity money to collect, and if after two years they wanted to go home that could be arranged" (as cited in, Williams &Macdonald, 1985, p. 341).

Colonial officials then confronted the Banabans with the news that it would be impossible for them to reoccupy Banaba for at least two years, owing to the absence of food supplies and the destruction of all four villages. The proposal

73. Rabi settlers unloading rations in 1945 (F. Christopher Collection 1946).

was that the Banabans would settle temporarily on Rabi, where food and housing could be provided, with a guarantee that they would be returned to their homeland at the end of two years should they so desire. As Maude explained, officials hoped that after two years, the Banabans:

"... would have recognised the superior advantages of Rabi and in their own interests, decided to remain there; if not, the period should be enough to enable the Commission to import sufficient food reserves for their support on Ocean Island and for the provision of temporary shelters for them while rebuilding their former homes. They were assured that the removal would have no effect as regards their lands on Ocean Island or their privileges with respect to any of the Banaban Funds" (H.E. Maude, 1946, p. 14).

Banaban elders remember, however, that they were forced by the British government to go to Rabi. Their morale and spirits were at an all-time low. On 15 December, 1,003 people aboard *SS Triona* arrived on Rabi and landed at Nuku:

	Men	Women	Children	Total
Banabans	185	200	318	703
I-Kiribati	152	97	51	300
Total	337	297	369	1,003

(See Appendix 12: For the list of Rabi Pioneers 'Honour Roll' who arrived on Rabi 15 December 1945).

The accommodation and provisions supplied by the British government were a far cry from what had been initially promised by the officials in Tarawa. The accommodation was army tents that had been hastily erected and were indeed no match for tropical downpours during Fiji's annual cyclone season. Two months' supply of army rations was likewise inadequate.

Was There Truly 'Only One Solution'?

For nearly three years, Banabans had suffered ill-treatment at the hands of the Japanese. They lived through the heartache of being physically taken from their homes, their villages, and their island, leaving their handful of worldly possessions behind. Then, just as that tragic episode ended, they heard they could not go home. The Banabans were frustrated because they could not travel from Tarawa to Banaba. Not one Banaban elder could return to Banaba to review its state. They only had the word of government officials. Over 50 years later, after other facts have come to light, new questions need to be raised:

- A Rabi elder returned to Banaba on an official trip in the 1960s while mining was at its peak. He reported that he was shocked to discover his family house still standing in Tabiang village. His house and others were occupied by I-Kiribati company employees. The Banabans had been told the Japanese burnt their villages, but here was proof that not all houses were destroyed. Undoubtedly the British deliberately lied, saying that all four villages were burnt to the ground.

- By the time of the Japanese invasion in 1942, many of the Banaban houses were made of timber and corrugated iron like other European style houses built on the island. Obviously, the British deliberately misled the Banabans even if some of the traditional houses had been destroyed.

- The British also lied about the extent of food resources on the island. The Banabans' diet consisted mainly of the island's natural resource of coconuts and fish, and they could have returned and survived.

- The British also lied about the destruction being widespread and devastating. The government and BPC got the mining facilities up and running quickly after the cessation of war.

- The British also lied about their intent. Clearly, they intended to resume mining immediately because on 10 October 1945, only ten days after the Japanese surrender of Banaba to Australian troops, 49 I-Kiribati labourers arrived aboard the HMAS *Kiakia* to work for the BPC.

The war provided the British with the opportunity to solve the 'Banaban Problem' by completely removing long-standing, contentious landowners who, in British terms, stood in the way of development of "working of the deposits to the best advantage of the Commissioners ... without restrictive terms and conditions" (See Appendix 6). A recent 1996 Kiribati government report (see Chapter 27) includes many first-hand accounts from Banabans who were forcibly removed from the island in 1943. All reported that their houses were intact when they left. In the testimony of Kabunare, the only survivor of the massacre two days after the Pacific war was over, never mentioned the destruction of

Banaban villages by Japanese forces. In fact, in an official Australian Army interview, Kabunare makes several references to Banaban villages:

"3. During the Japanese occupation, I was employed as a fisherman and lived at TABWEWA VILLAGE.

9. About five months before the end of the war our section of fisherman at TABWEWA was transferred to UMA village. We were not told why we were transferred to UMA village. There were only three of us at TABWEWA – myself, ERIM and ABERAM ...

27. Then we walked on down the track across the road and on down to the cliffs below TABIANG village ..." (original capitalisation).

During further interviews for the Kiribati committee hearings in 1996, Kabunare was asked detailed questions about Banaban villages, the village layouts, and how the buildings were constructed. As the only survivor of the

74. Aftermath of phosphate mining Banaba (Williams Collection 1901-31).

occupation to be on Banaba when the allied forces arrived, his evidence is compelling. In an official Australian army document ('31/51 Australian Infantry Battalion (AIF) Nauru – Ocean Island Force
– Ocean Island Force Intelligence Report 1, Covering the surrender and occupation of Ocean Island, Gilbert Island Group, on 1 October 1945, and activities of Occupation Force to 6 October 1945'), the following statement appears in 'Section VII – Buildings':

> "Most of the houses are undamaged, although only a few have been used. A few houses have been fitted with electric light, with power supplied by the Japanese power station."

The evidence of BPC's Assistant Civil Engineer at the time, Peter Anderson, also supports this statement (see Chapter 32):

> "When I arrived back on Banaba after the war my job was to assist in the repairing and building of damaged plant and equipment, this included the (BPC) houses. I found that the Japanese had left the houses in a reasonable condition, and had mostly used some of the houses, especially in Tabwewa, for storing pumpkins. The Banaban villages were virtually gone by the time I arrived back, except for a few scattered huts" (Peter Anderson interview with Raobeia (Ken) Sigrah 1998).

It is clear that the British report that the Japanese destroyed the villages was part of a propaganda programme to move the Banabans off the island.

What Happened to Village Land Holdings?

After the war, BPC went about systematically mining the whole island. Its activities raise more questions as to how it was able to mine these sites:

- Did the BPC get the signatures of every Banaban (now living on Rabi) to mine these areas?
- When the BPC attempted to mine the sacred village site of Te Aka in 1964 in the already extensively mined region of Te Aonoanne, why did they stop mining to allow an Australian anthropologist to remove important Banaban artefacts and skeletal remains?
- Why did the BPC decide to cease all mining in Te Aka site after the mysterious death of the head overseer?

One of the major grievances for Banaban elders was the destruction of Banaban burial sites, an issue raised in subsequent court cases with the British government in the 1970s. Banaban elders still lament that their ancestor's remains were crushed by the miner's bulldozers, shipped off, and scattered over farms in Britain, Australia and New Zealand.

75. A view of Banaba "topside" (central plateau) twelve years before mining ceased in 1979 (R. Anderson Collection 1967).

29: ARCHAEOLOGICAL INVESTIGATION: TE AKA VILLAGE 1965

The Launching of an Investigation

In 1964, BPC employees discovered an old village site in the interior of Banaba while they were preparing the area for mining by clearing overlying vegetation. Typically, this process would involve completely removing the land surface, which could destroy the village site. The BPC postponed mining activities in the immediate area and informed the Bishop Museum in Honolulu and the Australian National University in Canberra of its discovery. Both institutions agreed to sponsor an archaeological investigation by Lampert early in 1965. He was assisted by Professor John Golson of ANU's Department of Anthropology and Dr K.P. Emory from Bishop Museum. Lampert spent three weeks excavating the site with a full-time labour force of two I-Kiribati, a Tuvaluan and Mrs Lorraine Thwaites, along with volunteers among BPC's European staff.

Lampert conducted an archaeological investigation of Te Aka site, Ken Sigrah's clan's sacred ancestral village. A report of his findings was published in *Archaeology and Physical Anthropology in Oceania* in April 1968. Although now retired, Dr Lampert made time to discuss the dig at the Australian National University, Canberra, in 1997. He was amazed to hear that Te Aka site was considered sacred and taboo by the Banaban people. Before his investigations, he had not been made aware of this information. He only knew that the BPC had uncovered an old village site and was concerned that Banaban relics and artefacts be removed for safe keeping before it began mining in the area.

Lampert was further shocked to hear that mining of the area had been cancelled not long after he had finished his investigations due to the mysterious death of an overseer involved in the mining. When told of a visit to Te Aka in 1997, Lampert was surprised about the almost impossible conditions endured to climb through the mined-out phosphate fields which completely encircled the old site. A virtually impregnable fortress of towering limestone pinnacles cut off access to the ancestral birthplace to all but the very fit and adventurous. During a meeting, Dr Lampert kindly donated his files, documents, photographs, maps and field notes from the original investigation. Much of this material is being used as supportive evidence regarding the existence of Te Aka as Banaba's indigenous people.

76. Banaban representative, Kaiekieki Sigrah (Lampert 1965).

Initial findings

After the initial rediscovery, the Banaban Representative (a member of the Rabi community appointed post-war to live on the island) identified the site as Te Aka. A subsequent Banaban Representative, Kaiekieki, who had taken up his position before Lampert

77. Te Aka site – with mining area in background (Lampert 1965).

arrived, also confirmed the site's identity. Lampert noted these different sources of identification. Lampert also found a BPC map from 1907, which showed six 'native houses' then surviving at the location of Te Aka. Following its rediscovery of the site, the BPC mapped the building floors in detail (Figure 4.8). From this map and Lampert's examination of the site, a dozen buildings were identified, although not all these buildings would necessarily have been standing at any one time. One of the building sites was identified as a *maneaba*. A large part of it had been accidentally bulldozed before Lampert's arrival. He found its floor dimensions were approximately 14 by 12 metres, a size which distinguished it from the other village buildings whose floors averaged 6.5 by 4.5 metres. The locations of other building sites were easily recognisable by the slightly raised floors of broken rock and coral shingles, which were retained by low walls of partly buried, vertical slabs of water-worn coral rock. Lampert was advised that in constructing such buildings, it was customary to carry both slabs and shingles to the village site from the beach.

A typical Banaban *maneaba*

The typical Banaban *maneaba* was an open-sided building with "a high-rectangular roof of pandanus thatch supported on large stone pillars" (Maude and Maude, 1932, p. 27), the eaves projected considerably beyond the rectangle defined by the support post. Therefore, the corner posts found at Te Aka *maneaba* did not necessarily represent the very corners of the original building. Approximately 7 metres north-west of the *maneaba*, there were three coral pillars about 100 centimetres in height. Lampert thought they might mark the former outline of a different type of building, though neither coral shingle floor nor stone supports for a raised wooden floor were present. A large coral pillar (310 by 72 by 54 centimetres) was lying 30 metres to the west and could have been a *maneaba* corner post. It had later been used as a pounding bench. He could find no direct evidence to link it with his investigations of the *maneaba* site.

Banaban domestic buildings were constructed like a *maneaba* but on a much smaller scale, with their roofs supported by wooden posts. As it was an inland settlement, Lampert found records of three domestic buildings: family sleeping houses, small sheds for cooking and storage, and small houses where women stayed while menstruating. At Te Aka, all buildings other than the *maneaba* were presumed to be domestic. However, the function from the surface evidence, including the one that had been fully excavated, could not be determined.

In his report, Lampert said that if more time and labour had been available, he would have preferred to strip the

78. Te Aka site - Massive coral limestone pillar, not in situ: found 30 metres SW of *maneaba*, with mining area in background (R. Lampert 1965).

entire site horizontally. With limited resources, he could only strip areas that he felt were of potential importance. Beginning with the *maneaba*, he began working in a southwest direction through an adjacent building (A), then through a seemingly vacant area adjoining both buildings. It left enough time for Lampert to make a cutting through another building (B) and adjoining ground in another part of the site. In this way, Lampert excavated one-fifth of the total area.

Because later quarrying would destroy the area, he took steps to ensure that no other significant features were left undetected.

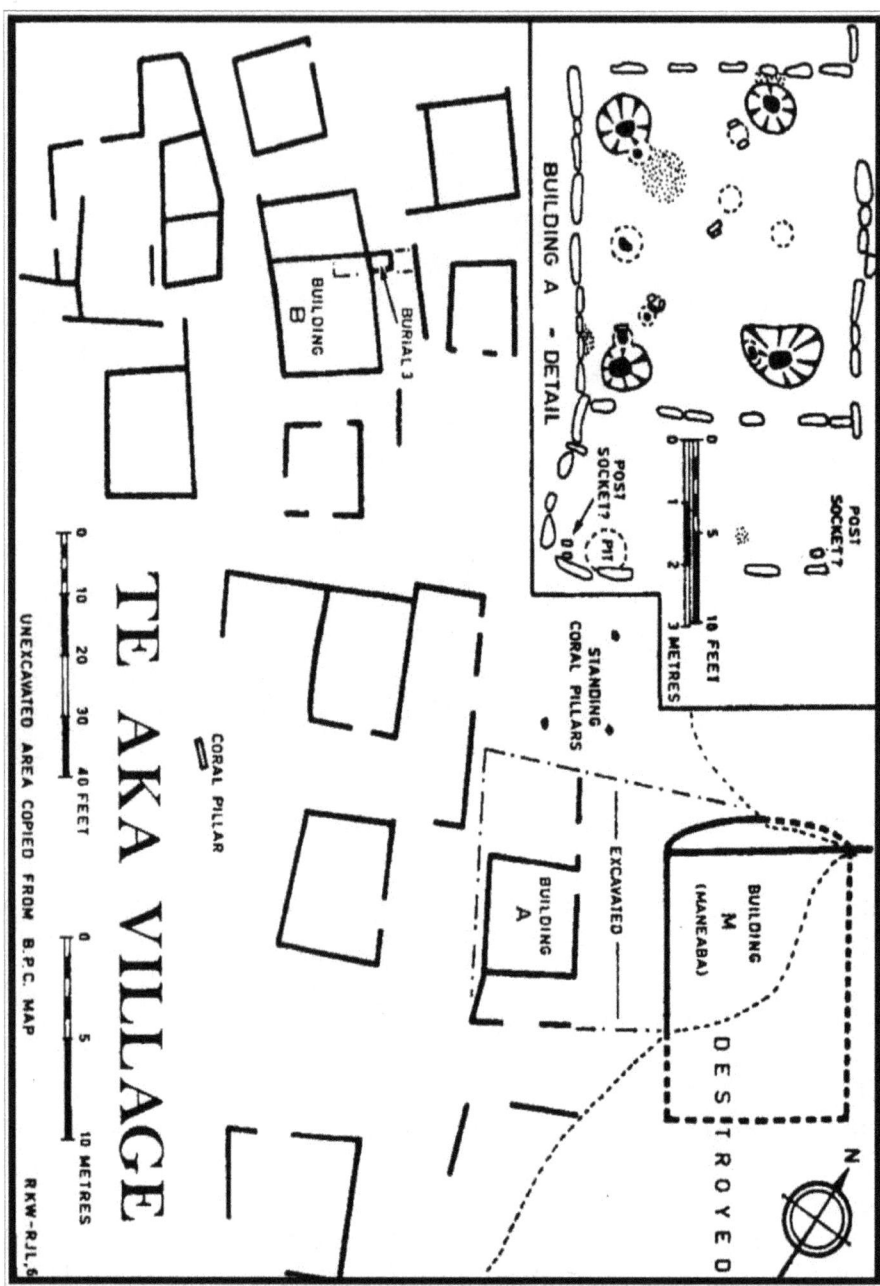

Figure: 4.8. Te Aka village map (Source: R. Lampert).

A bulldozer lightly cleared the scrub and boulders, and then, a grader removed successive, shallow layers until natural phosphate was reached. During this latter process, no noteworthy pits or other features were uncovered, although one burial site was disturbed.

After the preliminary clearing of the material disturbed by the earlier BPC bulldozer, the top 5 centimetres of floor shingle was removed by trowelling. The main floor of the *maneaba* consisted of rough phosphate boulders, which averaged a depth of 20 centimetres, interspersed with coral shingle. On further investigation, Lampert discovered that there was no trace of the seat or foundation rocks for the stone corner pillars that were usual for this type of building. He assumed that the pillars were not sunk any distance into the earth. Indeed, he later discovered that these pillars were packed around with stones and capable of standing upright on their own weight, usually penetrating only the top 15 centimetres of soil.

Below the rocky construction of the *maneaba* floor was dark, almost black, soft soil containing a sparse scattering of coral shingle. Lampert believed this was topsoil that had been buried under the floor. Post holes and cooking pits began to appear at this level. Post holes ranged in diameter from 40 to 50 centimetres. Five of the seven post holes ended with a smooth, horizontal stone slab (see Figure 4.9). All were filled with a mixture of coral shingle and medium brown soil. The cooking pits had depths around 5 centimetres and contained pieces of blackened phosphate rock and a mix of dark soil and charcoal fragments.

Building A

The raised floor of building (A) was southwest of the *maneaba* and separated from it by about 5 metres. Rectangular in form, it had dimensions of 6 by 5 metres. At its southeast border was a smaller (5 by 2.5 metres) adjoining floor of a similar structure, which appeared to be an extension of the main building. The floor was excavated by stripping horizontally. Unlike the *maneaba*, there were no rock phosphate boulders, and the shingle floor was laid directly on topsoil. On the other hand, the vertical border slabs were buried as far as the top of the natural phosphate.

The four corner posts appeared to have been replaced

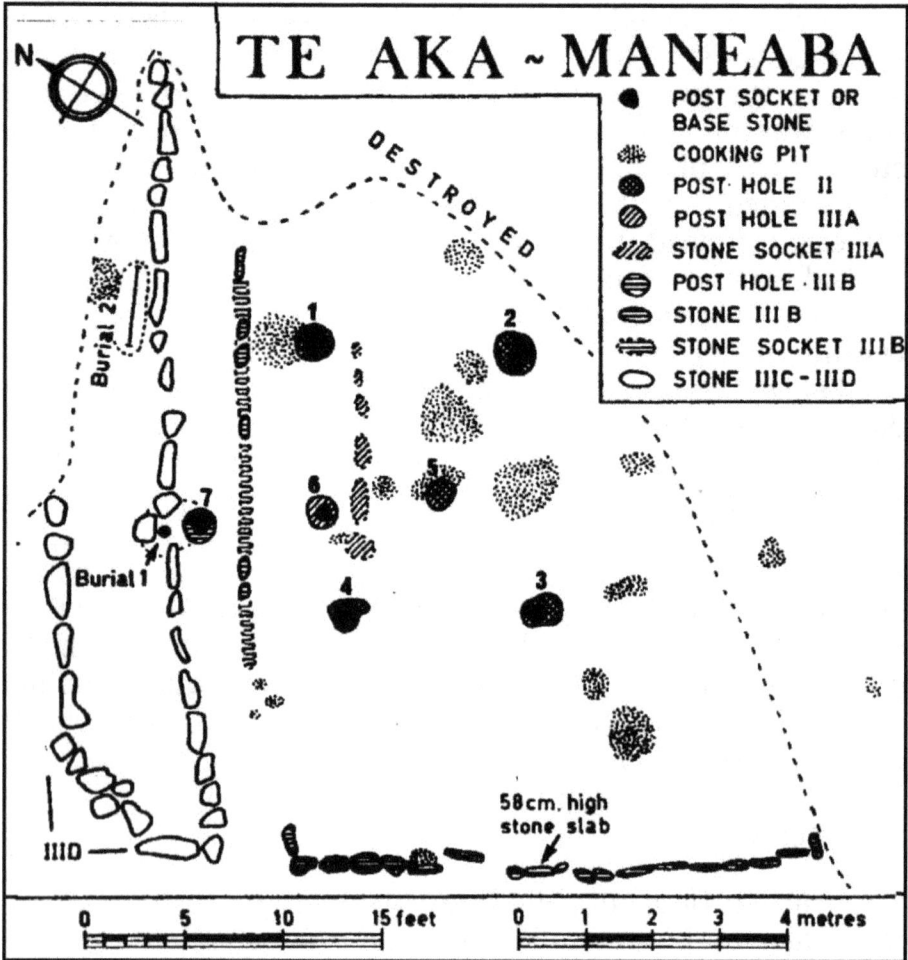

TE AKA ~ MANEABA

N

DESTROYED

	POST SOCKET OR BASE STONE
	COOKING PIT
	POST HOLE II
	POST HOLE IIIA
	STONE SOCKET IIIA
	POST HOLE · III B
	STONE III B
	STONE SOCKET III B
	STONE IIIC - IIID

Burial 2

1
2

7
6
5

Burial 1

4
3

IIID —

58cm. high stone slab

| 0 | 5 | 10 | 15 feet | | 0 | 1 | 2 | 3 | 4 metres |

Figure: 4.9. Map, Te Aka maneaba Source: R. Lampert).

many times. Post holes and some lined post sockets had been cut through one another, leaving a complex mixture of stones and shingle in each corner. There was no evidence that the coral shingle floor had been renewed. In common with the *maneaba*, building (A) contained several cooking pits cut into the phosphate surface before its construction. Another pit had been cut into the floor at a higher level. It was the only pit that Lampert was sure had been used while the building was occupied. However, building (A) was not used for cooking during its more recent history because the pit was covered by at least 5 centimetres of shingle. The floor of the small adjoining structure to the southeast suggested that a lean-to had been attached to the main building. Apart from the *maneaba*, all other buildings at Te Aka, whatever their function, were roughly the same size. Size could not be used to determine the function of building (A) (Figure 4.8).

Building B

Lampert chose to excavate building (B) for two reasons. First, it was at the opposite end of the site from building (A). Secondly, adjoining its northeast wall was a small structure bordered by slabs and was 120 centimetres square, a size making it unique on the site. The floor of this building was identical in construction to the floor of building (A). No postholes were encountered within the excavated area. Lampert discovered that the slab-bordered square was a grave.

Burials

The skeletal remains of two individuals were found in the earth-filled extension of the *maneaba* (Figure 4.9). The first remains consisted of a skull only, buried under a coral slab forming part of the northwest border of the *maneaba*. The earth-fill at this point was noticeably disturbed at a high level, indicating that the floor had been cut through and the burial was relatively recent. A piece of iron wire and a fragment of bottle glass well down in the grave fill provided further evidence of its recency. The bone was hard, though carbonised in patches on the outside. Concentrations of wood ash and large pieces of charcoal were found in the grave fill right down to the burial level, 18 centimetres below the surface. Although the skull was nearly complete, fragments of it appeared in the grave fill at a higher level, suggesting that the head was not buried in a 'fresh' condition.

The second burial site contained an incomplete skeleton 45 centimetres below the surface of the *maneaba*. The body had been dismembered at the time of interment. Ribs and vertebrae were in a normal anatomical position; the pelvic bone was at the end of the vertebrae but in a reversed position; the skull and long bones of the legs were completely

79. Te Aka site – partly excavated *mwenga* (A); Looking SE (R. Lampert 1965).

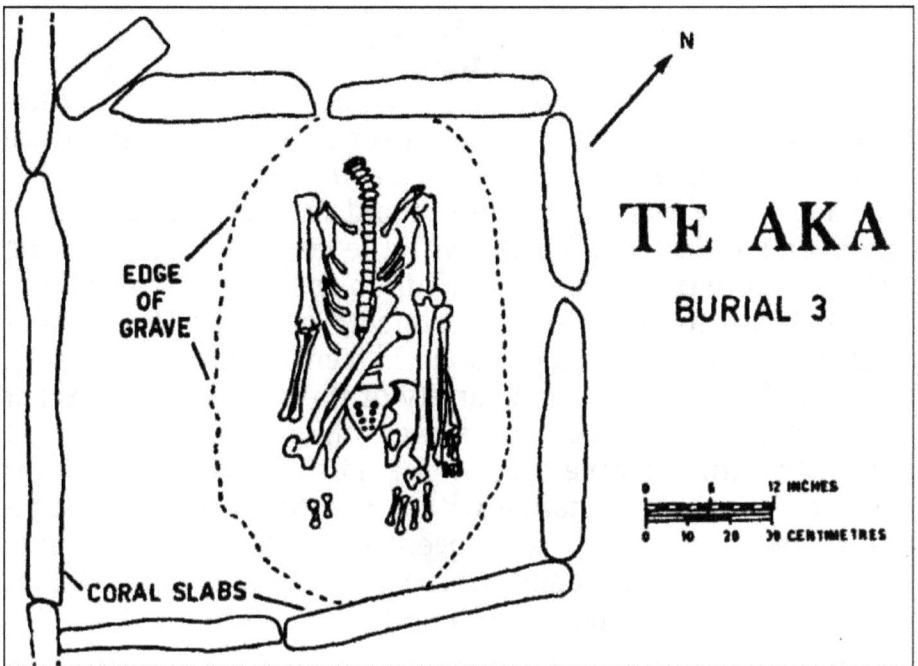

Figure: 4.10. Te Aka - Burial 3 (Source: R. Lampert 1965).

missing. The bones were in poor condition.

In the square enclosure adjoining building (B), a third grave had been dug from the present ground level, as shown by the continuation of loose, stony, dark soil down to a burial level 25 centimetres below the surface. Although the skull was missing, all other bones were in normal anatomical positions and in good condition. The body had been placed on its back with legs fully flexed and arms fully extended along its sides. In common with the other burials, no grave goods were present (Figure 4.10).

Te Aka Artefacts

Banaba has no clay for ceramics nor stone suitable to produce a cutting edge. Therefore, Banabans efficiently used their island's resources by turning to shell, bone and stalactite (found in the *bangabanga*). At Te Aka site, Lampert found two complete shell adzes, three fragments, four rough-outs and an unusual adze produced by flaking instead of grinding. Except for the flaked adze, all thicker specimens found were made from the shells of the *Tridacna gigas*. *Tridacna* are commonly referred to as clams found in Pacific reefs. There are seven species of *Tridacna,* with the largest clams reaching 30-40 centimetres in length and up to three times this width. The material for the thinner artefacts could be the smaller *Tridacna maxima* (usually about 10 centimetres in length), which is the most common variety of the giant clams. Except for the flaked adze, the adzes are similar in type. Lampert noted that this sample size was small and could not offer evidence of cultural change within the site's history. On all adzes, both surfaces have been ground, with one side producing a cutting edge. Six adzes were identified (see Figure 4.11 for corresponding items);

(a) A finished adze, taken from 15 centimetres below the surface of building (A).

(b) A finished adze taken from the *maneaba* floor construction.

(c) Adze taken from the surface near building (A).

(d) A finished adze taken from the *maneaba* floor construction.

(e) A rough-out adze taken from just below the shingle surface from the *maneaba* extension.

(f) An adze shaped by flaking. The cutting edge was formed by long, invasive flake scars. Steeply flaked concavities at opposite points on the two sides may form a lashing grip. Unflaked parts of the outer surface are smooth; they did not display the marking of either *Tridacna* or *Hippopus*, the only two genera of the giant clam whose shell is of sufficient thickness. Given that it is unlikely that the manufacturing process involved polishing and then flaking, we may assume that either a polished adze was reworked or, more probably, the raw material was a piece of shell naturally eroded by the surf. No exact comparable artefact was on record for this part of the Pacific.

Other artefacts included (see Figure 4.11 for corresponding items);

(g) Part of a lip of the shell *Cypraecassis rufa*, one end of which had been ground to a fine cutting edge while the other was pitted from hammering. It appeared to have functioned as a chisel. Taken from a deep post hole in building A.

(h) A partly drilled *te atau* (fouling line weight) of stalactite. Taken from the disturbed part of the *maneaba*. These lines were used in the sport of frigate bird snaring.

(i) (j) (k) & (l) Samples all taken from Nauru.

(m) A piece of smooth and relatively flat bone tapered by grinding, taken from the surface northwest of building A. An I-Kiribati informant advised that this could be *te a*, which was used in conjunction with a bone needle (*te rika*) for net making.

(n) This is one example of several partly finished but broken stalactite shanks of *te kaneati* (bonito fishing hook) found on the village surface.

(o) A ground and doubly perforated disc from the end of a *Conus* sp. shell is a type of Banaban and Kiribati pendant ethnographically recorded by Finsch (1914). The sample was found on the village surface, as were two others: a broken specimen, 21 millimetres in diameter, and a polished but undrilled one, 60 millimetres in diameter.

(p) A perforated shell (*Polinices* sp.) is one of six from the surface of Te Aka site. Finsch (1914) shows part of a Banaban necklace of a similarly modified small gastropod (*Natica lurida*) with the string passing through both the drilled hole and the natural opening.

(q) & (r) Taken from below the constructed *maneaba* floor were two pieces of split bone, probably human. Concavities in their sides appear to have been made by the gnawing of rats rather than filing.

(s)   An object with a round cross-section and one end pointed, both features produced by filing. The other end has been filed narrow, then broken. Taken from the surface northwest of building (A). When tested for phosphate with ammonium molybdate by Mr C.A. Key at the Department of Anthropology, ANU, the intensity of the reaction suggested that the material is tooth rather than bone. If so, this sample is probably a whale tooth, possibly part of a pendant. Banaban *te unaine* (women elders) have identified this object as a unique instrument once used by their female ancestors during marriage ceremonies, not a pendant, as Lampert suggested.

Other Artefacts

Lampert's investigation found other artefacts that are not illustrated here. From the *maneaba* surface, a porpoise tooth was found; it had been laterally drilled at the root, like examples from Kiribati (Finsch 1914). Scattered over the village surface were many centrally perforated shell- discs, 4 to 7 millimetres in diameter and identical to those strung together to form Banaban necklaces and belts. From 30 centimetres depth in the earth-filled *maneaba* extension came an *Amphiperas ovum* shell drilled halfway along its outer lip; this kind of ornament was usually used as an arm decoration as part of a dancing costume. From the village surface, several centrally drilled shark teeth were found, probably coming from the cutting edge of a Banaban weapon. Finds attributed to European contact included a bone button, clay pipe stems, bottle glass and five glass beads with diameters of 1.5 millimetres to 4.5 millimetres. Nearly all were surface finds. However, the smallest glass bead was found between rocks of the *maneaba* floor, where it may have intruded after the floor's construction. A clay pipe stem was found in the filling of a shallow post hole in building (A), where it had obviously been deposited at a later stage of the building's history.

Fauna

The following list of fauna were specimens taken from the surface of Te Aka village site. The shells were identified by Mr W.G. Buick, University of Papua New Guinea. The fish by Dr T. Abe and Mr Kaneko, Tokaiku Fisheries Research Laboratory, Tokyo. The rat by Dr J. Mahoney, Department of Geology and Geophysics, University of Sydney, and the dog by Mr L. Cramm, then of the Department of Anthropology, Australian National University.

The narrow reef encircling Banaba is the habitat of the shellfish, and most of the fish are found on the site. It can also be expected that there will be evidence of open sea fish (*P. glauca* and *Scombridae*) in the homes of people renowned for their expertise in trolling from canoes for bonito.

Shellfish

Turo sp.	*Tridacna gigas*	*Bursa sp.*	*Polinices sp.*
Manicinella sp.	*Cypraea (Arabica) scurra*	*Conus sp.*	*Nerita of Polita*
Tridacna maxima	*Amphiperas ovum*	*Natica lurida*	*Cypraecassis rufa* (Presented by artefact (g) only)

311

In many cases, the eroded and fragmented condition of the shells made species identification impossible.

Fish

Prionace glauca	Linne (blue shark), detached teeth	*Labridae*	(wrasses), premaxillary
Muraenidae	(moray eel), dentary	*Scaridae*	(parrotfishes), premaxillary
Scombridae	(mackerel and tuna including bonito), dentary	*Scarus sp.,*	dental jaw
Epinephelus sp., *Serranus sp.,*	(grouper or rock cod), premaxillary; premaxillary	*Scarops sp.,* *Balistidae*	upper pharyngeal (triggerfishes), dentary

Mammals

Rattus exulans	Peale 1848 (Polynesian rat), mandible
Canis familiaris	(either European or Polynesian dog), detached tooth and incomplete femur
Delphinidae	(porpoise), detached teeth

Summary of excavated materials

Context	Finds
General surface scatter, including top 5 centimetres in excavated areas and disturbed material	Shell necklace discs and complete shells; fowling line weight (k); two shell adzes (f) & (c); two adze rough-outs; three shell pendants (o); several broken or unfinished stalactite bonito hook shanks (h); pieces of an unworked stalactite; drilled shark and porpoise teeth; European introduced material.

Context	Finds
Maneaba area: below shingle surface and in the verandah floor.	Two adze roughouts (e); drilled A. *ovum* shell
Maneaba area: in and directly below floor construction.	Glass bead; two pieces of split bone
Building A, recent: below shingle surface and in shallow post holes	Clay pipe stem
Building A, early: in and below buried topsoil; in deep post holes	Shell adze (1); shell chisel (g); a piece of worked stalactite

Conclusions

The following conclusions are based on Lampert's findings. It was apparent that Te Aka village had been occupied up until European contact, as shown by the clay pipe stem found in a post hole of building (A). The age of wood surviving in another post hole of the pre-*maneaba* building suggests that the period of occupation was perhaps as far back as 200 years ago (dating determined with the assistance of Mr Polach from the C-14 Dating Laboratory, ANU). In 1997, at a meeting in Canberra, Dr Lampert and Professor Golson revealed that carbon dating tests have dated charcoal from one of the cooking pits as far back as 300 to 400 years ago. So, Te Aka existed when Te Aonoanne and Toakira districts were amalgamated to form Buakonikai, a time Lampert describes as 'recent.' He assumed that the Te Aonoanne *maneaba*, called Takanoi, was moved to Buakonikai around the same time. Still, Takanoi was almost certainly the excavated *maneaba*, which stood at Te Aka site until well into the early part of the twentieth century.

Lampert agreed that the form of burial suggested by the excavated skeletons was consistent with traditional practices recorded by Grimble (1921). The traditional burial was

313

postponed until an advanced stage of decomposition or due to preserving the body by embalming. Later the skull was often retained by relatives of the deceased, who also kept other bones for making tools such as fishhooks. The grave could be opened later to obtain bones as well. Such practices explain how the body in the third burial site is headless. Its vertebrae were undamaged and in a normal anatomical position suggesting the skull was removed at an advanced stage of decomposition. The incomplete remains at the second burial site could be interpreted similarly.

According to Grimble (1921), the Banaban practice of flexing the legs contrasted with the I-Kiribati practice of typically burying their dead with fully extended limbs. The body's position in the third burial site generally followed this Banaban practice. However, it differed from the traditional Banaban body orientation, which 'invariably lay with head east and feet west.' A femur bone taken from the third burial site was sent to G.C. Schofield, from the Department of Anatomy at Monash University, for extensive examination. He found that the bone was a right-sided femur of an adult female and was not Polynesian.

Although Lampert had limited time for his research on Banaba, he noted other sites that warranted further examination. One of these was behind Tabwewa village, on the high ground where several stone cairns existed as late as 1930. However, the land surface over most of this area had already been mined. No cairns were found in the untouched remnants. Of the constructed coastal terraces described by the Maude's in 1932, one called Te Tarine was still intact even though it had been severely disturbed by wartime gun emplacements and post-war European holiday campsites. Harry Maude had visited several land boundary markers and commented that they consisted of about 10-metre lengths of aligned stones situated at the corner of the various plots. Boundaries were recognised by sighting over the aligned stones towards certain prominent marked pinnacles of natural coral. In his conclusion, Lampert stated that Bob Williams, the BPC surveyor on the island, was still using these markers to determine land ownership in his time so that phosphate royalties could be correctly distributed amongst the Banaban landowners.

80. Te Aka site, headless skeleton in *mwenga* (B) area (R. Lampert 1965).

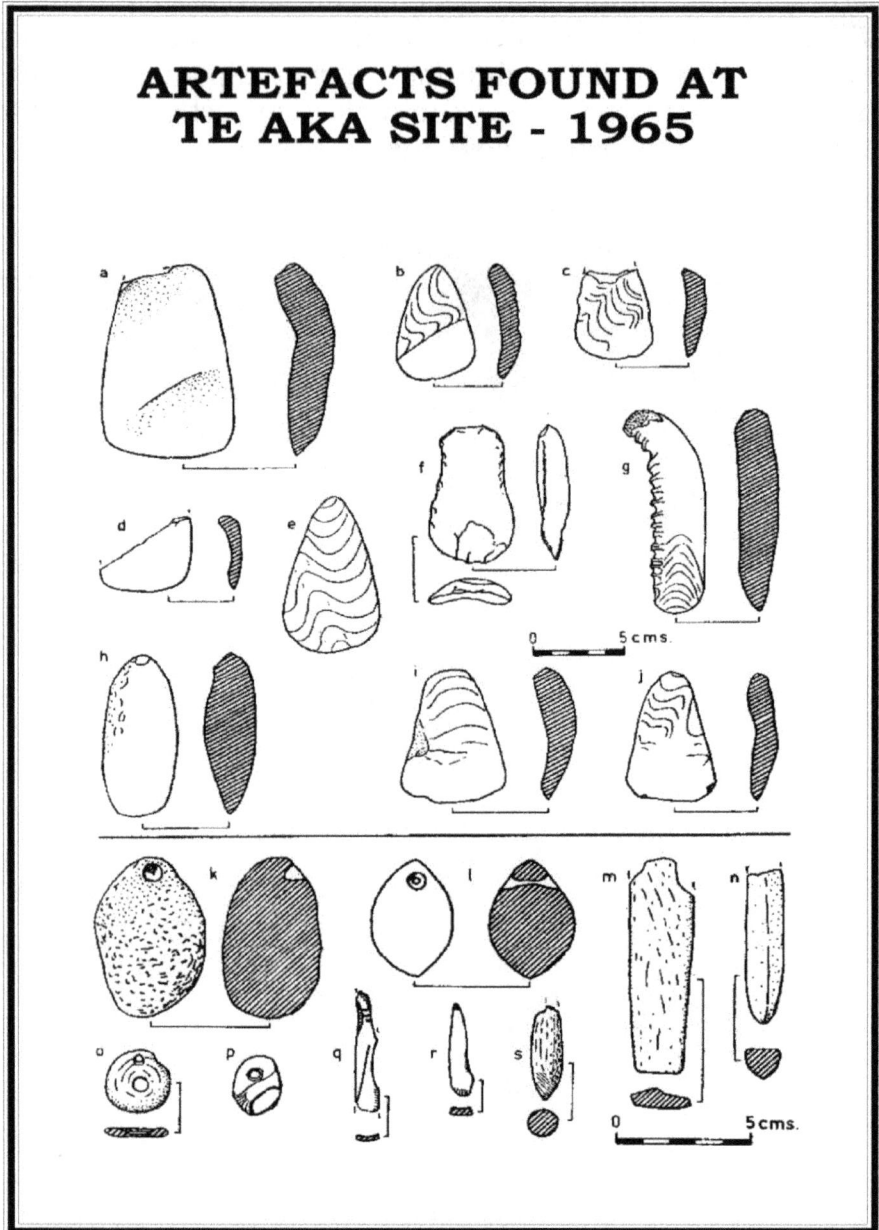

Figure: 4. 11. Artefacts found at the Te Aka site, 1965
(Source: R. Lampert).

30: THE LAST ARCHAEOLOGICAL DIG 1968

The following information was kindly supplied by Mrs Lorraine Thwaites, the wife of a BPC employee living on Banaba in 1968. Her story recounts the last archaeological investigation carried out on Banaba before the destruction of all Banaban village sites in the early 1970s. Mrs Thwaites assisted Lampert on his dig at Te Aka site in 1965 and learned some elementary archaeology. Before leaving Banaba, Lampert pointed out a site to her in the area of Tabwewa village, which he felt could be 'of interest under all that covering of cement.' A modern type of small building was on the site, which after Lampert's departure, was turned into a Scout hall.

In August 1968, Thwaites noticed that the phosphate mining was nearing the site Lampert had pointed out to her. She sought permission from the BPC Island Manager, Mr L. Withers, to look under the cement slab before the bulldozers cleared the site. Permission was granted for six weeks. Thwaites directed the investigation, assisted by Mrs Conrad, wife of another company employee. Conrad had no experience in archaeology and followed the instructions of Thwaites.

The site was reported to be that of a *maneaba* in Tabwewa village. Abitiai Tabore (about thirty-five years old) replaced Kaiekieki as the Banaban Representative in June 1968. Abitiai could not provide any information on the previous building or buildings. One Banaban, Tetebano, said he believed the site was once the house of a Banaban village elder or a trade store. With the surrounding area now entirely mined, the place looked very different from when Tetebano had lived on the island as a boy.

To the north was a wall, approximately 2.5 metres high, built of large pieces of coral rock and cement. On the other side of this wall was a water tank beside a large breadfruit tree. On the western side was a road between the site and the area which had already been mined. The site's eastern side rose steeply while the old village, remnants of which could still be seen in the undergrowth, stretched out towards the south, almost through to the district of Tabiang.

The area of cement which covered the site was removed with the help of the BPC staff. The retaining wall of the water tank was left, along with some other cement blocks on the eastern side, which constituted a wall of a recent building. Thwaites found it was hard work for two women with little experience to instruct working men 'how to remove cement very gently.' After they removed the cement, the women began to strip the area in horizontal sections.

Thwaites commented that as married women with commitments to children, homes, husbands and her son, she and her assistant could only spare time from 8.45 to 10.30 am to work on the site daily. As neither of them could drive, they depended on the island's bus service to travel to Tabwewa district, and then they had to walk about 400 metres up a steep grade to the site. At first, the BPC loaned the women a wheelbarrow and then provided a labourer to remove the soil that the women had scraped from the surface after removing the cement. The soil was placed in a pile so it could be sifted later. The soil varied in depth before it reached the coral shingle. The coral shingle was interspersed with rough phosphate rock and coral boulders, which in most cases, were permanent. They found that these large rocks and boulders were usually built around other large stones, perhaps to create a pillar to support a roof.

The women began working from a large flat coral rock which was in a vertical position aligned to part of the cement wall and which joined the retaining wall of the water tank in the north. As they were trowelling towards the west, four small post holes were revealed, consisting of four flat coral rocks in a vertical position, with a flat stone at the bottom. Pieces of old timber were in these holes, which Thwaites sent to Lampert for further examination. The post holes were approximately 1.2 metres apart and only 38 centimetres deep. In the same section, two ovens were uncovered. The only items of interest found when excavating the ovens were a few small shells, fish bones and two small beads. These items, along with a sample of the charcoal, were forwarded to Lampert. (These objects were in a Te Aka artefact collection held by ANU and returned to the clan in November 1997).

The next section was worked from the large flat coral rock towards the south. Two large postholes were uncovered in this section. At one time, they would have been complete pillars of stones, as many large stones were among the course coral shingle Thwaites assumed to be the floor level. Some of the rocks were permanent; other large stones had been added. Nothing other than small shells and fish bones were found along that side of the building.

Thwaites commented that there was evidence that a building, or buildings, had been there at one time. Both women, however, found it hard to determine what their findings meant. They began to trowel across the section to the western side. They discovered a long line of charcoal stretching towards the south. They trowelled to the bottom (natural phosphate level) of a section of this charcoal and found several beads, fish bones, and shells. They left the

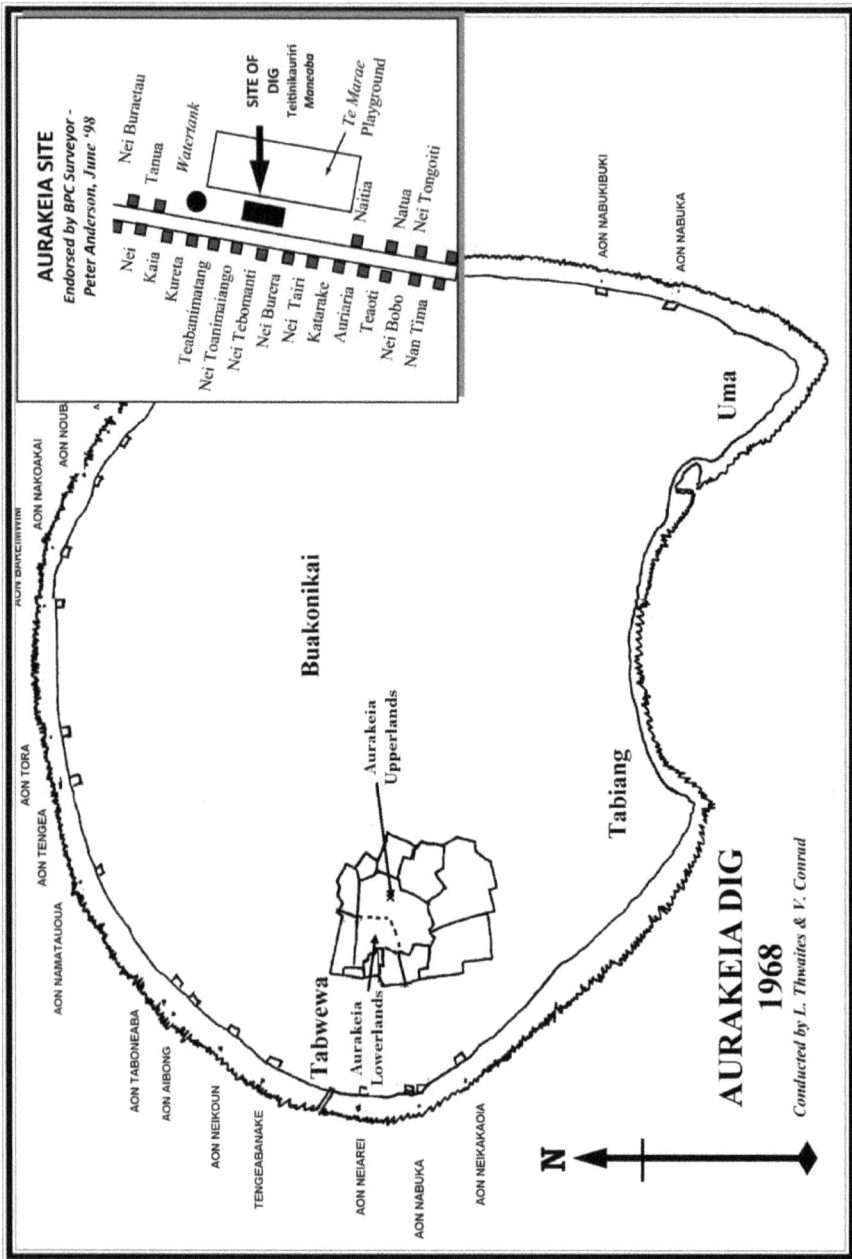

Figure: 4.12. Location of Aurakeia dig, Tabwewa Village 1968 (drawn by R.K. Sigrah).

81. Tabwewa Village (Miller Collection 1908-39).

cooking pits feeling it would be better to do them last, and continued through coarse coral shingle towards the west. In this section, they discovered a 'cairn', which consisted of a large heap of big stones. There was no indication that it was there from looking across the surface, as the coral shingle covering this area was quite deep at 20 centimetres. After working around this mound of rocks and stones for two mornings, they found one large human molar amongst the large pieces of rock.

The women then brushed all the dust off the cairn and took photographs to include with their report for Lampert. The women left the cairn intact and continued working towards the west. At a distance of 45 centimetres from the cairn, they uncovered one vertebra, although they had not reached the bottom of the disturbed soil. They discovered, at approximately 15 centimetres, an intact vertebra. The next part to come to the surface was a skull remains, but the women were puzzled to find the skull was facing east while

82. Tabwewa Dig Site (Thwaites Collection 1968).

the rest of the body was facing west. It was at this stage that Thwaites notified Withers, the BPC Island Manager, that they had discovered human remains.

The women ceased work for the day, roped off the area, and covered it with plastic sheeting. Thwaites asked R. Jorden, the company doctor, to look at the remains to help them identify from which part of the body some of the smaller bones came. He mentioned that three vertebrae from the neck were missing. The women used brushes on the fragile remains. The two shoulder blades were intact, but the women could not tell which way the arms had been placed as the bones were fragmented.

The following morning the Banaban Representative arrived at the site and took notes, presumably about the remains. The women were still working with a brush when they uncovered another part of the skeleton, this time the pelvis. Dr Jorden had told the women if they could completely uncover the pelvis and one femur, he could tell them whether the remains were male or female and the approximate age of the person.

By this stage, the women were working some afternoons, as their six weeks period was ending. They again packed up for the night, covering the exposed skeletal remains with plastic sheeting. However, some I-Kiribati workers visited the site while the women were absent and stood on the pelvis, causing it to break. The bones were fragile, and the women could not piece the pelvis together again, even trying hairspray in their vain attempt to mend the damage. Under the pelvis, the women found another skull, this time facing west.

Withers insisted that the women remove all remains from the site and place them in a box and have them delivered to his office. He asked the women not to return to the site. The women were very disappointed as much of their work was incomplete. They did not have time to excavate the cooking pits along the eastern side or the post holes. However, they completely excavated the cairn and found several interesting items. The following day the phosphate digging machines moved in, and no more 'finds' were reported by Thwaites.

Thwaites had uncovered three artefacts. Two she suggested were like the adzes taken from the Te Aka site by Lampert, but she was unsure. The other piece was of a stone that looked like it could have been worked. The women found several shark teeth, which they believed to be porpoise teeth, with holes drilled through some of each type of teeth. They also found numerous beads of different shapes and sizes and two pieces of stalactite. After finishing their work on the dig, the women made a drawing of the site, and its approximate location, with the assistance of Mr Williams (Figure 4.13). Thwaites noted other 'interesting spots' to investigate on the island, but the Island Manager did not grant permission to excavate these areas. Later she wrote to Lampert that these 'interesting spots' had been mined.

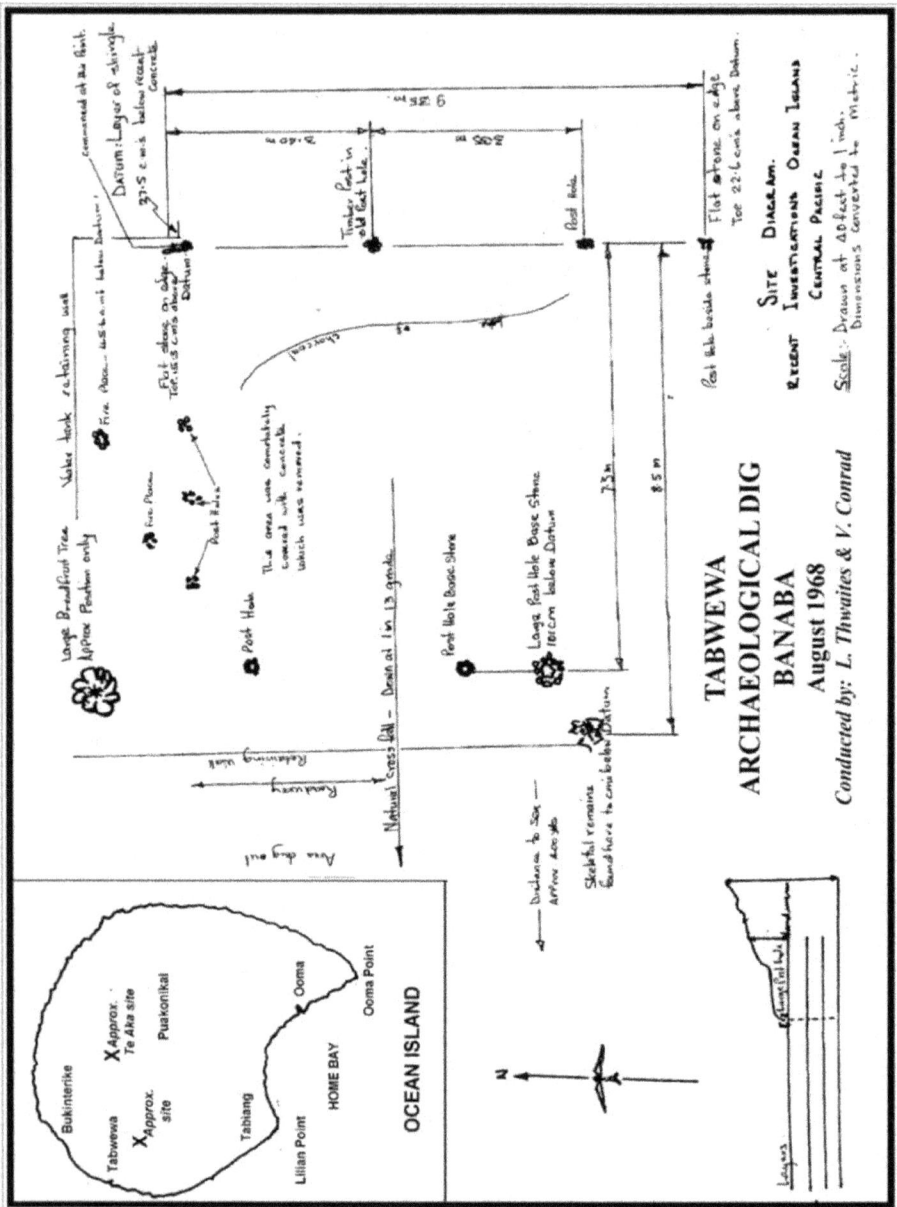

Figure: 4.13. Drawing of the archaeological dig of Tabwewa Village (Source: Williams and Thwaites, et al.).

Measurements of soil layers taken from cairn

Section 1	Coarse coral shingle	20.30cm
Section 2	Black earth	7.62cm
Section 3	Large pieces coral rock placed in a circular formation	10.18cm
Section 4	Coral shingle surrounded by large stones	20.30cm
Section 5	Bottom of the cairn. Large oval flat stone. Natural phosphate underneath the flat stone	

83. Tabwewa dig – 15-inch ruler alongside skull and another skull in the background (Thwaites Collection 1968).

Letter to Dr Lampert

Thwaites sent the following letter to Lampert from Victoria, Australia, on 20 November 1969. The letter followed her report on the Tabwewa dig she conducted on Banaba in 1968. She explained many of the problems she faced with the BPC management over her discovery of Banaban remains during her investigations. Her letter has been reproduced in its original form.

20th Nov 1969
To: Dr Ron Lampert, Department of Anthropology – Prehistory, A.N.U., Canberra, Australia.
Dear Ronald,
Reference Your Letter RL: IH, Cables 1st Oct. 1968 & 16th Oct 1968.
Basil, the children and I are about to leave Ocean Island permanently on the next "Triaster" (approx. 29th Nov). I haven't received a reply from you on my report of the excavation by Mrs Conrad and myself. As a matter of fact, the day I was about to post it the mail closed early without notice, so I gave the envelope to one of the passengers to post for me. This passenger was leaving permanently.
The thought had entered my head that the report may never have been posted so I am forwarding you another copy.
Things have changed on Ocean Island as you no doubt have read. Mrs Conrad (my companion in the excavation) and I were going along nicely. Of course, we had the usual curious onlookers, but things went quite smoothly until we found the skeletal remains. I notified the Island Manager, Mr L. Withers, who immediately changed from being helpful to someone I could not understand at all.
We were told that we were not to scrape any further until we had notified the Banaban Representative, Abitiai Tabore. This we went along with, but he would not give any explanation for his request.
The Banaban Representative visited the site and took notes down in a little booklet and left. Abitiai Tabore had been placed on Ocean Island by the Rabi Council to keep an eye on phosphate workings. Abitiai and Mr Withers then held a private meeting at Mr Withers B.P.C. Office to discuss the skeletal remains which Mrs Conrad and myself had found.

Mr Withers instructed us to lift the remains and place them in a special box which he had built in the Carpenter shop, and we were to deliver them to his Office. It was very difficult to lift the remains without them breaking up, and worse having to do it in a hurry.

At this stage, I insisted on knowing what all the fuss was about. After falling out completely with Mr Withers, and having also dragged my husband in to back me up, Mr Withers stated that there was not to be any more excavating on the Island. We were led to believe that the Banabans, in seeking independence through the United Nations, were using evidence against B.P.C., such as that the B.P.C. were 'Digging up Cemeterie's and spreading the dust of their ancestors over the ground of the U.K., Australia and New Zealand . The fact that we found these remains was just the evidence that Abitiai Tabore wanted. I know that this will sound rather stupid, but this was what happened.

Well, the remains were in the Manager's Office for a month or more. I approached Abitiai Tabore (Banaban Representative) and explained what I wanted the samples of the skeletons for. I made an appointment with him to discuss the whole affair, but he did not keep this appointment.

I don't know if you are aware that there are a number of Banabans from Rabi now working on the Island. One of them who is an 'old man' I got to know quite well, so I explained to him (Tetebano) how I had made an appointment with Abitiai Tabore to discuss the disposal of the bones, but that Abitiai had not kept this appointment. Tetebano possibly has some influence, because the next day Abitiai visited me to say I could have 'one bone' and that the rest were to be buried in the Banaban Cemetery. I asked may I have the skull to which he agreed. By the time I got it, just about everyone on the Island had had a 'peep and a poke in the box', which had broken the crumbling skull even more. Somehow, I could not get it through their thick skulls that these remains

327

were not buried just yesterday. I can't tell you how disappointed I am over the whole business.

I received your copy of 'An Archaeological Investigation on Ocean Island' for which many thanks. I wish I had received it earlier, as there are some figures and drawings in it which would have helped me. I think perhaps we could have tossed some things aside thinking they were not anything, when in fact they could have been. Also, your letter of instructions arrived too late. We had already taken the remains up. Mr Withers only gave us a couple of days to get ourselves off the site altogether. It seems so silly that he agreed in the first place that we could excavate, and then just because of the human remains, he changed completely. At one stage he asked me to change my mind about the bones being 'Human' and say they were that of a 'Pig.' I thought he was joking – but he wasn't.

Another thing Mr Withers was furious with me for sending a cable to you mentioning the 'find.' He said I should have asked his permission and that I was placing B.P.C. in a very difficult position. I know this will sound very queer to you. Now on a lighter note. Bob Williams has resigned and departed. He plans to settle in Western Australia. There are mainly young people with young families on the Island now. The Island itself really looks terrible now. The phosphate has been mined right along as far as the District Commissioner's and the school. The old Police lines have been moved to a new site. Must away now Ronald and hope to hear from you soon. Bill Gillespie said he would follow anything up for you if necessary. He was the fellow who took you down the caves. Signed: L.J. Thwaites, Victoria, Australia.

One of the skulls that Thwaites found was sent to Lampert at ANU, Canberra and arrived in a very poor state. To date, it has not been located. The other skull was put to rest and reburied in a secret location on Banaba by Abitiai, the Banaban Representative at the time.

31: PETER ANDERSON'S LEGACY

As the authors' work on this book drew to a close, even more questions began to emerge, especially about the later part of Banaban history and the deals struck between Banabans and British, Australians and New Zealanders over phosphate mining. Many of these questions have never been raised before, especially since most history books were written from an outsider's perspective. Rather than an inclusive approach, recent works by Katerina Teaiwa, Wolfgang Kempf, Elfriede Hermann, Jennifer Shennan, Tekenimatang and Makin Corrie, Julia B. Edwards and Jane McAdam address issues affecting Rabi and Banaba but have mostly tended to overlook the history of Te Aka as the original settlers. The complicated, unconscionable complicity of the British government over the mining of Banaba throughout the twentieth century has also been overlooked.

One man's name kept coming up in the authors' records: Peter Anderson. He had been a civil engineer and surveyor with the BPC on Banaba for nearly twenty-five years. Peter is one of the few company people who had played a significant role in liaising with Banabans to record their land titles. He first arrived on the island in 1939 and was evacuated along with other European company staff in 1942. He went into active service with the Australian Forces and

84. Raobeia (Ken) Sigrah meeting with Peter Anderson (King Collection 1998).

returned to Banaba in 1946, soon followed by his wife, Sue. Peter Anderson was the one European during the post-war period who knew virtually every square metre of the island. On his return, he was tasked to locate the bodies of six Europeans murdered by the Japanese during the war.

The other reason for meeting with Peter was his connection with the author's uncle, Kaiekieki Ueanimaraki (Sigrah), who had been a post-war Banaban Representative on Banaba and worked closely with Peter over the years. The Japanese had removed Kaiekieki and his family to Nauru during the war. They returned to Banaba when the Rabi Council appointed Kaiekieki as their Banaban Representative to keep an eye on Banaban interests and land holdings and to ensure that everything was done in line with the original agreements. Kaiekieki said that Peter knew everything there was to know about Banaban land matters, as well as about the BPC's role and its constant endeavours to take more land for mining. So, it was with much-excited anticipation that Peter Anderson and the authors finally met in Brisbane, Australia, in June 1998. The information he provided and the valuable Te Aka artefacts he has returned will be a lasting legacy to Banaba.

85. Te Aka artefacts and drilling tool from Peter Anderson Collection.

Over his years in the region, Peter collected many artefacts from Banaba and other Pacific Islands. He took Banaban artefacts mainly from the Te Aka site before any clearing of the area and before Dr Lampert's dig began. Peter explained that he found all his artefacts scattered over the ground surface in the dense undergrowth. Once bulldozers started to clear that surface, hundreds of ancient tools and relics were destroyed.

Items in Peter Anderson's Te Aka collection are as follows:

- Various types of fossilised shells
- Two adzes with wooden hafts (that Kaiekieki made for Peter from the island's *te itai* tree (see Photo 85)
- Various cooking implements used mainly for scraping coconuts
- *Te atau* – frigate bird fouling weight with sennit string attached
- *Te ati nimate* – coral pestle for pounding
- Various shells used for cultural ceremonies and purposes

Other Banaban items were given to Peter as gifts:

- *Te iriba* – Banaban fan 1941
- Wooden drilling tool – post-war
- *Te ramwane* – shoulder piece from Banaban dance costume 1941
- *Te waa* – a model of Banaban outrigger 1947

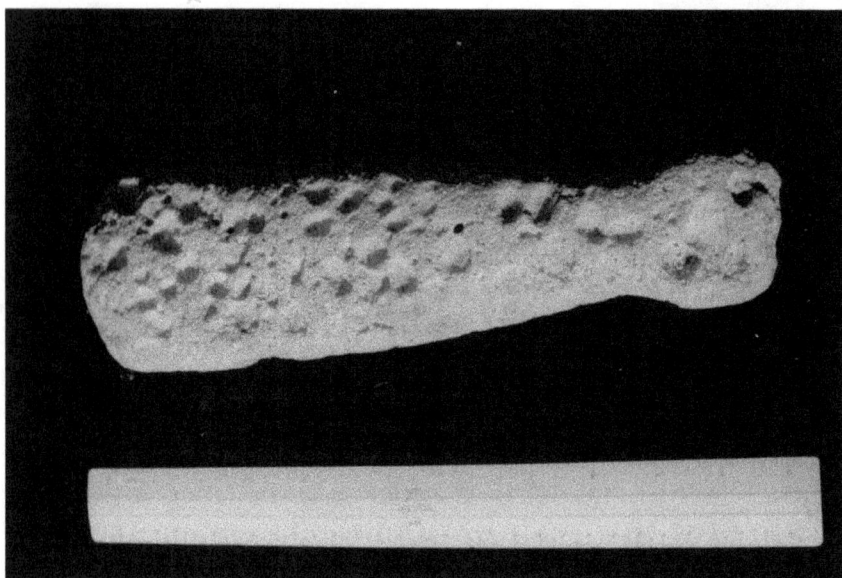

86. *Te ati ni mate* (coral pounder) found on the ground at Te Aka village by Peter Anderson (King Collection 1998).

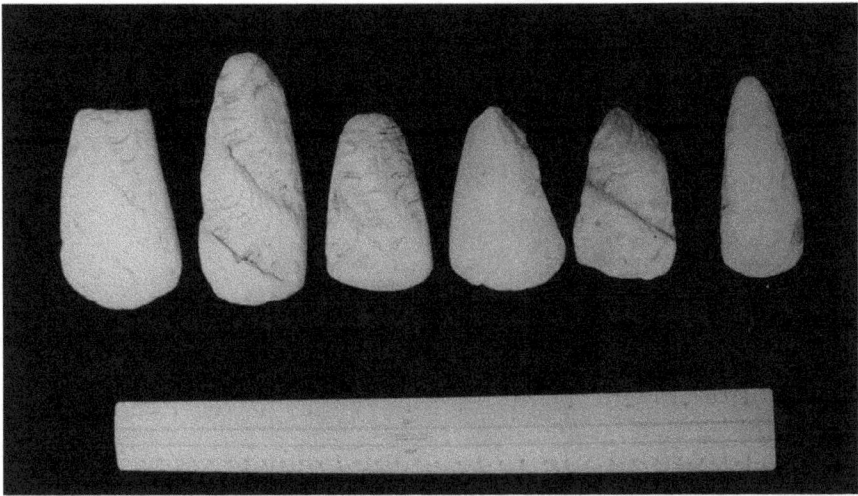

87. Various adzes found on the ground at Te Aka village by Peter Anderson (King Collection 1998).

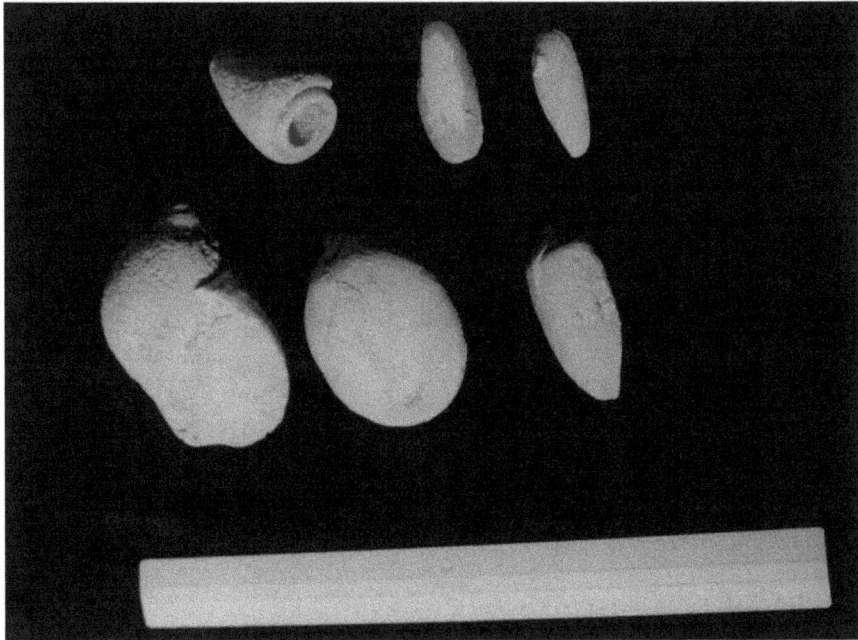

88. Fossilised shells found on the ground at Te Aka village by Peter Anderson (King Collection 1998).

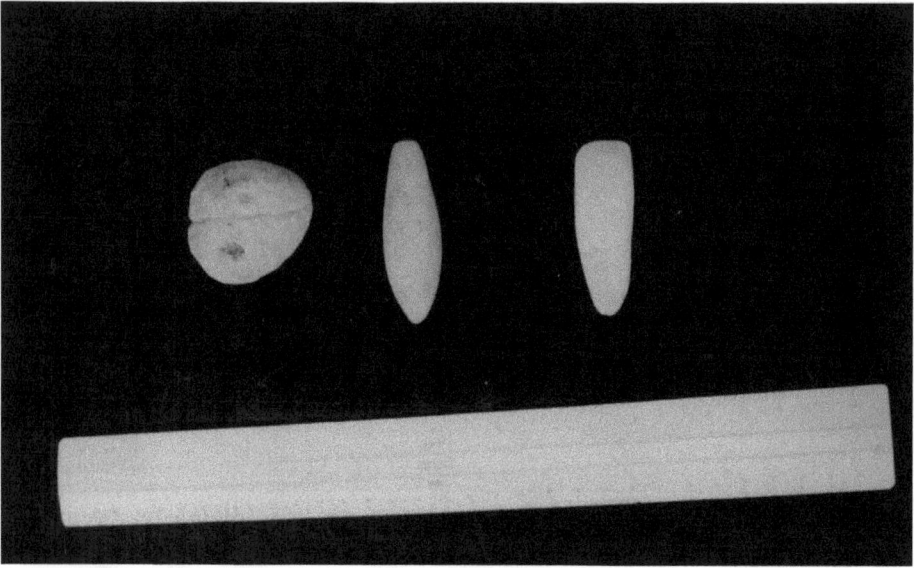

89. Back scratchers and *te atau* (half worked stone weight) found on the ground at Te Aka site by Peter Anderson (King Collection 1998).

90. *Te atau*, the fouling weight for frigate bird snaring, found on the ground of Te Aka site by Peter Anderson (King Collection 1998).

The following is the transcript of the interview with Peter in June 1998. The authors hope it will provide more information on events since mining began on Banaba in 1900.

Q. When were Banaban villages formed, and did this coincide with the arrival of the Europeans and phosphate mining?

A. Yes, after Albert Ellis arrived in 1900, Telfer Campbell, the Resident Commissioner for the Gilbert and Ellice Island Colony at the time, made a government order to form the villages. The mining company did not have the legal power to do this.

Q. Why did Toakira district and Te Aonoanne district merge into Buakonikai village?

A. The mining company did not like the crooked layout of the Banaban hamlets, especially through the northern region, which was the first area to be mined. They straightened the road through Te Aka area and moved the *maneaba* to a new site further eastward that would become known as Buakonikai.

Q. Today, Banabans are said to be I-Kiribati and just another island within the Kiribati group, yet all Banabans believe they have a separate identity from the I-Kiribati race. Do you think we are different?

A. Yes. Before the War, when we lived amongst the Banabans, everyone knew and accepted that the Banabans were different ... compared to the Gilbertese and Ellice workers. This was never an issue during all my years on the island.

Q. Do you believe the Japanese were responsible for destroying Banaban villages during World War II?

A. I did not return to Banaba until 1946 as I was involved in active service, but I do not believe the Japanese did. If the

335

Japanese destroyed any houses, it would have been for strategic purposes only.

Q. If the Japanese did not destroy the Banaban villages, who did?

A. This is a question you should ask the Australian Army Occupation Force.

Q. Do you believe that Banabans lost their land titles and holdings because of the BPC operations?

A. It is possible, but I cannot be sure.

Q. Can you tell us the approximate location of the land which you say was taken by the BPC that was not part of their mining agreement?

A. Mainly along the leased boundaries of the eastern mining area and in some cases, the central mining area.

Q. Where did you find the precious Banaban artefacts you are returning to our people?

A. Hundreds of them were scattered over the ground of the old Te Aka site. Lampert was digging for artefacts when there was no need. Unfortunately, with the surface clearing of the land by bulldozers before the commencement of mining, thousands of Banaban artefacts would have been destroyed. My Boy Scout troops helped me collect the artifacts I have in my collection.

Q. You have been given the description of Mrs Lorraine Thwaites Tabwewa village dig. Can you point out the actual site on our Tabwewa village map?

A. Yes, it was originally the Tabwewa *maneaba* building. Then after the war, with the return of the Banaban marking party, it was turned into their general store and later became the Scout Hall.

Q. We have heard many stories from former European staff about various 'haunted' places on the island. Do you know of any of these places?

A. Yes, certainly, my family and I have experienced it for ourselves. One place we know very well is along the road to Etani Banaba, where there is a huge raintree. A Chinese worker hung himself there, which always sent a chill through you when you had to drive through. Even our dog would cower in terror under the dashboard as we drove past.

Q. Was it you and Banaban representative Kaiekieki who initially rediscovered Te Aka village site?

A. Yes, I discovered an old foundation stone when I accidentally kicked it with my foot underneath heavy undergrowth. I then told Kaiekieki about it, and he told me the story about Te Aka and confirmed the site's location.

Q. Did you arrange to have mining stopped in this area and advise the Australian National University of the discovery of artefacts?

A. No, it was probably Mr Chapman (BPC manager) who was my immediate superior, as I had personally advised him of the discovery.

Q. In the UK court case, it was stated that the 'Phosphate and Trees Purchase Deeds' did not exist. Is this true?

A. Yes, they did exist – I have seen them.

Q. You were involved in locating the bodies of the murdered Europeans after World War II. Arthur Mercer's body was never found. What do you believe happened to him?

A. There were rumours that some Banaban friends unsuccessfully tried to help him escape by putting him to sea aboard one of their outrigger canoes. I believe he did escape. Before the War, Arthur, myself and a fellow BPC worker had discussed plans to make an escape from Banaba should the Japanese arrive. There was a large ocean-going outrigger that we planned to use it if we had to. Arthur was very experienced and skilled at sailing these outriggers. On my return to Banaba after the War, this large outrigger was missing, and the Banabans avoided discussing the canoe's disappearance.

Q. You mention that some Banabans returned to work as phosphate labourers on Banaba two years after the war in 1947. Where did they live?

A. A camp was set up for them with army tents behind Tabiang.

Q. Why were these Banabans unable to return to their old village sites and rebuild?

A. It would have been nothing to do with the BPC but a government matter.

Q. How do you think the company could get so much land in the old Toakira district for most of its plant and machinery?

A. That area was well and truly settled by the BPC before I began working on the island. I do not know how they obtained so much land in this area.

Q. What do you believe became of the sacred *bangota* and cairns from the Te Aka region?

A. This area was turned into the golf course between the Te Aka site and Bukinterike, where the new government headquarters were moved to and later destroyed by Japanese bombers in WWII. The golf course area was one of the last places to be mined before the BPC ceased operations in late November 1979.

32: A SAD STORY

At the end of the Pacific war, with exaggerated reports from the British government that all the villages on the island had been destroyed, the Banabans were gathered and taken to Rabi in Fiji, over 2,100 kilometres away. On 15 December 1945, seven hundred and three ill-treated and weary Banabans, of whom three hundred and eighteen were children, and three hundred Gilbertese arrived at their new home. Rabi was a freehold island owned by Levers Pacific Plantations Limited, which the British Government had bought at the beginning of the war using the Banabans' phosphate royalties. About 70 square kilometres in area, or ten times larger than Banaba, Rabi has a rugged interior that rises to 470 metres. Banabans found it hard to adapt to this strange new home.

Mining quickly resumed, and the BPC expanded its operations further across Banaba. The story of the next fifty years is a sad tale of two islands. On Rabi, the Banabans remained stuck, unable to return, and gradually assimilated to their new environment. Meanwhile, on Banaba, the BPC's authority and power were untrammelled, even though in 1947, they signed a new mining agreement with landowners. The 1950s and 1960s were halcyon years as royalties flowed to the Banabans back on Rabi. However, by the 1970s, the Rabi Council of Leaders was angry and investigated a now-famous court case against the British government over

91. BPC facilities Home Bay during the peak of mining (R. Anderson Collection 1967).

92. View of Home Bay seventeen years after mining ceased (S. King Collection 1997).

mining, rehabilitation, royalties and later over the question of sovereignty and independence. This also coincided with the independence of Tuvalu and Kiribati. Although Banaba is now under the nation of Kiribati, Banabans reoccupied their homeland after mining ceased in 1979 and BPC left the island.

After a twenty-year interregnum in 1997, a "Homecoming" group went from Rabi to Banaba. Today a small community maintains a presence. This chapter addresses these issues and brings the story to the present.

1947 Agreement

When mining resumed, Banabans had been granted permission to have a representative on the island to ensure there would be no encroachment onto Banaban lands that were not part of the current lease agreements. The representative's official role was to represent and protect the interests of the Banaban landowners who had been moved to Rabi. Over this post-war period from 1945 to 1979, five Banaban men undertook this vital role; their names are listed in order of their engagements: Kabanti, Kaiekieki, Abitiai, Taungea, and Kirite. It proved a difficult position as this lone Banaban liaised with the BPC and the GEIC, which had all the backing of the British government.

In 1947, a new agreement over mining leases replaced the agreements of 1913 and 1931. The new agreement covered an extraordinary area, virtually allowing the BPC to mine most of the island's phosphate deposits. This agreement disadvantaged the Banabans, who unwittingly agreed to a level of royalties set at a 1947 rate that could not be changed. It was well below the current world rate and remained in place for thirty-two years until mining ceased. With hindsight, we can see that the Banabans were tenacious negotiators but had limited business, legal or mining knowledge.

The 1950s and 1960s on Rabi

However, life was good as royalties flowed to the exiled community on Rabi. Based on the lands on Banaba that had been mined, individual landholders had a high level of access to disposable income on a principle established by Banaban elders that royalties would continue to be paid even though the actual land had been extinguished. In the 1950s and 1960s, as the road was built from Nuku to Uma, bicycles, motorcycles, cars, trucks, and buses began to appear. Home and village generators and refrigerators were installed. Homes had western-style furniture and imported timber frame houses, later, concrete-block became more common. A Co-Operative Society began, copra was being exported to Suva, and a new wharf was constructed at Nuku. Churches and *maneaba* were built in each village. Queen Elizabeth Hall, including a picture theatre and Council chambers, were built in Nuku. The original Lever Bros Managers House was converted into the official Council Guesthouse. The first schools were the Banaban School at Nuku and the Buakonikai Primary School. The Banaban High School opened in the 1970s together with Tabiang Primary School. Funds were readily available for further education scholarships and for the Banaban dancing groups to perform in Fiji and even overseas to Australia and the Pacific Festival of Arts. Transport to the Fiji mainland improved with the purchase of inter-island shipping. Funds also allowed for the purchase of a prominent headquarters in Pratt Street, Suva, known as Banaba House. Community spirit was enhanced by the annual December 15th commemoration, initially a beauty contest but changed into a week-long, inter-village sporting and cultural competition. The Banabans never realised the impact the cessation of mining would have, thinking that the annual interest on A$10 million dollars was a lot of money.

The Fiji government believed that the Banabans on Rabi had plenty of money, especially with respect to other Fijians. However, as one of the past Banaban Administrators said, "Banabans have no idea where their money comes from. They just think it's an endless pit". The Banabans, in the 1970s, composed a song recalling how they wished they had known the value of money as far back as when Albert Ellis arrived in 1900. Money had never been part of a Banaban's culture, and they have learned the hard way how to manage monetary affairs in a cutthroat business world. One of the major problems in the 1950s and 1960s was that Banabans had to overcome the cost and reliance on imported food. Since moving to Rabi, they had to adapt to new skills and life in a new environment. The Banabans were now relying increasingly on shopping at the Banaban-owned Cooperative and cans of tinned tuna and fish (ironically caught on a nearby Pacific Island and canned in China).

93. Banabans seeking justice in UK Courts (Source unknown) 1975.

While visitors to Rabi in the 1970s were impressed with the community spirit and the charm of the Banaban at people, they were also greatly alarmed by the amount of processed foods the Banabans were eating. By the 1980s, not much was heard of the Banabans and life on Rabi or Banaba. Visitors to Rabi decreased, and contact with the outside world diminished.

UK Court Case

After 221 days and 10,000 documents had been examined in the British High Court, the judge finally handed down his verdict on the Banaban case. He found that the BPC had failed to keep their promise to replant the Banaban's land, and the Banabans should get damages, but just how much he could not bring himself to say. He instructed the Banabans to reach a settlement with the British Phosphate Commission. For the failure to restore the ravaged land, he said, "The damages shall not be token, not minimal, but not large." He discounted the argument that mined land must be legally restored, adding, "However potent such arguments may be in political or social fields, they cannot affect the law of contract."

The second case on the breach of trust issue was finely balanced and could have gone either way. Judge Megarry eventually decided the British Government was not, in fact, trustees for the Banabans. The British were, therefore, not technically liable for the injustices committed in their name. The judge concluded with a most unusual recommendation:

> "I am powerless to give the plaintiff any relief, but in litigation against the Crown, I think a judge must direct attention to a wrong that he cannot right and leave it to the Crown to do what it considers proper. The Crown is traditionally the fountain of justice, and justice is not confined to what is enforceable in the court. The question is not whether the Banaban should succeed as a matter of fairness or ethics or morality. I have no jurisdiction to make an award just because I conclude they have a raw deal" (Binder 1977:165).

During the court case, the Banabans took their cause to a dramatic and physical level when the Banaban Elders on Rabi decided to send 100 young men from Rabi to the homeland to regain the island and halt mining. The arrival of the Banaban contingent on the island had forced the BPC and GEIC government's hand by insisting that their group be permitted to land. Until this period, any Banabans trying to visit their homeland had to have written approval from the GEIC. After reluctantly being given permission to land the Banabans received a 'cool reception' from BPC officials and staff who had been told by management not to mix with the 'Banaban troublemakers' (Lennon 1992).

94. Tabonaba, (Island Point), Banaban camp 1975 (Source: Go Tell the Judge, BBC).

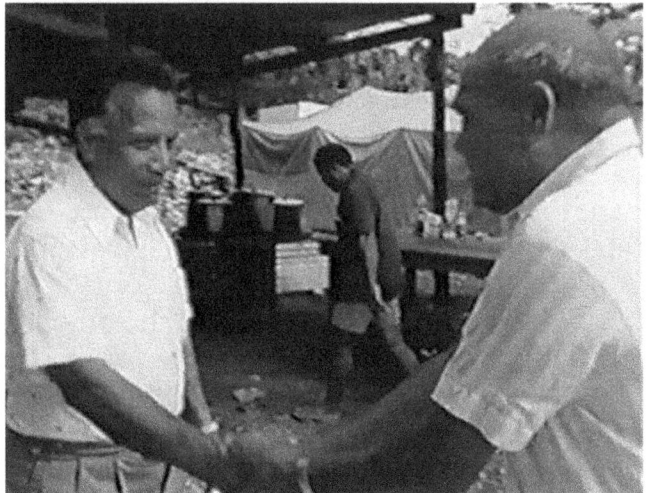

95. Tito Rotan greeting Tito Christopher at Tabonaba camp 1997 (Source: Go Tell the Judge, BBC).

The Banabans began to set up a camp behind the previous site of Uma village on the southeast coast in an area known as Tabonaba, meaning 'Island Point'. Tensions on the island grew as the BPC and GEIC brought in more I-Kiribati (Gilbertese) to act as local Island police and build up the police presence on the island. During this period, the BPC began doubling their production levels while its team of lawyers countered the Banaban's legal actions in London.

By 1979, with court proceedings still, underway, another contingent was sent from Rabi to reinforce the Banaban numbers on the homeland. The mood of the Banabans by this stage had become more defiant and radical in terms of their usually well-mannered and gentle nature. Elders back on Rabi made a monumental decision to send this new contingent of young Banabans prepared to 'die for the cause'. As tensions grew, these young Banabans began to be arrested and beaten. The skirmishes resulted in a fatal injury to Tabare Biara, aged twenty-one years, who was struck by a tear gas canister and hit over the head with a baton. He became paralysed and died of brain damage a few months later. The Ellice workers with the BPC would not involve themselves in these actions and assisted Banabans during this time of conflict. This tension fuelled the Banabans more, and they planned a protest march targeted at the BPC management to stop mining. Only hours before the scheduled march, word came through from Ellice Island labourers that the I-Kiribati police had been issued side-arms and given orders to 'shoot to kill'. It was only after Elders on Rabi received this news, and after much consideration, they issued instructions for their people to 'stand down' (Teai 1997). The thought of their beloved homeland becoming a violent battleground was abhorrent to them.

Note: Ken Sigrah was 23 years old and one of the young men in the first contingent. He was arrested with other Banabans during the skirmish when Tabare Biara was mortally wounded and ended up imprisoned in a jail cell on his homeland.

The Banabans court case against the British Government and the British Phosphate Commission (BPC) finally ended in 1979. It became known as one of the most protracted court cases in UK history. In their case against the British Phosphate Commissioners for their failure to replant their island, the Banabans were awarded derisory damages of UK£9,000 and made to pay their own court costs, which amounted to over UK£300,000. As a result of political pressure, the British Phosphate Commission offered UK£780,000, which the Banabans knew was insufficient and would not provide enough funds for restoring their island.

In their other action against the British Government for breach of trust, the Banabans lost. The judge held that even though they had been given a 'raw deal', in law, there was nothing that he could do to help them. However, he made it plain that there were grave breaches of government trust, which his court was powerless to remedy. He made an unprecedented appeal to the British Government to act accordingly. As a result of press and radio coverage in the UK culminating in the BBC television program, "Go Tell it to the Judge", and political and parliamentary pressure, the British Government offered (provided the Banabans did not appeal their action against the Crown) to set up a trust fund to produce a pension for the Banaban community. They insisted that the capital, which amounted to UK£6.5 million (A$10 million), be taken from the BPC reserves and put into a trust fund with only the interest paid to the Banabans. After four years of 'holding out', thinking the settlement was unfair, the A$10 million was accepted.

Independence for Kiribati and Rabi

While the legal proceedings were still underway in London, the Banabans took up another major challenge that would see them knocking on the doors of the United Nations, seeking separation from the GEIC. The British planned to dissolve the GEIC and return sovereignty to the people under two new Island nations of Kiribati for the former Gilbert Islands and Tuvalu for the Ellice Islands. By 1970 the Banabans had realised that the British government had no intentions of looking after their affairs. Frustrated by decades of constant disputes over their land leases back on Banaba and inadequate royalties, in January 1974, the Banabans extended their fight for justice by lodging a petition to the British Government for the legal separation of Ocean Island (Banaba) from Gilbert and Ellice Islands Colony. Their quest for independence fell on deaf ears as the British once again washed their hands of the Banaban issue and declared they were handing over responsibility to the newly formed GEIC Council of Ministers. The Council of Ministers unsurprisingly concluded that Banaba was an integral part of the Gilbert Islands and added that it would oppose separation and independence for Banaba then or in the future.

In November 1979, the last shipment of phosphate left Banaba, and this sad phase of Banaban history finally came to an end. At the breaking up of the GEIC, the British had decided to excise Banaba and include it in the new nation of Kiribati.

Note: The British were careful to include in the Kiribati Constitution a protective clause that stated that the UK Privy Council, *"Has jurisdiction to hear appeals from any High Court decision involving the interpretation of the Constitution where application to the High Court was made on the basis of contravention of the rights of any Banaban or of the Rabi Council under Chapter III or IX of the Constitution."*

Cessation of mining

With public opinion mounting, the BPC's last phosphate

shipment left Banaba's shores. As a final parting gesture and to show their appreciation to the newly emerging Kiribati nation, BPC donated all removable fittings and equipment to the Kiribati government (Teai 1997). This action resulted in further tension between Banabans and the new Kiribati government. BPC may have done the honourable thing with this gesture, but in reality, it was avoiding the cost of removing their mining machinery, plant and industrial debris, saving them millions of dollars in rehabilitation or removal of asbestos. Banabans, after seeing the island's hospital completely stripped bare and not wanting to hand over everything to the Kiribati government, who were sending the spoils to other islands throughout the Kiribati group, began to destroy various items, including medical equipment, medicines and machinery. (Note: Except for the

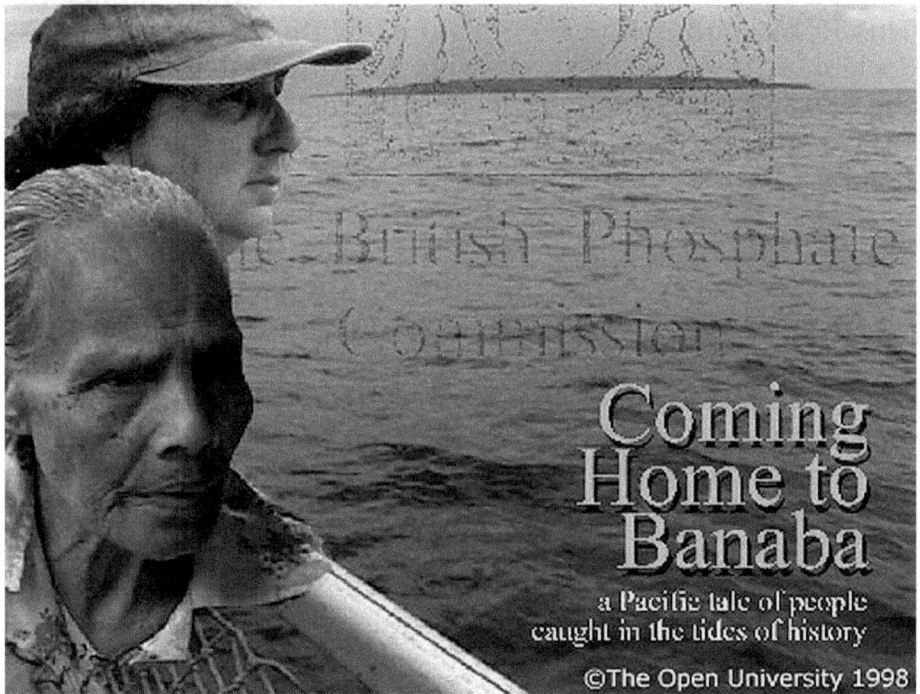

96. Coming Home to Banaba filmed during Homecoming 1998 (J. Cooper, BBC, OU, UK).

large operating light in the theatre, which had refused to budge!) The landscape at the end of mining was catastrophic as the BPC's accelerated mining production towards the end had proved very effective as the only unmined area was the ground under the buildings they had left behind. Even along the island's roadways, mining had encroached right to the edge of the bitumen, and it was dangerous to wander away from these thoroughfares. The island was now covered with razor-sharp coral pinnacles, in some areas reaching a depth of up to 18 metres.

Homecoming

In July 1997, three chartered yachts headed towards Banaba carrying the I-Matang descendants of mining families and Banabans keen to place their feet again on their homeland. This Homecoming had been planned by the Banaban Heritage Society, organised by Stacey King. The aim was to investigate the state of the island some twenty years after mining had ceased and to raise public awareness for the plight of the Banabans, who now mainly resided in Fiji and purely for nostalgic reasons, to visit the sites where they and their families had lived and worked. The Banabans, especially the elders on the trip, were returning to the land of their birth. While others were visiting their homeland for the first time. This was the first return for Banaban elders to the island from which they had been forcibly removed by the Japanese and exiled by the British. The visit, in three groups, lasted a week and included two weeks staying with the Banaban community back in Fiji. The outcome of this adventure, other than the emotional and spiritual thrill of standing on Banaba itself, was a BBC documentary, "Coming Home to Banaba", produced by Jeremy Cooper, various ABC radio interviews taken on Rabi, Fiji, and multiple media reports in Fiji. The significant impact was the televising of the story throughout the UK, Europe, and Japan, raising global awareness of the environmental, political and cultural situation on Banaba.

Uncertain Future

After four years of holding out against the offered A$10 million UK court settlement and the various conditions attached, Banabans finally caved in under financial pressure. Today the Banaban people find themselves in a grim situation. The Trust Fund was created without proper policies that would guarantee the security for the real monetary value of investments or take into account the rate of inflation over the years that would follow. By 2000, the interest was just enough to provide for all Banabans and the ongoing costs of maintaining and administrating communities on both Rabi and Banaba. Today more than forty years after the cessation

97. Hospital theatre light, the only removable fitting left behind by the Kiribati government in 1979 (S. King collection 1997).

of mining on Banaba, nothing has been done to rehabilitate the island. On Banaba, the Banabans live amongst the crumbling ruins left behind by the BPC. Lack of water supply during persistent droughts is a major problem.

During a visit to Banaba in 1997, the population was 500, but today it has dropped to around 350. There is no regular shipping to the island, no airstrip, and except for the fish stock which the islands' surrounding reefs and waters provide, most food is imported. When rain falls, Banaba can produce green vegetables and crops. Today only a handful of food trees remain, not enough to sustain the Island's community as it did over the centuries.

In 2002, the Banaban Trust Fund, which at one stage had reached the impressive figure of A$15 million, had declined and was no longer meeting the annual operating budget of around A$300,000 per year. Some additional funds were generated by Fiji Government grants and profits from business. In a UNESCO Report in 2002, Hindmarsh noted the interest was not a lot of money when the Banabans were expected to administer two islands 2,100 kilometres apart, and a cost of around A$14,000 per month just to maintain public works for the Banabans currently resettled back on Banaba. Over the past years, both islands' financial and physical situation has deteriorated rapidly. With no mining rehabilitation on Banaba, no public works, maintenance, or development, survival for the Banabans on Banaba is becoming increasingly difficult. It is also challenging to channel aid to Banaba or Rabi as it must go through the two governments involved. Fiji for Rabi based projects, and Kiribati for those on Banaba. When approaches have been made in the past, for example, direct to the Australian government, the sovereignty of the Banabans proved to be a major hurdle, blocking any direct approach to the respective governments.

Uncertain times lie ahead. Between 1945 and 1979 was a tragic period marked by a campaign for a fair deal on royalties, a call to end mining, and a post-war struggle while adjusting to life on a new island home - Rabi. The next forty-year period, 1979 to 2019, was a period of adjustment as royalty monies ceased. Banabans had to survive on decreasing dividends from their Trust Fund while being increasingly isolated on Rabi, within Fiji, far from Kiribati and expensively separated from the Banaban homeland. Banabans on both Rabi and Banaba have been forced back to a subsistence lifestyle and living off the land, with limited funds for development, education and health. This, indeed, has been a sad story.

98. Asbestos ridden buildings now reduced to rusting steel (S. King collection 1997).

99. Young Banaban generation on Rabi performing traditional dance at 15 December Celebrations (A. Quanchi 2008).

33: TO THE NEXT GENERATION

The authors hope through this book that future Banaban generations and general readers and scholars will understand and appreciate the complexities of the culture and history of Banaba. Much of the information they gathered was accumulated from knowledge passed on in the verbal form for generations by Banaban Elders, along with their personal written records dating back as far as 1923. This information is supported by photographs and documents kept in private collections by early phosphate pioneers and their families. How could the Banabans ever have foreseen that the white rock under their feet would be the very reason for the devastation of their island?

The authors hope the next generation acknowledges that Banabans lived on Banaba after the war. They included a handful of labourers working for the BPC, the official representative appointed by the Rabi Council of Elders, and a small group that had approval from the Rabi Council of Elders and BPC. They lived in an isolated camp called Tabonaba, meaning 'Island Point' behind the old Uma village site. After the cessation of mining in 1979, volunteers with Rabi Council of Leaders (RCL) approval gradually repopulated the island, and three hundred people moved from Rabi to uphold the Banaban presence on the homeland (today, the RCL have set a population limit of approximately 300). Due to distance and lack of a direct sea and air link, there is little movement between Rabi and Banaba. The Kiribati government are only providing minimal infrastructure and financial support. The Banabans as a community on Banaba are struggling, with only ten percent (60 hectares) of the island left unmined. While there is a church, a primary school, a basic store, and an administration presence from Kiribati, the people now occupy old asbestos mining buildings instead of their traditional sites. The promised rehabilitation has not occurred, which is an issue the next generation needs to address.

A further complication today is that of the original settlers sent to Rabi in 1945, one-third of the arrivals were I-Kiribati which means that to be a "Banaban" in modern times is confused and contested because of intermarriage and adoption. Through all this, Banabans throughout the world struggle to maintain their identity and be proud of the heritage of their homeland.

The authors also hope this book will be a voice for Banaban people everywhere. They want to inspire young Banabans to uphold their rich culture and traditions for future generations. The Banabans face many social and financial problems now that Rabi and Banaba fall under the jurisdiction of two separate Pacific nations - Fiji and Kiribati. Australia, New Zealand and Britain also need to be implicated in any future Court proceedings. It is up to all Banabans to ensure they uphold their elders' teachings as the new generations merge with modern western-style society. The evolution of the people on Rabi to lean more towards Fijian culture is perhaps inevitable, just as the Banabans were influenced by Kiribati culture after the arrival of Nei Anginimaeao from Beru in the late seventeenth century. The threat of continued assimilation is real if Banabans on Banaba cannot resist incursions and influences from Kiribati or if Banabans on Rabi are not able to resist influences from

Fiji and elsewhere. A pessimistic approach suggests it is not inconceivable that "Banaban" as an identity may disappear. However positively, the authors assert that Banaban identity will indeed remain and strengthen. There will always be Banabans.

100. Future Banaban generations, Rabi, Fiji (S. King collection 2003).

This book is the first to record and express the past from a Banaban perspective. The authors have covered important issues that have great cultural significance for Banabans today and future generations. They hope that the questions raised here will increase awareness of issues embedded deep in the hearts of the community's beloved elders and the whole global Banaban community. Much has been endured in the struggle to save Banaban identity and homeland. This book is for future generations.

GLOSSARY

I-Kiribati	English
A-nte Rua-rua	below the pit
aba	land
aba ni butirake	land of the asking
abo	fishing line
ae	that
aii	coconut crab
aika	which were
Aka	first hamlet
ana	belonging to
anti	spirits
anti n aomata	half human, half spirit
anti ni mate	pounder made of wood or coral, used for preparing pandanus
ao	and
Ao kabiram te ba	and of oil for your anointing
Ao kanam te amarake	and your right to partake of the food
Ao kanam te ika te urua	and your right to eat the stranded fish (travelly)
Ao katikani koran aon te aba	and of drawing the measuring cord across the land
Ao mwaem te kaue	and your right to garland the stranger who arrives
Ao ruoiam	and your right to direct the *rouia*
Ao taekan aon te aba	and to decide on land matters within your boundary
Arana am Kainga!	Name your hamlet!
ati ni mate	pounder made of wood or coral,

	originally used as a weapon, now used for pounding pandanus leaves
atia	things that have been done
Auriaria te Tabu	Auriaria the Holy
ba arom ni bane aikai a bon tiku iroun teuaei	for all these your customary rights indeed remain with this man
ba e uotia ba te mane	for he takes them, being a male
bakarerenteiti	the lightning strike
bana	boxing gloves, woven from coconut sinnet with spikes on knuckles
Banaba	land of rock
bangabanga	water cave
bangota	ancestral shrine
baobao	tall wooden frames for frigate birds to sit on
bareaka	canoe shed
bata	sleeping house
batere	cultural dancing
bau	headpiece worn for Banaban dancing
baurua	large ocean-going outrigger canoe
binobino	coconut shell water containers
bonito	skip jack tuna
boti	sitting place in the *maneaba*
bua	lost
buki	Kiribati style of swaying hip dance
Bukiniwae	forerunner clan for the elder clans
bunna	sacred garland made of certain leaves
bure	belt made of plaited pandanus leaf and shells, worn for Banaban dancing
Burita	war canoe of te Aka clan

butirake	asking of special favours for social standing or to inherit land
butu	thumb thrust stance in Banaban boxing
bwaa	coconut oil
bwaai	things
bwaene	plaited coconut leaf baskets
E maoto naona!	His waves have broken!
Ea baka karaun Nei Kabuta!	Kabuta's rain has fallen! (an idiom for 'Life is back again!')
enta	neckpiece with amulet, worn for Banaban dancing
fatele	Tuvaluan style of dance
I bukin	because of
I nanora	in our hearts
I-Matang	European
ibi	hardwood tree, native to Banaba
ikabuti	smaller fishing scoop for catching schools of sardines along the seashore
inaki	sitting places in the *maneaba*
Inaki ni Buiniwae	sitting place of the forerunner, right-hand man to the elder
Inaki ni Karimoa	sitting place of the eldest
iroura	us
itau ni Banaba	Banaban boxing
Itimoa	name of canoe of protection for te Aka clan
itimoa	first lightning
itinikarawa	heavenly lightning
kabwane eitei	frigate bird snaring
kaekeko	acting on behalf of an elder
kai ni katua	oblong shaped hand throwing weapon for men made of wood or rock, now used as a weight for the game of *katua*

kai-ni-karemotu	tossing stick used by women in the game of *karemotu*
kaimatoa	Kiribati style of set pattern dance
kain roa	fishing pole
kainga	hamlet consisting of family dwellings
kaitau	special word of thanks
kakii	neckpiece made from human hair, worn for Banaban dancing
kakoaki	bleaching process
kakoko	first shoot of the coconut leaf
kakuri	Kiribati game
kamakama	sea crabs
kaneati	stalactite fishing hook
kaoti n Engiran	uprising of England
kaoti-n aine	woman's arrival
karanga	war spear dance
karanga are e uarereke	short stick war dance
karemotu	tossing the stick game
karetika	Kiribati style of throwing of *babai* plant stems
Karia	lowland in Tabwewa district
Karia te ang	waiting for the wind
Karietadestroy	upland in Tabwewa district
karo ten	style of braiding used especially for fishing lines
katabara	open stance in Banaban boxing
Katea rikim?	What is your genealogy?
kati	Kiribati game of bow and arrow shooting
katua	putting the weight game
kaunga	slave
kaunrabata	Kiribati style of men's wrestling
kauoua n raeaki	second partitioning of Banaba
kauti	rituals to evoke magic

362

kibena	fishing scoop net for catching flying fish
koro karewe	cutting coconut toddy
kouti-n aine	small mat worn around the shoulders
kua	porpoise
kunkun	*Terminalia catappa*, wild almond
mai	Breadfruit
mai	from
maie ni kauti	dancing magic ritual
makauro	hermit crab
malo	Polynesian word meaning a short skirt of leaves strung around the hips
manai	land crab
manai	land crab
maneaba	traditional Banaban community meeting house
mangko ni Banaba	wild mango
mao	*Scaevola kownigi*, bushy shrub found amongst rocks around the shoreline
mata-bou	a new face or eyes
matoa	Continuous or strong
maunei	dried treated grass skirt, worn for Banaban dancing (on Rabi)
motu	coconut markers used in the game of *karemotu*
mwemweneitei	upward flight of the frigate bird
mwenga	House
Na Areau	male spider god
Na Tabakea	male turtle god
naki toki	forever, non-stop
nati-n-atei	adopted child
nei tere	head marker in the *karemotu* game

Nei Tituabine	female stingray god
ngea	*Pemphis acifula*, coastal bloodwood useful for tool and weapon making
ni	for
non	*Morinda citrifolia*, commonly called Noni throughout the Pacific
oon tabakea	a certain species of turtle
oreano	Kiriabati style of ball game
ramwane	crosspiece ornament for men, worn for Banaban dancing
ren	*Tournefortia argentea*, plant
riri	dried coconut leaf skirt, worn for Banaban dancing
roa ati	tuna pole fishing
rouia	Kiribati sitting dance
tabakea	a certain species of turtle (also name of Kiribati totem)
tabo ni kauti	private terrace for magic ritual
Tabo-n te Rengerenge	edge of the cliff
tabunea	performing of sorcery
Taeka	word
tairua	foreigners or outsiders
taitai	tattooing
takataka	a piece of coconut
tangiraki	beloved
tani Bekan	pagans
tani Kiritian	Christians
tatae	fishing for flying fish
te	the
te Aonoanne	That place! (another name of te Aka adopted by newcomers to Banaba)
te ati ni kana	Kiribati custom of hair cutting and offering ceremony

te be	cloth wrapped around lower half of body, also known throughout the Pacific as a sarong or lava lava
te Burita	an enchanted place in te Aonoanne district
te moa n raeaki	the first partitioning
te moa ni kainga	the first hamlet
te rii ni Banaba	the backbone of Banaba
te waa	outrigger canoe
Te wa-ni-Kaiowa	the canoe that accompanies the two boarding canoes from the Karia clan
Te Wantieke I	canoe, which takes out the elder who boards foreign vessels from the Karieta clan
Te Wantieke II	the other canoe, which takes out the elder who boards foreign vessels from the Karia clan
tei	uphold
Te itai	*Calophyllum inophyllum*, also known as the ship tree by the te Aka people
Tera taum?	What is your family's inherited role?
tia itau	boxer
tia kabo	goodbye
tibu	grandmother or grandfather
tibu babako	great-great-great-grandmother or great-great-great-grandfather
tibu mamanu	great-great-grandmother or great-great-grandfather
tibu taratara	great-great-great-great-grandmother or great-great-great-great-grandfather
tibu toru	great-grandmother or great-grandfather

tie	Kiribati style of swinging game
tiribenu	shadow smash stance in Banaban boxing, used by women only
toa ma I-matang	foreign giant or giant from Matang
Toka ni Mane	seat of the man
tou	pandanus fruit
uea	king or high chief
uma	home stance, in Banaban boxing
uma n anti	spirit house
uma n roronga	young man's sleeping quarters
uma n teinako	house for menstruating women
uma ni kanaiai	cooking house
unaine	old women
unimane	old men
uri	*Guettarda speciosa*, a plant with small scented white flower
uringakia	for their remembrance
urua	type of fish (travelly)
utu	immediate family or next of kin
wawi	death magic

BIBLIOGRAPHY

Books; Manuals; Documents

Anderson, Peter. 1963. *Tropical Architecture*. Melbourne: Melbourne University Press.

Arundel, John T. 1865. Papers of John T. Arundel. National Library of Australia: https://bit.ly/2MeUk6F

Barrar, Wayne. 1995.*Fields of vision: Photography, phosphate and landscape from a Pacific History,* (Unpublished thesis), Master of Design, Massey University.

Barrar, Wayne 1992. *Pacific Traces; Nauru Portfolio*, Exhibition, Te Papa, Wellington.

Bauldry, G.F. 1873 Report of Bark *Armelda. The Friend,* 1 December 1973.

Bellwood, Peter. 1979 *Man's Conquest of the Pacific.* New York, Oxford University Press.

Benaia, Temaka. 1991. The History of the Protestant Church in Banaba and Rabi. BD-MA Thesis, Pacific Theological College, Suva, Fiji.

Bingham, Hiram. 1908. *A Gilbertese-English Dictionary*, Cambridge, USA.

Binder, Pearl. 1977. *Treasure Island – The Trials of Ocean Islanders.* London: Blond and Briggs.

Boldrewood, Rolf. 1894. *A Modern Buccaneer.* London and New York: Macmillan.

Cantieri, Janice. 2015. Our Heart Is on Banaba: Stories From "The Forgotten People of the Pacific". *National Geographic*: https://bit.ly/2UiTPHx

Cantieri, Janice. 2016. A History of Displacement, Remembered in Dance. *National Geographic*. https://bit.ly/2IuBfd4

Cantieri, Janice. 2016. When Supporting Your Family Means Losing Your History: A Banaban Elder Reflects. *National Geographic*. https://bit.ly/2XbA4Uo

Cantieri, Janice. 2016. Living on a Tropical Island—and an Asbestos Wasteland. *National Geographic*. https://bit.ly/2VK2t3b

Cantieri, Janice. 2016. Journey into Te *Bangabanga*: The Sacred Caves of Banaba Island. *National Geographic*. https://bit.ly/2DhymZY

Cantieri, Janice. 2016. Life in a Harsh Paradise: Surviving Drought on Banaba Island. *National Geographic*. https://bit.ly/2GnLvmb

Cooper, Jeremy. 1998. *Coming Home to Banaba,* (Video), London: BBC open University Productions.

Cranston, Belinda. 18 Feb 2015. An island destroyed: From tropical paradise to ghostly mining town. *SBS News*: https://bit.ly/2P9NJIC

Day, Grove A. *Louis Becke*. New York: Twayne.

Douglas, Norman and Douglas, Ngaire. 1989. *Pacific Islands Year Book, 16th Edition*. Sydney: Angus and Robertson Ltd.

Eastman, Rev. G.H. 1948. *An English-Gilbertese Vocabulary of the most commonly used words.* The London Mission Press, Rongorongo, Beru, Gilbert Islands.

Edwards, Julia B. 2014. Phosphate mining and the relocation of the Banabans to northern Fiji in 1945: Lessons for climate change-forced displacement. *Journal de la Société des Océanistes*, 138-139, 121-136.

Eliot, E.C. 1938. *Broken Atoms.* London: Geoffrey Bles.

Ellis, Albert F. *Diary of Visit to Ocean Island,* 13 May 1900 – 25 May 1900. PMB. 497, Canberra, Australia.

Ellis, A.F. 1936. *Ocean Island and Nauru.* Sydney: Angus and Robertson Ltd.

Field, M. 1999. Man with a Past – interview with a massacre survivor, Tarawa, Kiribati: https://bit.ly/2HJHid5

Finsch, O. 1914. Südseearbeiten. Gewerbe- und Kunsteiß, Tauschmiel und Geld der Eingeborenen auf Grundlage der Rohstoe und der geographischen Verbreitung. Humburg: L. Friedrichsen & Co.

Grimble, A. 1921. From Birth to Death in the Gilbert Islands, *Journal of the Royal Anthropological Institute.*

Grimble, A. 1947. *Return to the Islands.* London: John Murray.

Grimble, A. 1952. *A Pattern of Islands.* London: John Murray.

Grimble, A. 1989.*Tungaru Traditions.* H.E. Maude, ed. Melbourne: Melbourne University Press.

Grimble, A. n.d. "Sketched History of Banaba", MS in Grimble Papers in the University of Adelaide Archives.

Hermann, Elfriede. 2017. Climate Change and Worries over Land: Articulations in the Atoll State of Kiribati, *Environmental Transformations and Cultural Responses,* 10, (49-73).

Hindmarch, Gerard. 2002. One Minority People: A Report on the Banabans Apia, Samoa; UNESCO.

Irwin, Geoffrey. 1992. *Prehistoric Exploration and Colonisation of the Pacific.* Cambridge, Cambridge University Press.

Karutake, Iokaba, Stacey King and Raobeia Ken Sigrah. 2004. Cultural Identity of Banabans, *Islands of the World VIII International Conference. 1-7 November 2004*, Kinmen Island (Quemoy), Taiwan:https://bit.ly/2Iw9cKp

Kempf, Wolfgang. 2003. Songs cannot die: Ritual composing and the politics of emplacement among the Banabans resettled on Rabi Island in Fiji. *Journal of the Polynesian Society* 112 (1): 33-64.

Kempf, Wolfgang & Elfriede Hermann. 2005. Reconfigurations of place and ethnicity: Positionings, performances and politics of relocated Banabans in Fiji. *Oceania* 75 (4): 368-386.

Kempf, Wolfgang and Taomati Teai, 2005. Banaban routes and roots – a dialogue. *In One and half Pacific Islands; Stories the Banaban people tell of themselves*, edited by Jennifer Shennan and Makin Corrie Tekenimatang, 124-7, Wellington: Victoria University Press.

Kempf, Wolfgang. 2011a. "The first South Pacific Festival of Arts revisited: Producing authenticity and the Banaban case", *The challenge of Indigenous peoples: Spectacle or politics?* Ed. Barbara Glowczewski and Rosita Henry, Oxford: Bardwell Press.

Kempf, Wolfgang. 2011b. Social mimesis, commemoration and ethnic performance: Fiji Banaban representations of the past", in *Changing context shifting meanings: Transformations of cultural traditions in Oceania,* edited by Elfriede Hermann, Honolulu: UH Press, 174-91.

Kempf, Wolfgang. 2011c. *Translocal Entwinements: Towards a history of Rabi as a Plantation island in colonial Fiji,* Gottingen: GOEDOC, Dokumenten, und Publikationservere de Georg Augustt Universitat Gottingen: https://bit.ly/2VXErRA

Kennedy, Major D.G. 1946. Progress Report on Banaban Settlement Scheme. 23 October 1945 – 28 January 1946. (unpublished)

King, S.M. 1993-1998. *Banaba/Ocean Island Newsletter.* Gold Coast: Banaban Heritage Society. Issues:1–29.

King, S.M. 1900-1980: *Banaba/Ocean Island Chronicles.* Database (unpublished).

King, Stacey. 2006. Australia-Banaba Relations; the price of shaping a nation is now a call for recognition. *AAAPS conference. Brisbane,* Australia 24 to 27 January 2006. https://bit.ly/2Ilhzci

King, Stacey. 2008. Recognition of Banaban Contribution to Australia's Prosperity as a Farming Nation. Submission to Australia 2020 Summit, Topic 10. Canberra Australia. https://bit.ly/2GnkmiY

Kiribati Government. November 1996. *To investigate the Death, Injury, Damage and Other Atrocities which happened in Kiribati during the Second World War.* Tabled in the Kiribati Maneaba Ni Maungatabu, House of Assembly, Bairiki, Tarawa. (In I-Kiribati language).

Kitaguchi, Manabu, Paulo Vanualailai, Stacey King and Ken Raobeia Sigrah. 2004. Economic Vulnerabilities - Banaba Japanese Relations Islands of the *World VIII International Conference. 1-7 November 2004, Kinmen Island (Quemoy), Taiwan:* https://bit.ly/2UDZfBS

Kumar, Sunil, Teata Terubea, Vincent D. Nomae and Andrew Manepora'a. 2006. Banabans Living in Poverty. *Fijian Studies - A Journal of Contemporary Fiji.* Vol. 4, No.1

Lampert, R.J. 1965. Anthropological Investigation of Te Aka Village, Ocean Island: Preliminary Report. Canberra, Department of Anthropology, Australian National University.

Lampert, R.J. 1968. An Archaeological Investigation on Ocean Island, Central Pacific. Archaeology and Physical Anthropology in *Oceania*, Vol. III, No. 1. April.

Langdon, Robert. December 1965/January 1966. The Ocean Islanders, A Quite Scandalous Document. *New Guinea and Australia, the Pacific and South-East Asia.*

Mackay, John. 1875. Jottings of a Labour Cruise from Queensland to the Equator, in Brig *Flora,* of London. Sydney, Mitchell Library Newspaper Cutting, Vol. G98815.

Mahaffy, Arthur. 1910. Ocean Island. *Blackwood's Magazine*, November.

Maude, H.E. 1946 Memorandum on the Future of the Banaban Population of Ocean Island; With Special Relation to their Lands and Funds. Auckland.

Maude, H.E. 1968. *Of Islands and Men - Studies in Pacific History.* Melbourne: Oxford University Press.

Maude, H.E. 1975. "The Relationship Between the Banabans and Gilbertese." Statement given in civil lawsuit against the British government.

Maude, H. E.1981. *Slavers in Paradise; The Peruvian labour trade in Polynesia, 1862-1864.* Stanford University Press and Australian National University Press.

Maude, H.E. ed. 1991. *The Story of Karongoa.* Suva: IPS.

Maude, H.E. and Lampert, R.J. 1967. The Stalactite Fish Hooks of Ocean Island. *Journal of the Polynesian Society*, Vol. 76, No. 4, December.

Maude, H.C. and Maude, H.E. December 1932. "The Social Organization of Banaba or Ocean Island, Central Pacific." *Journal of the Polynesian Society.* No. 164, pp 262.

Maude, H.C. and Maude, H.E. 1994. *An Anthology of Gilbertese Oral Tradition.* Suva, University of the South Pacific.

McAdam, J. Under Two Jurisdictions: Immigration, Citizenship, and Self–Governance in Cross–Border Community Relocations, *Law and History Review*, 34, pp 02.

Moldovan, A. The Black Knight and the Iron Maiden, ABC News, Australia: https://ab.co/2JOnxDD

Moldovan, A. Banaba: Podcast: The island Australia Ate, Ear Shot, Radio National ABC. Australia: https://ab.co/2HKbrZI

Pacific Phosphate Company (PPC). Confidential Correspondence Letter Books. Australia Archives (Melbourne) No. 63, 25 February 1911. Series No. MP 1174/1:https://bit.ly/2vSD263

Quanchi, Max. 1994. A trip through the islands; the photography of T.J. McMahon. *Meanjin*, Vo 53, No 4, pp. 715–22.

Quanchi, Max. 1995. T.J. McMahon; photographer, essayist and patriot in colonial Australia, the Pacific and empire, in Max Quanchi and Alaima Talu, eds, *Messy Entanglements*, Brisbane, Pacific History Association, pp. 49–62.

Quanchi, Max. 1997. Thomas McMahon; photography as propaganda in the Pacific Islands, *History of Photography*, Vol 21, No 1, pp. 42–53.

Quanchi, Max & Grant McCall. "December 15: Tragedy, Commemoration and Youth on Rabi Island". (Unpublished paper) presented School of Social Science Seminar Series, March 2011, USP, Suva.

Raobeia, Ken Sigrah and Stacey M. King. 2006. Paper: Banaba-Ocean Island Chronicles: Private collections and indigenous record keeping proving fact from fiction. *AAAPS conference. Brisbane*, Australia 24 to 27 January 2006: https://bit.ly/2UzUOba

Sabatier, Ernest. 1971. *Gilbertese-English Dictionary*. Translated from the French edition by Sister Oliva. Sydney: South Pacific Commission.

Shennen, Jennifer. 2006. The Banaban of Rabi. *National Geographic New Zealand*. Issue July-Aug 2006: https://bit.ly/2X6sdaU

Sigrah, Raobeia K. (and Ancestors of) 1923 - 1999. Banaban Genealogies. Four unpublished manuals. Copies held under 'closed access' PMB, Canberra, Australia.

Sigrah, Raobeia Ken and Stacey King. 2004. Legacy of a Miners Daughter and Assessment of the Social Changes of the Banabans after Phosphate Mining on Banaba. *Islands of the World VIII International Conference 1-7 November 2004, Kinmen Island (Quemoy), Taiwan.* https://bit.ly/2UzW26g

Sigrah, Raobeia Ken and Stacey King. 2004. Essentially Being Banaban in Today's World: The role of Banaban Law "Te Rii ni Banaba"(Backbone of Banaba) in a *Changing World, Islands of the World VIII International Conference 1-7 November 2004, Kinmen Island (Quemoy), Taiwan.* https://bit.ly/2UjH8wa

Sigrah, Raobeia Ken and Stacey King, 2007. The Banaba-Ocean Island Chronicles: Private collections indigenous record keeping, fact and fiction. - *Hunting the Collectors: Pacific Collections in Australian Museums, Art Galleries and Archives*. ed. Susan Cochrane and Max Quanchi. Cambridge Scholars Publishing. Newcastle, UK.

Silverman, M. G. 1970. "Banaban Adoption", in *Adoption in Eastern Oceania.* Edited by. Vern Carroll. *University of Hawaii Press.* pp. 209-235

Silverman, M. G. 1971. Disconcerting issue; meaning and struggle in a resettled Pacific community. Chicago: University of Chicago Press.

Stanley, David. 1992. *Micronesia Handbook.* Moon Publications, California.

Tatham, David. "Dickson, John Quayle 1860-1944," *Dictionary of Falklands Biography.* https://bit.ly/2JJ1qyl

Teaiwa, Katerina Martina. 2014. *Consuming Ocean Island - Stories of People and Phosphate from Banaba.* Indiana, Indiana University Press.

Trimble [Grimble], Arthur. Ocean Island - Remarkable Droughts. Seven-Year Cycles. *Sydney Morning Herald.* 21 August 1925

Walkup, Alfred. 1885. Report of the *First Voyage of the Missionary Barkantine 'Morning Star' to Micronesia, 1885.* Boston, American Board of Commissioners for Foreign Missions.

Webster, John. n.d. [1851] *The Last Cruise of the Wanderer.* Sydney, F. Cunninghame.

Williams, Maslyn and Macdonald, Barrie K. 1985. *The Phosphateers.* Melbourne: Melbourne University Press.

Wilson, John 1991. The Cruise of the 'Gipsy': The Journal of John Wilson, Surgeon on a Whaling Voyage to the Pacific Ocean 1839-1843. Honore Forster, ed. Washington: Ye Galleon Press Fairfield.

Wood, C.F. 1875. *A Yachting Cruise in the South Seas.* London, Henry S. King and Company.

Photograph Collections

Anderson, Peter; Collection. 1960s. Professional photos of Te Aka artefacts taken by Mark Stryzik. Donated by P. Anderson, Brisbane, Australia.

Anderson, Roger; Collection. 1969. Colour photos and colour slides, donated by R. Anderson, Melbourne, Australia.

Broadbent, Len; Collection. 1923. Donated to S. King by Len Broadbent (Jr) Sydney, Australia.

Doutch, Fredrick William; Collection. 1914. Donated to S. King by Honor and Harry Maude, Canberra, Australia.

Hobson, A.J. Collection 1932. Donated to S. King.

King, Stacey M.; Collection. 1992-2019. Colour photos and slides were taken on Rabi and Banaba islands, Gold Coast, Australia.

Kitaguchi, Manabu; Collection. 1997. Taken while on a research trip to Canberra, Australia and donated to R.K. Sigrah and S. King.

Lampert, R.J.; Collection. 1965. Taken during archaeological investigations of Te Aka village, donated to R.K. Sigrah.

Mander-Jones, Margaret; Collection. 1997. Taken on Banaba during 'Homecoming Trip' and donated to S. King, Brisbane, Australia.

Maude, Harry. 1932. Photographs from Maude's notebook held at Barr Smith Library, University of South Australia, Adelaide.

Maude, Harry and Honor; Collection. 1934. Donated to S. King by Honor Maude. Photos taken while the Maude's lived on Banaba and published in various articles by Harry Maude.

Maynard Collection. 1945. Taken on Rabi Island during the first settlement of the island.

Miller, John; Collection. 1908–39. Copies supplied to S. King by Frank Miller, Bribie Island, Australia.

Quanchi, Max Collection. 1908–1912. Original photos Rabi.

Thwaites, Lorraine; Collection. 1968. Original photos were taken of Tabwewa archaeological dig and donated to S. King.

Williams, John Francis.1900–1931. Great grandfather of S. King, family photographs were taken on Banaba during the first 30 years of mining. Gold Coast, Australia.

Interviews

Anderson, Peter and Sue. Various Interviews with Sigrah and King Brisbane, June 1998.

Bakanebo, Kaiea. Provided the words of Te Karanga 1997.

Christopher, Frank. Banaban elder. Recorded interview and transcript with S. King. Rabi Island, Fiji, 12 October 1992.

Elders of Te Maiu clan. Interview with Sigrah, Rabi Island, Fiji, 22 September 1997.

Elders of Te Aka clan. Interview with Sigrah, Rabi Island, Fiji, July 1998, and 28 August 1998.

Elders of Aurakeia clan, elder of Karieta. Interview with Sigrah, Tabwewa, Rabi Island, Fiji, 24 September. 1997; Suva, Fiji, 10 October 1997; and Rabi Island, Fiji, 24 July 1998.

Elders of Aurakeia clan, elder of Karia. Interview with Sigrah, Tabwewa, Suva, Fiji, 10 October 1997.

Golson, Professor Jack. Interview with Sigrah and King. Pacific Studies, ANU, Canberra, November 1997.

Konanerio, Naiewalker. Old Banaban elder from Tabiang village. Recorded interview and transcript with S. King. Interpreter: Kaioka Nanton, Rabi, 14 Oct 1992.

Lampert, Dr Ron. Interview with Sigrah and King. Pacific Studies, ANU, Canberra, November 1997.

Langdon, Robert. Interview with Sigrah and King. Pacific Studies, ANU, Canberra, November 1997.

Lennon, Edna. Various interviews with S. King. Gold Coast, 1992.

Marston, William (Bill) OBE. "The Evacuation of Ocean Island Prior to World War II." Former General Manager for British Phosphate Commission. Recorded interview and transcript S. King and Statement, Melbourne. 18 March 1993.

Marston, William (Bill) OBE. "The Defence of Ocean Island and Nauru by Heron and Wren Force Prior to Japanese Invasion during World War II." Former General Manager for British Phosphate Commission. Written statement, Melbourne. 10 May 1993.

Marston, William (Bill) OBE. "The Design of BPC Houses on Ocean Island." Former General Manager for British Phosphate Commission. Written statement, Melbourne. 2 June 1993.

Maude, Harry and Honor. Canberra. Various Interviews with S. King 1993-1994. Recorded Interview with Sigrah and King, Canberra. November 1997.

Miller, Frank. Born on Banaba, the 1920s. Son of John Miller, 1908-39. Bribie Island. 1993.

Naiwalker and (his wife) Nei Mata. Elders of Tabiang Village. Recorded interview and transcript with S. King. Interpreter: Kaioka Nanton. Rabi, Fiji, 14 October 1992.

O'Sullivan, B. "His Early Visits to Oceans Island as a Child with his sister Annie (Bridges) 1923-25." Recorded interview and transcript with S. King. Gold Coast, Australia, 1991.

Tarariki, Nei. "Arthur Cozens Story", Arthur Cozens aunty. Recorded interview and transcript with S. King. Interpreter: Kaioka Nanton. Rabi, Fiji, 12 October 1992.

Teai, Thomas. Various Interviews with S. King, Banaba and Rabi, February 1997.

White, Maureen. Various interviews with S. King. Melbourne, 1993 and Sigrah and King, Melbourne, 1998.

Documentaries, Videos

1975. Episode, Four Corners, Australia Broadcast Commission. English language filmed on Rabi.

1978. Episode, Four Corners, Australian Broadcast Commission. English language filmed on Banaba.

1979. Go Tell it To the Judge (the legal battle of the Banabans of Ocean Island). Producer: J. Barraclough. BBC Productions. UK. English language filmed on Rabi, Banaba, UK. https://youtu.be/VS99b9qMTvI

1991. Title: Nauru Island Planet. Documentary. Producers: Jean-Michel Cousteau et Jacques-Yves Cousteau Society, France. Russian language filmed on Banaba and Nauru. https://youtu.be/Kdj607OFlek (Also available in French and English).

1993. Title: Exiles in Paradise. Producer Alex Hodgkingson. Episode, Sixty Minutes, Nine Network Australia. English language filmed on Rabi and aerial view Banaba.

1994. Oh God Help Us. Compilation video by S. King. Sixty Minutes, Nauru Island Planet, Go Tell the Judge.

1995. Title: Banaba. Producer: Sarah Armstrong. Episode, Foreign Correspondent, Australian Broadcast Commission. English language filmed on Rabi and Banaba.

1997. Title: Missing Paradise in the South Pacific. Documentary. Producer: Aoata. Pink Noise Ink Productions, NHKTV, Japan. Japanese language, filmed on Rabi, Fiji, UK: https://bit.ly/2EE6j7y

1980. Title: Coming Home to Banaba. Documentary. Producer: J. Cooper. BBC OU UK. Filmed on Banaba during Homecoming 1979: https://bit.ly/2K9jwsA

2012. Title: Teimanaia, der Gottmensch der Banabans Episode Religionen im Pazifik, Fidschi. Producer: Barbara Kren, ORF, Austria. German language filmed on Rabi.

APPENDICES

Appendix 1: Approval Letter from Aurakeia Clan Elders of Karieta Clan, Tabwewa, 24 September 1997

ANA KARIAI KEN TORO NI BIRIAKI IBUKIN TE UTU

Aio nanora ngaira kain te Kainga ae Aurakeia - Tabwewa aika kanoan Naning man te Karieta ba ti anga are kariai ba ti a mwiokoa Ken Tororo ae utura naba ba e na katabwanin rikira na rongorongon ara Utu ni kabane mani kakoi inanon bain ara Kauntira n Rabi ao tabo ake e etaku ba ana ako iai.

Aio ara moti are ti motikia n ara botaki ae karaoaki n ana auti Meri Tawate 1 Nuku ni bongin namakaina ae 24/9/97.

Rikira aikai ana tiku ba ai rikiia naba kanoara nakon roro aika ana roko na aki manga bitaki.

Signed:

Appendix 2: Approval Certificate from Aurakeia Clan Elders of Karieta and Karia Clans, Tabwewa, 10 October 1997

Authority of Consent

Awarded to

Ken Sigrah

To Include Authorised Family Information in Proposed Book
&
Prior to Publishing must further obtain final Consent of Authenticity of information used.

Presented by

Heirditary Decendants of Aurakeia Clans

Friday, 10 October 1997

Mary T'Kenny,,   Aren Baoa,,   Baeang Kanimea,,   Nawaia Touakin

Appendix 3: Approval Letter from Karieta Clan Elders, 24 July 1998.

ANA BOWI TE KARIETA AE KARAOAKI I RABI
24 TH JULY '98

Ngaira aika kain te Karieta tia kariaia koreakin rongorongon ara utu ae inanon te boki aei "TE RII NI BANABA" ba eti raoi.

Ngaia ae tia kariaia Raobeia Sigran ao Stacey King ba ana toma te makuri ni kabane mani karaoi b'ai aike anori oa a kaeti ma te utu aei.

Bwai ni kabane aika ana karaoaki ena manga rinanoaki naba inanon te utu.

KARIETA CLAN MEETING HELD AT RABI ISLAND
24TH JULY '98

We the following members of the Karieta Clan hereby endorse the historical information and recording in this book "TE RII NI BANABA" regarding the Karieta Clan as being a correct record or our Clan history.

We therefore endorse Raobeia Sigrah and Stacey King to continue their work on all matters concerning our Clan.

Appendix 4: Approval Letter from Te Maiu Clan Elders, 22 September 1997.

Ami Tiaina ke Arami

Your Signature or Name

Kanoan Naitinua man te Maeu, Tabwewa

The Descendants Of Naitinua From Te Maeu, Tabwewa 22nd September 1997

Appendix 5: Approval Letter from Te Aka Clan Elders, 28 August 1998

TE AKA CLAN MEETING RABI IS, FIJI 28/8/98

We the recognised elders and representatives of
the TE AKA have endorsed the historical facts
and recording of our Clan history in this book
"TE RII NI BANABA" to be a correct record of our Clan.

We therefore endorse Raobeia Sigrah and Stacy King
to continue their work on all matters on behalf
of our Clan.

Signed:

    Naraobeia

    Namotintaeka

    Nei Kabuta

Appendix 6: Letter from Governor-General's Office to Secretary of State for the Dominion Affairs, 22 October 1927.

COMMONWEALTH OF AUSTRALIA.

GOVERNOR-GENERAL'S OFFICE

DECODE of telegram despatched by H.E. the Governor-General to the Rt.Hon.
the Secretary of State for Dominion Affairs, dated 22nd October, '27

S.

Following from Prime Minister begins —

British Phosphate Commission. Australian Commissioner has informed us regarding course of negotiations for land at Ocean Island required by Commissioners. They consider basis for acquiring 150 acres phosphate land proposed by Commissioners in letter to you of 16th December 1926 was equitable and even liberal and they might reasonably have declined to improve their offer but in July last an amended basis was agreed at Ocean Island between the Resident Commissioner and the Chief Representative of the British Phosphate Commissioners which was approved by the Commissioners in order to show their desire to meet as far as possible the views of the Banabans as represented by the Resident Commissioner. Understand this amended basis was approved also by you and represented the maximum payments to which the Commissioners could agree. Phosphate is vitally important to Australia and as the phosphate from Ocean Island is urgently required now and will in future be required in progressively increasing quantities for use in Australia and other countries within the Empire it is important that no restrictions shall prevent the development and working of the deposits to the best advantage by the Commissioners. The terms offered by the Commissioners are in excess of those recently agreed at Nauru and amply cover the differences in conditions between that Island and Ocean Island providing both for the present and the future welfare of the Banabans. As all the phosphate on Ocean Island will eventually be required it appears to Commissioners advisable that steps should be taken to secure another island or islands for the use of the Banabans when Ocean Island is no longer suitable for their habitation and the Commissioners have expressed their willingness to co-operate in this matter. The question of immediate removal to another island can be avoided if the land now required is made available without restrictive terms and conditions. As the Banabans are asking excessive payments for other land which the Commissioners now require to lease for the construction of new works urgently necessary to ensure increased output it is desirable that equitable terms and conditions

(2)   β

should now be agreed for at least 20 years as at Nauru for leasing land required for purposes other than phosphate mining.

Commissioners therefore request that

(a) phosphate mining land at Ocean Island be made available without delay for use as required by the British Phosphate Commissioners upon terms not exceeding those agreed at Ocean Island early in July and approved by the Commissioners and the Colonial Office;

(b) terms and conditions for leasing land at Ocean Island for purpose other than phosphate mining be arranged for 20 years on the same basis as at Nauru;

(c) that it be recognised that the whole deposit of phosphate at Ocean Island must eventually be worked;

(d) that arrangements be made for the acquisition of another island or islands suitable for eventual occupation by the Banabans.

As you have doubtless been advised in similar terms by United Kingdom Commissioner shall be glad to hear your views. My Government concurs generally with recommendation but considers the suggested transfer of Banabans to another island raises somewhat serious issues. We do not consider we are justified in making such a recommendation as this matter is one entirely within the province of British Administration. Ends.

Copies sent to Prime Minister's Dept
25 / 10 / 27

Fill
JHP 9/11/27.

Appendix 7: Acknowledgement Letter for the Return of Te Aka Artefacts and Relics – Professor J.M.A. Chappell, Head of Division of Archaeology and Natural History, ANU, Canberra, 10 November 1997.

THE AUSTRALIAN NATIONAL UNIVERSITY

THE RESEARCH SCHOOL OF PACIFIC AND ASIAN STUDIES

REFERENCE:

CANBERRA ACT 0200 AUSTRALIA
TELEPHONE: +61 6 249 5111
FACSIMILE: +61 6 257 1893

Division of Archaeology and Natural History

10 November 1997

TO WHOM IT MAY CONCERN

This is to certify that a box of skeletal remains and a box of artefacts excavated on Banaba (Ocean Island) in 1965 by Dr R. J. Lampert, then a member of this University, have been handed over to Mr Ken Sigrah for repatriation to the Banaba community of Rabi and Banaba

John Chappell

Professor J. M. A Chappell
Head of Division

Appendix 8: Acknowledgement Letter for the Return of Te Aka Artefacts from Peter Anderson, 16 June 1998.

Peter Anderson
P.O. Box 373,
Beenleigh. Q. 4207

TO WHOM IT MAY CONCERN

This is to certify that I have returned these various Banaban Artefacts collected by me from the site of the old *te Aka* Village on Banaba, Central Pacific to Ken (Raobeia) Sigrah as Representative for the *te* Aka Clan, Rabi Island, Fiji. Therefore I have given to him the responsibility to look after and preserve for posterity these items for the benefit of the entire Banaban Community.

Peter Anderson

Fomer Civil Engineer & Surveyor

for British Phosphate Commission

1940 -1969

Appendix 9: Words for *Te Karanga* War Spear Dance (Old Banaban Dialect and Kiribati Language).

Maua tia nako! E nira ni kaina ea toua mea teke rara

Te anti temanna, katiboua ibana I-abana I karawa

Na tiri motika kaibibia   Nna korokoreia na oraoraia

ba kanau ba te aan nanou

Teein angiu ba riariau tanotanon au kai

Ba te toa ma I-matang

Ma katatake biri, ma katatake tooa, makatake tua

Te mate ngai

Ike te koto Ba ti na mangaria koreia ni butou

Ma koreia n atu-u ei tutu ei bora

Tabera ni ngaina ni mainiku

Teei n angiu ma riariau

E wewete n tang Auriaria Ma iteran karawa meang

Ti tokia ti rebua

Mea mantinti Mea maiai Mea maenako Ia toua

Appendix 10: Words for the *Te Karanga are e Uarereke*, War Club Dance (Old Banaban Dialect and Kiribati Language).

Ma-ua. Tia nako!!!
E mananga
E manangananga
Te ka titiro uakina
Te anti te manna
Te Ina Itibubua

Kona ira boan au kai
ma karereka nako irarikin karawa
Kongo neana ma bukina ma tokitokina
Ia Ia ebo
Ia Ia e mate

I koreia e makoro
I koreia e makoro
Ia- Ia-Ia-Ia-Ia
M! - M! - He!

Appendix 11: Those Who Died on Banaba During World War II. Evidence from the committee appointed to investigate the death, injury, damage and other atrocities. This list includes causes as told literally by Banabans to an inquiry in 1996.

NAME	AGE	REASONS FOR DEATH	NAME	AGE	REASONS FOR DEATH
Aareke Taubwerei	37	Killed by Japanese			
Abetenoko Kabunginteiti		Killed by Japanese for being leper.	Bateriki Uriam	35	Died at sea
Abitara Abetenoko		Killed by Japanese for being leper.	Batia		Killed on Banaba
Aminiati Rota		Died during time of War	Batiua		Died of hunger on Banaba
Amota		Died of hunger on Banaba	Batuao Tioboa		Died of hunger on Banaba
Amota		Died of hunger on Banaba	Bauia Atanieru		Died during World War 2
Angang Kobae		Electrocuted by Japanese	Bauro Karuru		Shot by Japanese
Angkam Taebo		Beheaded by Japanese	Bauro Terebu		Died from Japanese
Anterea		Burnt in launch at Nauru	Bauro Wanikaie		Shot by Japanese at Lillian Point
Anterea Tokaati		Died at sea	Beau Metai		Killed by Japanese on Banaba
Aratika U.	38	Beaten by Japanese	Bebentau (Amota)		Killed on Banaba
Areke Taubwerei	40	Died of hunger on Banaba	Beia		Killed on Banaba
Aretana		Died of hunger on Banaba	Beianibuariki Tamuera		Shot by Japanese
Ari		Killed by Japanese because of leprosy	Bere Teitia		Died during World War 2
Aroito		Died of hunger	Berenti Timon		Died
Ataera Taaba		Died of hunger on Banaba	Beretaita		Killed by Japanese
Atera Taoieta	21	Killed by Japanese	Beretiata Eeteri	19	Shot by Japanese
Atia Kamaata		Killed by Japanese	Betero Teekea		Killed by

Name	Age	Cause	Name	Age	Cause
		bombing.			Japanese
Auatabu Ramanga		Killed on Banaba	Betero Teiwaki		Died from Japanese
Autiaong		Killed by Japanese	Betero Tuake		Killed by Japanese
Baaroum Takatau		Died from bombing	Betio Taaba		Died of hunger on Banaba
Baibuke		Killed on Banaba	Biribo Eria		Died from Japanese
Baita Taubwerei		Killed by Japanese during Second World War	Birirake Koriri		Shot by Japanese at Lillian Point
Baitau		Killed by Japanese	Biroto Biroto	38	Died of hunger on Banaba
Baitke Tangitang		Died from hunger on Banaba	Bitaki	56	Shot because he was hungry
Bakaia		Died from hunger on Banaba	Bobu Taukaro		Killed by Japanese
Bakoaun		Died of hunger on Banaba	Boribou Bwakai		Killed by Japanese because he was leper
Bangao		Electrocuted by the Japanese	Botaraa		Died of hunger on Nauru
Banimone Mangoua		Accidentally died on Banaba during the War	Botiara Takeke		Killed by Japanese
Baniuea B.	36	Died of hunger by Japanese	Boua		Beheaded by Japanese
Bannei		Beheaded	Bouatemari		Killed
Banro Kauaba	37	He was killed because he was wrongly accused of stealing food.	Bouatemari Kauabuina		Died of hunger
Banuea		Died on Banaba	Bouatoa		Can't prove reason of his death
Barekiau		Died from being beaten by Japanese	Bouatoa Taniana		Shot by Japanese at Lillian Pt.
Bataka		Died of hunger	Boubou Bakai		Killed by Japanese
Buatia Beniamina	37	Beheaded by Japanese	Itaia		Died of hunger on Banaba

Name	Age	Cause of death	Name	Age	Cause of death
Bure T	68	Hunger	Itemaera Koito		Died during World War 2
Burentoun		Killed	Itienang		Shot by Japanese
Butintoa Arekibo	30	Died when shot by Japanese	Itinikua		Died in jail on Banaba
Bwaita Taubwerei	38	Beheaded by Japanese	Itinneita Ieru	33	Beheaded By Japanese
Bwataka Babaki		Shot by Japanese	Itintoki Nariaki		Killed on Banaba by Japanese
Bwebwetake Tekaie		Died of hunger	Ititaake Kuuta	25	Shot by Japanese
Enete Moote		He was killed by Japanese	Iuta Ietii		Killed on Banaba by Japanese
Ereata		Killed by Japanese	Kabaea		Died from bombing on Banaba
Ereniti		Nobody knows the reason of his death	Kabaki Uriam	21	Shot by Japanese
Eria		Beheaded by Japanese	Kabatia Uatire	28	No evidence of his death, recruited from Nonouti
Eria		Killed by Japanese	Kabiri Tewawa		Shot by Japanese
Eriakim Obera	25	Killed on Banaba	Kabotau	45	Shot by Japanese
Erim Anterea		Shot by Japanese	Kabureia Bakanebo	27	Shot by Japanese
Eritai Ioane		Died from Japanese bombing	Kabwaki Uriam	17	Beheaded by Japanese
Eritara Takanang	18	Shot	Kaeia Teuea (Teaba)	32	From hunger by Japanese
Eriu		Killed by Japanese on Banaba	Kaiaia		Killed
Etekia Reebo	26	Shot by Japanese	Kaiaia Motiua		He was bitten by a shark trying to escape from Japanese
Etekiati Reetio		Killed by Japanese	Kaimatang Iobi	37	Killed by Japanese
Etekiati Tetio		Killed by Japanese	Kaiua Batake	27	Shot by Japanese
Etete K.	58	Shot at Lillian Point by Japanese	Kaiwa		Killed on Banaba
Etuare Timon		Died of hunger on Banaba	Kakaua Batake		Died of stomach ache caused by

			hunger
Iaekana Iatua		Killed by Japanese on Banaba	Kamainga (Kabiua)	Died of hunger on Banaba
Iaokiri Metako	29	Killed by Japanese on Banaba	Kamatua & Tanentoa	Killed on Banaba
Iareta Tione	13	Hunger	Kamoti Tabuu	Killed by Japanese
Iebeta		Died of hunger on Banaba	Kanan	Beheaded by Japanese
Ieeru Karoba		Beheaded by Japanese	Kantarawa Tekaai	Killed by Japanese because he was leper
Ientau		Killed on Banaba	Kareman	Died of hunger on Banaba
Ieu		Killed by Japanese on Banaba	Karibaua Tabwebwe	68	Died of hunger
Ioane Arame	28	Shot by Japanese	Kataba Terama	Hunger
Ioera Kamaata		Died of hard labour	Katarake	Died of hunger on Banaba
Iona		Died of hunger on Banaba	Kaua	Died of hunger on Banaba
Ioreme Batongabiti	39	Beheaded by Japanese	Kauaba Boata	Electrified
Iote		Killed by Japanese	Kauabatonga	Death unknown
Iote Iote		Killed by Japanese on Banaba	Kaumai Teakin	Killed by Japanese
Ioteba Kaumai		Died of hunger on Banaba	Kaumiti	Killed by Japanese
Iotua Airu	45	Killed	Kauongo	Died of hunger on Banaba
Iou Mareko (Nanonna)		Died from Japanese	Kautu	Killed on Banaba
Iram Etekiera		Died from Japanese	Keke Taukai	Killed because he was leper
Irannau		Killed	Kewekewe Moatau	Shot by Japanese
Irata Bine		Killed on Banaba	Kiakia	Died from hunger on Banaba
Irata Teweru		Died of hunger	Kiatoa Kaumai	Killed by Japanese on Banaba
Kiatoa Tatau	23	Killed by Japanese	Nautuao	Killed on Banaba

396

				by Japanese
Kiteon		Died of hunger in Banaba	Nawaine Pine	Shot by Japanese
Koakoa Baitongabiti	22	Shot at Lilian Pt. by Japanese	Neemia	Died of hunger on Banaba
Kokia	34	Japanese killed him while repairing buoy in Harbour	Nekita T	53	Hit by bullet
Koriri A	38	Shot by Japanese	Neneuri		Killed on Banaba by Japanese
Koura	30	Died of hunger on Banaba	Ngaia Timea	35	Died of hunger
Maata T.	28	Shot	Ngarontaake Tikunteiti		Killed by Japanese because he was leper
Maemae		Killed by American bombing in Nauru	Nonouri Anterea		Shot by Japanese
Maene Rii	19	Died of hunger on Banaba	Nuea Tabwi	39	Beheaded
Maibintebure	3	Died of hunger	Nuete Nuete		Killed on Banaba by Japanese
Maningare Atauea		Died of hunger on Banaba	Nukai Aurane		Killed on Banaba
Mannaua Tabakarawa		Shot by Japanese	Numaia Intia		Killed by Japanese
Maraea Airu	41	Shot	Obena (Maera)		Killed on Banaba
Maraea Tekoriri	2	Died of hunger	Obeta Redfern	30+	Burnt to death by Japanese
Mariano Tekaai		Killed by Japanese because he was leper	Omeri	19	Shot
Maron		Died of hunger on Banaba	Oteta		Killed by Japanese
Mataroa Matakite		Died by Japanese	Oteti Reema		Died of hunger on Banaba
Matata		Died of hunger on Banaba	Penipelite Salanoa	20	Shot by Japanese
Matin Mweia		Died during World War 2	Penisula Falesau		Killed by Japanese
Meeti	43	Hunger	Ramten		Killed by Japanese
Mereki Miti	27	Shot by Killed	Raoboia		Killed by Japanese

Name	Age	Cause	Name	Age	Cause
Metutera Tiira		Killed by Japanese	Rebaio T	30	Shot
Minataba Timwea		Killed by Japanese during the War	Rekau Teekea		Died during the War
Miriama Tito		Died of hunger caused by Japanese	Renren		Killed on Banaba
Mitire Mekieru	23	Killed (recruited from Onotoa)	Rerewa		Shot by Japanese at Lilian Point
Moteti Tiotebwa	6	Injected by Japanese and died later	Reuera		Killed at sea while trying to escape
Moutu Tokiauea	32	Shot	Ribai		Killed by Japanese (shot)
Mwaake Rianako		Beheaded by Japanese	Ribine		Died of hunger on Banaba
Mwaerere Tekatau		Killed by bomb	Ribinine Taaba		Died during the War
Mwariko		Died from desperation of hunger caused by Japanese	Riboriki Tara	3	Shot by Japanese
Mweretaka	45	Admitted to hospital, but Japanese didn't feed him.	Riria Itienang	42	Died of hunger
Naatia Ribaai		Shot by Japanese by being leper	Ritang Keebwa		Died during Second World War
Nabari		Died of hunger on Banaba	Riuai Teunaia		Killed because he was leper
Nabere Ribantaai	40	Died from hunger	Riwa Uriamti		Killed on Banaba
Nabutau Teaniwai		Shot by Japanese	Roau Timwea		Killed by Japanese during the War
Naiti		Died of hunger on Banaba	Roboam Terebo		Killed on Banaba
Nakarua	40	He was poisoned by Japanese	Rokoua Teimone	34	Killed on Banaba by Japanese
Nakekea		Died of hunger on Banaba	Ronikanimeang		Shot by Japanese
Namoriki Kaitangare		Shot by Japanese	Roota Bakatokia	10	Beheaded by Japanese
Naniten		Died during Second	Rooti Kairo		Died during the

398

Name	Age	Fate
Aretana		World War
Nariki Teubei		Shot by Japanese
Nataua		Killed by Japanese because he was leper
Ruoitao Tiaoti	34	Shot
Taam Botibara		Died of hunger on Banaba
Taam Taam		Killed on Banaba
Tabanga Kaitano	34	Died of hunger on Banaba
Tabea Reo		Died on Banaba
Tabenaba		Killed (Recruited from Onotoa)
Tabewaa Tibaua		Beheaded by Japanese
Tabikarawa	54+	Died of hunger
Taboia		Killed by Japanese
Tabonteren (Doctor)	42	Stabbed by Japanese bayonet when he refused to inject children with poison
Tabore Teuea	40	Shot
Taboua		Died at sea while fishing for Japanese
Tabua Tekaiwa		Died of hunger on Banaba
Tabuaki Baketi		Killed by Japanese
Tabuariki		Killed (recruited from Tabiteuea)
Tabuatoatau		Killed on Banaba
Tabuia		Died of hunger on

Name	Age	Fate
		War
Ruka Kauaba		Died of hunger on Banaba
Rukai Maika		Died during the War
Taom Eria		Shot by Japanese
Taoroba		Killed by Japanese
Tarae Ribaai	19	Shot because he was a leper
Tarakabu Tebau		Died from Japanese
Tarakia		Died of hunger on Banaba
Taratai	46	Died of hunger
Tareti Maio		Died of heart attack when bomb exploded
Tatoa		Died of hunger on Banaba
Tauamarawa Beia		Killed by Japanese
Tauantang		Died of hunger
Tauantang Aakori		Electrocuted by Japanese
Taukaro Kauaba		Killed by Japanese
Tauna		Died of hunger
Taunii Airu	28	Died of hunger by Japanese
Taura	26	Killed by bombing on Banaba
Tauro Romania	38	Killed by Japanese
Tautebua Taebo		Beheaded by

Name	Age	Cause
		Banaba
Tabuia Iete		Electrocuted by Japanese
Tabuke Tuen	27	Shot by Japanese
Tabutoatau Iokara	45	Beheaded by Japanese
Tabwanin	1	Hunger caused by Japanese
Tabwewaa Tibaua		Shot by Japanese
Tabwiia Naeuta	34	Died from electric shock
Taebo Koura		Died at sea
Taeka		Died of hunger
Taiau Tabeaua	40	Died of hunger caused by Japanese
Taivasa Siose	23	He was bayoneted by Japanese
Takaingutu		Killed (recruited from Tabiteuea)
Takaio Tekeua	26	Shot by Japanese
Takanoi		Killed on Banaba
Takaria Tauoua		Killed by Japanese
Tamaiti Kiratururu	48	Hunger
Tamuera Teaon	37	Shot by Japanese
Tamwennang Tebo		Died of hunger on Banaba
Taneai		Killed by Japanese
Tanentoa Tautebwa		Killed by Japanese
Tanentoa Temaiana		Died of hunger and eating leaves
Tangaroa Tengakia	20	Shot by Japanese

Name	Age	Cause
		Japanese
Tautebwa Kauarawete		Shot by Japanese
Tautua Tuiko		Died of hunger in Banaba
Tawake		Killed by Japanese
Tawita		Died of hunger on Banaba
Teaeki Taukai		Shot because he was a leaper
Teaiwa Tebuanna		Died of hunger on Banaba
Takin Nakua	18	Killed by Japanese
Teangabai		Died of hunger on Banaba
Teannaki		Died of hunger on Banaba
Teannaki Bokai		Killed by Japanese
Teanningo Taboia		Killed by Japanese
Tearau Rukio		Died of hunger on Banaba
Tearo		Killed by Japanese on Banaba
Teatao Matakite		Killed by Japanese
Tebanro Kauaba	23	Beheaded by Japanese
Tebara Tiwai	46	He was burnt
Tebau Tikauea		Killed by the Japanese
Tebauia		Killed at Banaba
Tebebe Korotabu		Died of hunger by Japanese
Tebetaio Ieremia		Killed by the Japanese
Tebikemone		He was killed because he was

			leper
Tanibanarata Mareko	Beheaded by Japanese	Tebionga	Died on Banaba from hunger
Tanna Kobae	Died of hunger by Japanese	Tebiri Tamuera 24	Shot by the Japanese
Tannang Beiaruru	Killed by Japanese	Teboitabu 28	Killed by the Japanese
Taoieta Tatabwano	Died after being beaten by Japanese	Tebwaebwa Nakau 35	Left hungry by the Japanese
Tebwara Tiwai	He was burnt by Japanese because he was leper	Temango	Killed by Japanese
Teebora K. 60	He was shot	Temataake Taam	Hit by bomb
Teekea Teeu 24	He was shot by the Japanese	Temoa	Beheaded by Japanese
Teeta Biribo	Beheaded by the Japanese	Temoai Kamata 38	He was shot
Teibeiki Koura	He was killed by the Japanese	Tenanai Tione 9	He died of hunger by Japanese
Teibira Timoteo 24	He was beheaded by the Japanese	Teneabing T 54	He was hit by a bullet
Teibora Timoteo 38	He was beaten by the Japanese	Tenieta Nuete	He was shot by Japanese
Teieru	He died at sea	Tennang Kakau	He was killed by Japanese
Teikaabua Tekaua 48	He was beheaded by the Japanese	Tentau	Died of hunger on Banaba
Teikabua	He died of hunger on Banaba	Terangabure 38	Shot by Japanese
Teikaoti Teimone 32	He was killed by Japanese on Banaba	Teraoi	Beaten to death by Japanese
Teikarawa	He was killed on Banaba	Terara 60	He was killed for being leper
Teimaiana	Died of hunger on Banaba	Terawea 38	He died during Japanese time because there was no food
Teimarane	He was killed on Banaba	Teretia	He was taken out to sea on a barge and shot by Japanese

Teinai Tabore	Killed by the Japanese	Teretia Nuea	Burnt by Japanese because he was leper
Teinamoroa	Killed on Banaba	Teriboriki	Died of hunger on Banaba
Teitao Teubaa 26	He was shot by the Japanese	Terikano Obaia 34	Died of hunger
Teitawana	He died in Banaba	Terikaua	Killed on Banaba by Japanese
Tetibwebwe Kabiriera	He died of hunger on Banaba	Terikiai (Tion)	Killed
Teitikai Tabutoua	Killed by the Japanese	Terokouea	Died of hunger on Banaba
Teitoi	Died of hunger on Banaba	Teruaa Atanieru	Died from the Second World War
Tekaai Kanone	He died of hunger because the Japanese feeding only on leave	Teruka 18	Shot Stabbed by Japanese
Tekaai Ribauea	He was killed by the Japanese because his child had leprosy	Tetabo	Died of hunger on Banaba
Tekai	Died of hunger on Banaba	Tetange Tongaii 56	Beheaded by Japanese
Tekamino Temone 18	Shot by the Japanese	Tetanibea (Teburimai)	Killed Stabbed by Japanese
Tekanan Kariaa	Killed on Banaba	Teteka	Beheaded by Japanese
Tekatara Ionikara 38	Shot by a Japanese	Teteki Baewe	Beheaded by Japanese
Tekau	Killed on Banaba by Japanese	Teteki Baintoun	He was shot by Japanese for no reason
Tebautu M. 38	Shot	Tetieuea	Killed on Banaba by Japanese
Tekea	Died of hunger on Banaba	Tetuai	Died of hunger on Banaba
Tekeabuti Tion 7	Died of hunger during Japanese time	Teuanang Bureua	Died of hunger by Japanese
Tekeuea Tieka 25	Killed on Banaba by Japanese	Teuarai	Beheaded by Japanese

402

TE RII NI BANABA –BACKBONE OF BANABA

Tekiera Teaeaki		Killed by Japanese	Teuati Amatia		Shot by Japanese
Tekimai Tetita		Killed by Japanese	Teuea Aata		Shot by Japanese
Tekinene Boua		Beheaded by Japanese	Teukera Tiuere	25	Beheaded by Japanese
Tekirai Taiau	15	Shot by Japanese	Teuta Ereaatara		Beheaded by Japanese
Tekonaba		Beheaded by Japanese	Tewae		Died of hunger on Banaba
Temaiana		Died while under force labour by Japanese	Tewaiti		Died of hunger on Banaba
Temaiana Tiroi	40	Beheaded by Japanese	Teweaniti Ribaai	21	Shot because he was a leper
Teweia Aata		Died of hunger and Japanese feed them on leaves	Toakarawa Teaero		Killed by Japanese
Teweru Awiu		Died of hunger on Banaba	Toatoa		Beheaded on Banaba
Teweti Abiuta	59	Died of hunger on Banaba	Tokaaba		Died of hunger on Banaba
Tewiatabu Amuera		Died by Japanese	Tokaia Mweaua		Killed by Japanese
Tewita Eritai		Died of hunger (He came from Tamana)	Tokiauea Tem		Shot by Japanese
Tiaon Tarau	25	Killed by Japanese	Tominiko Tauroba		Killed by Japanese
Tibwere Meia		Shot by Japanese (Came from Nonouti)	Tongabiri		Killed on Banaba by Japanese
Tibwere Rotoman	35	Blindfolded and beheaded by Japanese	Tongabiri		Died of hunger on Banaba
Tikunteiti		Killed because he was leper	Tongoiti	40	Died of hunger
Tim		Killed by Japanese	Tooti Kauoto		Shot by Japanese
Timaio		Killed by Japanese	Tooti Tooti	34	Shot by Japanese
Timaio Bateka	21	Shot	Torata		Killed by Japanese
Timi		Beheaded by Japanese	Torua		Killed on Banaba by Japanese
Timoteo Teaero	24	Shot or beheaded by Japanese	Toteai Tooa		Died of hunger

403

Name		Fate	Name		Fate
Timun Araba		Killed by Japanese	Touati Amatia		Shot by Japanese
Tinabora		He worked hard	Tuanikai		Shot by Japanese
Tekaie		and had no food except the leaves on the trees	Teuriaki		
Tinga		Died of hunger on Banaba	Tubua Rokea		He died in the War
Torata		Killed by Japanese	Tubua Tiua		He was hit by the American bomb
Tion Tarau		Died in the Second World War	Tuenge Tuengeri		Killed by Japanese during the War
Tiong	40	Died of hunger on Banaba	Tuengeri Ieete		Died of hunger on Banaba
Tioti Koraubara	24	Died of hunger by Japanese	Tuewi Tuiko		Killed by Japanese
Tirae Tabeaua		Died from the Japanese	Tutu	40	Died of hunger by Japanese
Tiri		Killed by Japanese because he was leper	Uakeia Nawere		Died on Banaba
Tiribo (Oriawa)		Killed on Banaba	Ueanteiti Teiabure	49	Died of hunger on Banaba
Tiribo Rekau		Beheaded by the Japanese	Urete		Killed by Japanese because he was leper
Tiroia		Killed on Banaba by Japanese	Uriam Baaka	39	Died of hunger on Banaba
Tiroia Kaumai		Shot by Japanese	Uriam Tamueru		Shot by Japanese (Came from Beru)
Titanre Tongai	56	Beheaded by Japanese	Utia Ribae		Killed by Japanese
Tito Tarau		Killed by Japanese	Utiate Buake	35	Died during the Second World War
Tiuta		Killed at Banaba	Vanro Kauaba	32	Killed by Japanese
Toa		Killed by Japanese on Banaba	Wareri		Died of hunger on Banaba
Toa (Tentoa)		Killed on Banaba	Winuea Tarua		Killed by Japanese

404

Appendix 12: The First Pioneers listed on Arrival in Rabi on 15 December 1945 "Rabi Honour Roll" as provided by Interim Administration of the Rabi Council of Leaders (as published 'Banaba/Ocean Island News'–Special 50th Anniversary Edition, December 1995).

RABI HONOUR ROLL

I-BANABA			I-KIRIBATI		
Mane (Man)	Aine (Woman)	Ataei (Child)	Mane (Man)	Aine (Woman)	Ataei (Child)
Akeriba	Atentati	Arobati	Aukitini	Aute	Banaba
Aki	Aurane	Aranuea	Alefaio	Ana	Binataake
Aron	Aibonga	Abiuta	Aba	Ana	Burenga
Aneri	Atara	Aotai	Asielu	Angiruru	Baia
Amon	Awaki	Areke	Atauea	Aribo	Boutu
Airu	Ataruru	Atera	Antiba	Arabo	Boniti
Abakuka	Akineti	Atiri	Abere A	Aarake	Batiua
Akata	Abitara	Aroito	Bakateke	Aro	Biamaroti
Abetai	Aribo	Aotai	Barabara	Baintaake	Eren
Bureitetau	Aita	Ani Baraime	Baraimo	Bwebwe	Erona
Boata	Auti	Abitiai	Benaia	Beia	Ekeniman
Betero	Abanei	Atera	Bonebati	Bereti	Etita
Barereka	Atibure	Ata	Biribi	Beretati	Esau
Biribi	Astara	Abisaloma	Bouatoa	Boboua	Ebiri
Burataake	Abane	Amitara	Baia	Beruro	Fanfofango
Binaoro	Borataake	Beretiata	Bio	Baroi	Feruaina
Bakoa	Bobo	Beronika	Boia	Eritabeta	Ioane
Beiata	Bukauea	Bobo	Biara	Ekewi	Itintebure
Biremon	Beia	Bureka	Buaua	Ekebure	Kautuntarawa
Boua	Bouatetaake	Bone	Bitoi	Fipe	Katata
Buaka	Bakaineaki	Kanati	Barai	Kamarawa	Kaitetara
Bureti	Beta	Bukauea	Bauro	Karo	Kurae
Beiaun	Birori	Bureti	Bakoaiti	Katita	Maria
Burangitara	Benerike	Bakaua	Betueru	Kaiamakin	Meri
Baakai	Beretakira	Banian	Ben	Katarina	Nnari
Beniamina	Bateteba	Burentau	Binauea	Kaitiro	Nauru
Bebeia	Biriata	Baitere	Bureti	Karaete	Nanoiaki
Burentetabo	Bakuao	Baira	Binataake	Karubea	Raine
Baneta	Emima	Babai	Ekeuea	Kateia	Robin
Baiana	Eritabeta	Betero	Eria	Kaeroa	Rewi
Bakoa	Eritabeta	Buka	Etei	Mikara	Rona
Barere	Eritabeta	Bebe	Iobi	Marima	Riteri
Beti	Iti	Baeang	Iona	Matereta	taake
Burebure	Kabebeiti	Bianeke	Itaia	Maure	Take
Baure	Kaekoa	Bwebweia	Ioane	Mere	Teruakai

I-BANABA			I-KIRIBATI		
Mane (Man)	Aine (Woman)	Ataei (Child)	Mane (Man)	Aine (Woman)	Ataei (Child)
Betere	Kureiti	Beteri	Karekenna	Maere	Tamara
Enoka	Kaue	Beibeti	Kairaei	Mata	Turia
Ieteba	Katiria	Beatebure	Kaburere	Marikarita	Tibeti
Itinteang	Kabuatea	Batibubua	Kaiarake	Merea	Tikauti
Ikamawa	Kataaua	Bititema	Kamon	Mita	Teringa
Itintarawa	Kataea	Burenimaneaba	Kuriri	Naomi	Teitibwebwe
Itaaka	Kabwebwea	Baure	Karekenano	Ngaia	Kaianano
Iete	Kaititake	Burenimatang	Ketua	Ngauming	Tokarawa
Kutunibanaba	Kaua	Betero	Keakea	Nanoua	Tarona
Karore	Kauae	Benieri	Kokoria	Nnere	Tawita
Kirennang	Karianna	Beia	Korotabu	Nnaua	Tokanikai
Kureta	Kuturoroa	Baoa	Kamarie	Oreba	Tekarutaake
Kautu	Keang	Bato	Karotu	Otobina	Tom
Kaitu	Kinati	Birateiti	Kataenano	Rete	Uba
Kaiekiekia	Katua	Buraoranti	Kantati	Ruita	Uabong
Kataobure	Kamarawa	Enere	Kaitarawa	Rara	
Kaintong	Kiebu	Eketaake	Karebanga	Ritia	
Kareaiti	Kiraua	Ereti	Kirata	Riteba	
Kaitangare	Karinea	Ewekia	Koina	Reren	
Keangibo	Katanga	Ekeniman	Kanana	Tatu	
Kiritian	Katenaitina	Eneri	Kourabi	Takaue	
Katarake	Kaia	Eriu	Kinono	Taua	
Keangibo	Kautu	Eribereta	Kiribati	Tarimwe	
Kakiaman	Kakebo	Eketi	Mote	Tamarawa	
Kition	Manranga	Eria	Matia	Tabita	
Kabanti	Maere	Etita	Mange	Teaibo	
Kiritama	Mimi	Eritabeta	Mataa	Taoia	
Kaiekieki S.	Mone	Ereno	Mote	Teruamaere	
Korauea	Mine	Itieta	Makanga	Tekeke	
Kaibati	Makimaki	Itinimaneaba	Matibeia	Tenta	
Karaiti	Maria	Itinaaba	Mote	Tebarai	
Kariatabwewa	Mareta	Itimaera	Mareko	Tongauea	
Kabuta	Mareta	Itinaorua	Maretino	Tuanna	
Kautuntaake	Maaka	Itinimatang	Mikaere	Tokaniti	
Kabanei	Maeten	Iareta	Nataua	Teuota	
Karueteiti	Makin	Iobi	Nakara	Tibeia	
Kawate	Metian	Iuta	Nutira	Tiria	
Kaimata	Mitara	Itinokuaki	Nanton	Teburenga	
Kaiaba	Mereara	Itinrerei	Nakabere	Tebitanatu	

I-BANABA			I-KIRIBATI		
Mane (Man)	Aine (Woman)	Ataei (Child)	Mane (Man)	Aine (Woman)	Ataei (Child)
Karotu	Me	Iorim	Nome	Tamarawa	
Matio	Meruta	Inoki	Nete	Tanari	
Moutu	Maewe	Kiritome	Nabu	Teuea	
Maata	Marea	Kairaoi	Noa	Teangua	
Mataro	Mere	Kabwebwenimarawa	Otiong	Tote	
Nakura	Meri	Kaewa	Rerebu	Teramanaba	
Naiwaka	Naomi	Kiata	Ruria	Tuaba	
Naikara	Ntarie	Kaekematang	Tietaria	Tota	
Nakau	Ntea	Kurititina	Takita	Tuka	
Nabure	Naomi	Kaewanimone	Taake	Terengaiti	
Natua	Ngeaua	Ketia	Tekenimeang	Taunari	
Namai	Nnera	Kaotinaea	Tarieta	Temoaiti	
Obaia	Namoriki	Karo	Tabora	Tikenati	
Reo	Nnaua	Kora	Tataua	Temaranga	
Rotan	Notue	Kaotia	Tareta	Toauatereke	
Rui	Nuaru	Kabunare	Tabore	Tue	
Rowi	Namo	Katangaua	Tanu	Taruma	
Ribantai	Orega	Kauongo	Kekiau	Takeiti	
Rewi	Ruta	Kaua	Tekai	Uareta	
Ringa	Rakena	Kirite	Teairo	Uneke	
Ribauea	Rote	Kaoma	Tetabo	Wineta	
Tebuke	Reiti	Katabukia	Tebaka	Wae	
Tekewa	Riria	Kabure	Tebureie		
Tito	Rutira	Kaokia	Tewe		
Tororo	Raitinibure	Koaua	Teaitua		
Tekaaki	Rawatu	Kirata	Tekinene		
Tinarubena	Ruiti	Keitiro	Teitikai		
Tubara	Routamone	Korati	Tina		
Tebetanga	Rakaba	Kaetea	Towaki		
Tenaera	Ririan	Kananoa	Terubea		
Timeona	Roe	Kaitiata	Teuanna		
Tuteariki	Rutiana	Kataunati	Taake		
Tione	Rianua	Karawa	Tekairaba		
Tamoa	Rube	Karuruko	Teburea		
Tabuariki	Raeterenga	Kiritiano	Teinimaki		
Tebungai	Rebeka	Kabumarou	Takamwe		
Timau	Temanibwebwe	Kiraraiti	Temarua		
Teai	Takeiti	Kuta	Tikeru		
Teekabu	Tina	Kabunimatang	Tebubua		

I- BANABA			I- KIRIBATI		
Mane (Man)	Aine (Woman)	Ataei (Child)	Mane (Man)	Aine (Woman)	Ataei (Child)
Tekoruru	Tamaiti	Kabwebwea	Teba		
Toaiba	Tarakita	Karinea	Tieke		
Taebontoun	Tabauea	Korieta	Toba		
Tonamo	Tentabuariki	Keangimawa	Taboia		
Tiaeke	Tokamaea	Kabuati	Tio		
Tamaroa	Taeboa	Keke	Toaia		
Tekintekai	Tebora	Kirata	Teriaki		
Taati	Teure	Mote	Turi		
Tamton	Takawau	Matu	Tokintekai		
Tamton	Tereua	Mereba	Tabeti		
Terarikinnang	Terea	Mere	Tekaie		
Tetebano	Turenga	Makei	Takoto		
Teinimaki	Teaoia	Makin	Toti		
Tekatau	Tatau	Mabubu	Toromon		
Tenikomumun	Toaua	Meruta	Teariki		
Tatake	Tarai	Mina	Terabwena		
Teikake	Tongobo	Mone	Tuari		
Tikaua	Tairi	Meri	Tokoia		
Tauakitari	Teanau	Mebon	Tabe		
Tengara	Tauea	Merita	Tiaterenga		
Tikoro	Tekaure	Mariano	Tonoua		
Tomo	Taake	Marikita	Tione		
Taukai	To	Mangoua	Teaboka		
Tekaai	Tatabo	Matou	Tetaake		
Teangoa	Tekiakia	Miriam	Teboitabu		
Tourakai	Tebomanti	Mereki	Tekoriri		
Taorereiti	Tetangare	Makin	Takabwebwe		
Tekennang	Tabuariki	Manibure	Tewai		
Tiare	Teburentang	Monika	Tiare		
Tekaobwere	Tebaara	Merina	Taomati		
Tokabeti	Tebwebwenikarawa	Moataake	Tarakai		
Terakau	Temariti	Marae	Taurarai		
Tamton	Teebora	Matauea	Teweia		
Teiannang	Taara	Mikara	Toma		
Teakai	Teang	Mere	Tebero		
Tamueru	Teaibure	Noa	Uarete		
Teaoua	Teraieta	Nareantabuariki	Wiriam		
Terama	Tokamarewa	Nakau			
Tion	Tauea	Noa			
Teai	Temoa	Namaua			
Taukarawa	Tion	Nabure			
Teera	Titoa	Obati			
Tekenimatang	Taem	Reiati			

I- BANABA			I- BANABA		
Mane (Man)	Aine (Woman)	Ataei (Child)	Mane (Man)	Aine (Woman)	Ataei (Child)
Tabunawati	Terenga	Rabaere	Ioteba	Tibeti	Teroata
Taukatea	Tanana	Ruti		Terutara	Tebike
Tebiraki	Tanuanteiti	Rubena		Tearei	Tawita
Taarakai	Tirouma	Raeri		Tataba	Tarantaake
Teremita	Tioua	Rita		Tekeinnang	Terane
Teburetau	Teraiti	Reia		Tekaruontaake	Taonibeia
Teikabua	Tekima	Reone		Tauraoi	Teingira
Taremon	Timou	Ratinu		Teinamawa	Terautete
Terakoro	Terubea	Rere		Tauantabo	Temate
Tiomaia	Tebwewe	Riritara		Tenekeata	Tebiriro
Tiare	Tebabuti	Rekau		Taberananginiti	Twane
Taakai	Tamara	Raitiera		Uata	Takabi
Tawaka	Tebwea	Rara		Waka	Teatirei
Taraing	Tiriobo	Riti		Wawa	Temarin
Tutara	Tebureai	Rita		Waumua	Tarame
Tamueru	Teneboieta	Rabinoniti		Watati	Teaitoa
Tematenako	Terira	Rabaua			Teanimatang
Tamia	Taraniman	Rise			
Tarau	Tekotara	Rimon			
Tokinteiti	Teraumwemwe	Tearintong			
Teitiaki	Tauta	Tebwebwani...			
Urebano	?	?			
?	?	?			
Uakirerei	Tebetia	Tebuari			
Uriaria	Teruia	Tawita			
Uereti	Tabita	Tikawa			
Iotua	Toanimaiango	Tekaie			
Ietera	Tare	Tebuaiti			
Ioteba	Tibeti	Teroata			
	Terutara	Tebike			
	Tearei	Tawita			
	Tataba	Tarantaake			
	Tekeinnang	Terane			
	Tekaruontaake	Taonibeia			
	Tauraoi	Teingira			
	Teinamawa	Terautete			
	Tauantabo	Temate			
	Tenekeata	Tebiriro			
	Taberananginiti	Twane			
	Uata	Takabi			
	Waka	Teatirei			
	Wawa	Temarin			
	Waumua	Tarame			

I-BANABA			I-BANABA		
Mane (Man)	Aine (Woman)	Ataei (Child)	Mane (Man)	Aine (Woman)	Ataei (Child)
	Watati	TeaitoaTeanimatang			
Ataei (Child)	Ataei (Child)	Ataei (Child)	Ataei (Child)	Ataei (Child)	Ataei (Child)
Teanimatang	Tura	Teue	Tabotari	Tebana	Toataake
Teina	Takirara	Terekita	Taneriwe	Tamau	Toaua
Teitirere	Tema	Taniera	Tabetaake	Tibe	Tebwe
Taati	Tekerau	Tumairang	Tarike	Tebakoia	Tekatoa
Tonganariki	Tarabito	Tabwebwe	Tawita	Taboua	Tebikea
Teiakarawa	Tekinoa	Tekanan	Taunebo	Tabukintarawa	Taketit
Tion	Tera	Teiti	Teneita	Tebwebwenikai	Tokiteba
Tebutiaki	Tetiro	Teretia	Timeri	Tauamarawa	Toreka
Tabure	Tatoka	Teaitinimatang	Tekoieta	Tautere	Tenanikabuti
Tengauea	Tenamoiti	Tereikabu	Teuia	Tebwebwenikarawa	Tebaiti
Tabwere	Tebakarere	Tetake	Tekoniti	Tangaroa	Teibiaro
Tekabu	Tewe	Tiebe	Tekanabu	Tereitaake	Tenna
Teretitake	Tawata	Tione	Tutara	Takie	Tute
Teraka	Takeke	Teuenimatang	Teikata	Torongi	Tabeta
Takabwebwe	Teribabaiti	Tenana	Tete	Tekoti	Tebuke
Teingira	Tarome	Tekabwebwere	Tokaniman	Tubaina	Teiti
Taumarea	Teretia	Taaboraua	Tarota	Tokonikarawa	Temarin
Teientinaniku	Tekimaua	Tekanu	Tekanikai	Takea	Uatu
Tiribo	Tinaua	Tetera	Uere	Rurunterenga	
Takaro	Tematang	Taburon			

INDEX

manai, 35, 63
maneaba, 16, 41, 45, 46, 85, 87, 119, 121, 122, 124, 129, 151, 153, 169, 179, 224, 227, 229, 239, 298, 299, 302, 305, 307, 308, 309, 312
  floor, 310
Maneaba, 124
Mangati, 9, 27, 90, 91, 92, 127, 214
  elder, 90, 147
Mangaua, 124
Manicinella sp, 310
Maninimate, 19, 39, 101, 124, 136, 141, 147, 171
Manx, 215
mao, 29, 64, *261*
map, 119, 297, 335
Maraeea, 240
Marakei, 127
Maranikaomoti, 128
Marata, 214, 224
Marawa, 199
markers, 314
Maro, 217
marriage, 19, 55, 161, 162
Marshalls, 14
massacre, 181, 184, 294
Mata Bou, 121, 122
mats, 162
Maude
  claim, 230
  list, 122
  List, 216
  notebook, 217

papers, 217
writing, 115
Maude, H.E., 2, 9, 13, 14, 15, 16, 17, 18, 19, 20, 21, 22, 25, 26, 27, 33, 37, 90, 92, 93, 96, 107, 113, 114, 115, 116, 117, 119, 122, 127, 129, 130, 134, 135, 141, 147, 158, 163, 168, 169, 176, 181, 185, 186, 189, 194, 196, 197, 198, 208, 215, 216, 223, 224, 225, 228, 229, 230, 249, 250, 263, 288, 290, 299, 314
McAdam, J., 328
McClure, H.W., 203
Meai, 124, 132
meat, 186
medical
  equipment, 348
  officer, 31
medicinal, 261
  plants, 29
  powers, 70
Melanesians, 16
Melbourne, 21, 246, 247
Memorandum, 263
menstruating, 28, 299
  house, 236
  women, 30, 66, 161, 239
Mercer
  body, 284, 336
  death, 285
  died, 285
  escape, 285
  lover, 285

ABOUT THE AUTHORS:

RAOBEIA KEN SIGRAH

Raobeia Ken Sigrah was born on 18 January 1956 on Rabi, Fiji. He identifies as a Banaban but is a Fiji passport holder now living in Australia.

Raobeia, or Ken (as he is known to his friends), started his education when he was seven years old at the Buakonikai Primary School in 1962 and continued at the Banaban Primary School until 1967. After passing his Intermediate exams, he was sent to Niusawa Methodist High School (a Fijian school on nearby Taveuni). In 1980, he attended Fulton College, Fiji, to study English for a year. In 1972, Ken was employed as a clerk for the Rabi Council of Leaders, Public Works Department. At the same time, he joined the Banaban Dancing Group, which officiated as the Council's cultural representative to perform in foreign countries. During the same year, Ken travelled with the Banaban Dancing Group at the invitation of the Australian authorities to perform at the official opening ceremonies of the Sydney Opera House. This opportunity came through the Fiji Arts Theatre, and the group also performed in Brisbane during this particular tour. In 1974, Ken toured with the dancing group to Nauru, Banaba and Tarawa while still officially working as a clerk for the Rabi Council. In 1975, Ken attended the South Pacific Festival of Arts in Rotorua, New Zealand. After this trip, he left the dancing group but still worked for Rabi Council. In 1979, Ken joined another group of young Banaban men and elders on an unforgettable trip to Banaba just before the cessation of mining. After nine months on Banaba, he returned to Rabi. By 1982, he was employed by the Fiji government as a clerk and a storeman, a job he retained for six years until 1989 when he resigned. He was then re-employed by the Rabi Council as Labour Officer and Inspector. He resigned again from the Council in 1990 and returned to a traditional Banaban life. Since then, Ken has studied Banaban culture and customs with Banaban elders as his tutors. Ken began to study Banaban culture and customs when he was 14 years of age. He undertook these studies as a responsibility according to Banaban custom and as a male clan member. He was tutored to be well qualified as a clan spokesman in general meetings concerning Banaban matters relating to culture, customs and genealogies. He has witnessed the turmoil that his people have endured. Ken has attended most general meetings representing individual clans to exchange ideas and plans with elders of the Banaban community. His first experience as a clan spokesman was in 1987, then in 1994, 1995, and 1996. In 1997, Ken asked Stacey King to assist with the writing of a history of Banaba. He aimed to promote and write about Banaban history, culture and customs. Still, in the past, he had difficulty finding a sponsor who could assist with editing and publishing such work. Many of the elders have died, and others are approaching their later years. The publishing of this material gathered over many years is for the benefit of the young Banaban generation, who are now being brought up in a different environment, to help them preserve their culture, heritage and identity as Banabans.

STACEY M. KING

Nei Titeiti Naking is the Banaban name of Stacey King, an Australian. At the turn of this century, four generations of Stacey's family were involved with the phosphate mining industry on Banaba. In late 1989, a photograph and document collection of Stacey's great-grandfather, John F. Williams, was uncovered. Through this discovery, the wonderful tales about their lives on Ocean Island (Banaba) became a reality. This material led her on a quest to research the history of Banaba and, at her mother's urging, to write a book on a story that had to be told. In October 1991, Stacey travelled with her mother and late aunt to meet with the Banabans on Rabi for the first time. This meeting was to change her life and that of her family forever. Because of her research on Banaban history, she already respected and admired the Banaban people and their once beautiful homeland. This admiration and love for the Banabans was also evident in her great-grandfather's photograph collection taken in the early 1900s. Her meeting with the Banabans on Rabi made her realise how much the people had suffered at the hands of the phosphate mining industry and the British, Australian, and New Zealand governments involved with this sorry saga.

During the first visit to Rabi, the Banabans asked Stacey if she could help. She felt it was impossible to walk away and not try to assist the community in some way. Stacey had worked in advertising earlier in her career before becoming a self-employed businesswoman in the early 1980s. She began to juggle her time between her business, raising her three children, and trying to help the Banabans. In 1992, Stacey started writing and publishing the *Banaba/Ocean Island News* and building a network of other interested people to try and rally worldwide support to assist the Banaban people. At the same time, she began preserving and recording Banaban historical material so it could be returned to its rightful owners. In 1993, Stacey formed the Banaban Heritage Society Inc, a non-profit organisation dedicated to preserving history and bettering the lives of the Banaban people. The opening of the first community library on Rabi and a much-needed communications and emergency network program were just two of the many community-based projects she helped implement through the volunteer services of Society members worldwide. In February 1997, Stacey made her first journey to Banaba and experienced the strong bonds her own family must have felt all those years before. On her second visit to Banaba in July 1997, while on the BHS Homecoming Trip, which took 60 people, including Banabans from Rabi, on an epic journey back to Banaba, she realised the homeland's significant cultural impact on its people. She became convinced, from her own experiences, that the Banabans were part of the very homeland itself and that the two could never be separated, even if the majority of Banabans were now living on Rabi. During this time, she was asked by Ken Sigrah to assist in the co-writing of this book. Stacey hopes that this book is only the beginning of many projects that will help right the wrongs of the past by assisting Banabans in realising their dreams and moving towards a much brighter future.

OTHER TITLES BY THE AUTHORS

Raobeia Ken Sigrah and Stacey M. King

Non-Fiction Chapter in a book
The Banaba-Ocean Island chronicles: private collections, indigenous record-keeping, fact and fiction. Chapter 17, *Hunting the collectors*. Cambridge Scholars, UK.

Non-Fiction Book
Te Rii ni Banaba. First Edition: IPS, Suva, Fiji. 2001

Historical Fiction
Nakaa's Awakening, Land of Matang. Banaban Vision Publications, Gold Coast, Australia, 2020 (Book 1; 4-book series. Blend of history, biography and fictional reconstruction)

Articles and Presentations

- Australia-Banaba Relations; the price of shaping a nation is now a call for recognition

- Banaba–Ocean Island Chronicles: Private collections and indigenous record-keeping proving fact from fiction
- Cultural Identity of Banabans
- Legacy of a Miners Daughter and Assessment of the Social Changes of the Banabans after Phosphate Mining on Banaba
- Essentially Being Banaban in Today's World: The role of Banaban Law, Te Rii Ni Banaba"(Backbone of Banaba) in a Changing World

(Copies of the above articles can be obtained at www.banabanvision.com)

Banaban Social Media sites by Authors

Abara Banaba–Come Meet the Banabans: banaban.com
Banaban Vision: banabanvision.com
Banaban Voice Facebook:
facebook.com/groups/banabanvoice
Banaban Blog: banaban.com/blog
Banaban Vision Blog: banabanvision.com
Banaban Vocal Media: vocal.media/authors/stacey-king-nu38u20qvz

Connect with Us:

Banaban Vision Publications

PO Box 1116 Paradise Point Qld 4216 Australia
Raobeia Ken Sigrah – Author's Page:
raobeiakensigrah.com
Stacey M. King – Author's Page:
staceymking.com
Email: books@banaban.info
Te Rii Ni Banaba –Facebook group:
https://www.facebook.com/groups/296299534653304/
Linkedin: Stacey King: https://www.linkedin.com/in/stacey-king-4ba68a76/

www.ingramcontent.com/pod-product-compliance
Lightning Source LLC
Chambersburg PA
CBHW051908090426
42811CB00003B/502